The
Lost Art
of Healing

§

The
Lost Art
of Healing

BERNARD LOWN, M.D.

Houghton Mifflin Company

BOSTON   NEW YORK   1996

For information about permission to reproduce selections from this book,
write to Permissions, Houghton Mifflin Company, 215 Park Avenue South,
New York, New York 10003.

For information about this and other Houghton Mifflin trade and reference
books and multimedia products, visit The Bookstore at Houghton Mifflin
on the World Wide Web at http://www.hmco.com/trade/.

Library of Congress Cataloging-in-Publication Data
Lown, B. (Bernard)
  The lost art of healing / Bernard Lown.
    p.   cm.
  ISBN 0-395-82525-3
  1. Holistic medicine. 2. Physician and patient. 3. Medicine and psychology.
4. Healing.   I. Title.
[DNLM: 1. Physician-Patient Relations. 2. Holistic Health. W62 L919L 1996]
R733.L684   1996
610 — dc20
DNLM/DLC for Library of Congress   96-18184   CIP

Printed in the United States of America

QUM 10 9 8 7 6 5 4 3 2 1

Book design by Melodie Wertelet

The names and initials of those whose cases are presented in this book
have been changed to preserve the privacy of the patients.

Lines from "The Unexpressed" by Yevgeny Yevtushenko are from *Almost at the End.*
Copyright © 1987 by Yevgeny Yevtushenko, Albert C. Todd, and Antonia W. Bouis.
Reprinted by permission of Henry Holt and Co., Inc.

Acknowledgments

Great teachers and extraordinary institutions enabled me to forge ahead in medicine and to evolve a philosophy of healing. In these pages the reader will often encounter the name of Samuel A. Levine, a physician who taught me the art of doctoring and started me on a lifelong love affair with medicine. My own skill as a teacher, which took decades to acquire, was refined by critical questions from more than two hundred postdoctoral fellows who spent two years working with me. From them I learned that a story charged with human interest is far more educational than a disembodied fact.

The support of close colleagues further honed my clinical proficiency, but none have played a more important role than my associates in the Lown Cardiovascular Group. They not only preach good medicine, they practice it daily. My closest and longest association has been with Thomas Graboys, a consummately skilled physician. As director of the Lown Group, he counsels advocacy for the sick as a doctor's uncompromising mission. Each of my other colleagues in the group, Dr. Charles Blatt, Dr. Shmuel Ravid, and Dr. Susan Bennett, has taught me to surmount some of the challenges of doctoring. My ultimate educators have been numerous patients, many of whom populate this book. They continue to inspire and sustain me.

Three institutions — the Peter Bent Brigham Hospital (PBBH), later to become the Brigham and Women's Hospital, the Harvard School of Public Health (HSPH), and the Lown Cardiovascular Center — have exercised a special vitality. When I arrived at the PBBH, it had not yet seen forty years of existence, but it was already a medical Mecca. Such recognition convinced me that an institution's dedication to innovative medical research need not diminish its capacity to provide excellent care for the sick.

My association with the HSPH enlarged my perspective on health and the primacy of its societal dimension. The HSPH above all provided me with a favorable environment for carrying out extensive research, some of which is reported in this book. These investigations would not have been possible without the unstinting support of Dr. Fredrick Stare, chairman of the Department of Nutrition, where all my investigative work was conducted.

Simultaneously, the Lown Cardiovascular Center constituted a testing ground for implementing the research advances as well as practicing scientifically sound yet compassionate medicine. It could not have been accomplished without a staff who shared the principles and were always ready to go the last mile.

Conversations with a number of friends, including William Davenport, Alan Dershowitz, Daniel and Anita Fine, John Kenneth and Katherine Galbraith, Jennifer Leaning, Prasannan Parthasarathi, Juliet Schor, Jerome Rubin, Patricia Fagen, and my agent, Helen Rees, encouraged me in the writing of this book and enabled me to rethink a number of issues.

Several editors contributed inestimably to the clarity of the language and to the organization of the content. At an early stage, Louis Berny and Sharon Hogan made invaluable suggestions. Much fine-tuning was provided by Houghton Mifflin editors, especially Harry Foster. With great sensitivity, he encouraged me to divest the pages of maladroit medical jargon. His searching questions enabled me to clarify the narrative and strengthen the thrust of my argument. Further refinement and exactitude were offered by manuscript editor Gerry Morse. No one, except me, read the text more often than my wife, Louise, who each time corrected and improved it.

To all, my profound gratitude.

Contents

Contents

Preface

MEDICINE IN THE United States is widely regarded as the best in the world. Hardly a day passes without a major scientific breakthrough. Many formerly fatal diseases are now curable. People are healthier and live longer than ever. Still, patient dissatisfaction with doctors has rarely been more acute. Although physicians are increasingly able to cure disease and prolong life, the American public is suspicious, distrustful of, even antagonistic to, the profession. Doctors, uneasy, astonished, resentful, and angry, universally acknowledge a crisis in health care. With the focus on colossal medical expenditures, amounting to a trillion dollars annually, most of the numerous solutions involve containing runaway costs. This book reaches a different conclusion about what is ailing our health care system.

Medicine's profound crisis, I believe, is only partially related to ballooning costs, for the problem is far deeper than economics. In my view, the basic reason is that medicine has lost its way, if not its soul. An unwritten covenant between doctor and patient, hallowed over several millennia, is being broken.

During my professional life I have seen medicine rise to an apogee of respect sometimes amounting to adulation, then watched in distress as it began a rapid downward slide, which is continuing. At midcentury a doctor's image outshone nearly every other profession or calling. Yet it appears that with each new medical miracle, the image of physicians shrinks and grows more tarnished. Doctors are held in lower repute than ever, except perhaps for biblical times when Ecclesiastes intoned, "He that sinneth before his Maker, Let him fall into the hand of the physician."

No significant social transformation results from a single or simple cause. Reflecting on forty-five years of medical practice, I see that something vital appears to be vanishing. It seems to me that medicine has indulged in a Faustian bargain. A three-thousand-year tradition, which bonded doctor and patient in a special affinity of trust, is being traded for a new type of relationship. Healing is replaced with treating, caring is supplanted by managing, and the art of listening is taken over by technological procedures. Doctors no longer minister to a distinctive person but concern themselves with fragmented, malfunctioning biologic parts. The distressed human being is frequently absent from the transaction.

The introduction of increasingly sophisticated technology is certainly one reason. Compared with the sharp images provided by ultrasonography, magnetic resonance imaging, computerized tomography, endoscopy, and angiography, a patient's history is flabby, confused, subjective, and seemingly irrelevant. Furthermore, it takes a good deal of time to elicit a full history. According to some doctors, technology has become a sufficient substitute for talking with a patient.

The decline in respect for doctors is also accelerated by the extraordinary hubris instilled in medical students. They are taught a reductionist medical model in which human beings are presented as complex biochemical factories. A sick person is merely a repository of malfunctioning organs or deranged regulatory systems that respond to some technical fix. Within this construct, the doctor, as exacting scientist, uses sophisticated instruments and advanced methods to engage in an exciting act of discovery.

Not only contemporary philosophic notions of illness, but powerful economic incentives reinforce these views. Society places a much higher premium on technology than on listening or counseling. Time spent in an operating room or performing an invasive procedure is rewarded tenfold more than conversing with patients or family. In addition to obviating discourse, current medical practice focuses on the acute and emergent and is largely indifferent to preventing disease and promoting health. Since preventive medicine, though recognized as the most cost-effective approach to illness, is time intensive, it is completely neglected. Diligent prevention invariably plays second fiddle to heroic cures.

I am convinced that the situation will not be corrected by economic fixes. The rot will continue until doctors reconnect with their tradition as healers. In moving words to his doctor, the essayist Anatole Broyard, shortly before his death from prostate cancer, wrote,

> I wouldn't demand a lot of my doctor's time. I just wish he would brood on my situation for perhaps five minutes, that he would give me his whole mind just once, be bonded with me for a brief space, survey my soul as well as my flesh to get at my illness, for each man is ill in his own way. . . . Just as he orders blood tests and bone scans of my body, I'd like my doctor to scan me, to grope for my spirit as well as my prostate. Without some such recognition, I am nothing but my illness.*

My aim is not merely to share interesting medical experiences but to present a message, a central idea vital to our troubled times. The practice of medicine with a human face is possible in this age of personal involution into the black hole of me-ism. Indeed, it is more necessary than ever.

I cannot emphasize too categorically that science must not be abandoned in order to heal. On the contrary, healing is best accomplished when art and science are conjoined, when body and spirit are probed together. Only when doctors can brood for the fate of a fellow human afflicted with fear and pain do they engage the unique individuality of a particular human being. A sick patient becomes more than his or her illness. This broader engagement ignites embers of clinical imagination, hones precision in judgment, and helps overcome the agony of decision making. A doctor thereby gains courage to deal with

* Anatole Broyard, *New York Times Magazine,* August 26, 1990.

the pervasive uncertainties for which technical skill alone is inadequate. Patient and doctor then enter into a partnership as equals. As the patient is empowered, the doctor's curing power is enhanced. More than a half century ago, Boston physician Francis Peabody counseled that the secret of care of the patient is caring for the patient.

A doctor establishes credentials as a caring practitioner during the very first visit by listening attentively. This, requiring engagement of all sensibilities, is the most powerful diagnostic device in the doctor's armamentarium. In fact, a doctor who takes a careful history reaches a correct diagnosis in 70 percent of cases. This is far more efficient than all the currently available tests and technologies. The reason is straightforward: the majority of complaints that patients present to doctors, even though focused on one or another organ, are functional, generally arising from the rough and tumble of living. Frequently stemming from an aching heart that is impervious to any modern instrument, they are not hidden from an ear cultivated to listen for the inaudible sigh, nor are they concealed from an eye sensitive to the unshed tear.

Cold-blooded realists may think this is all romantic blather, but even a realist does not remain long indifferent to large economic dividends. The most cost-effective way to reach a diagnosis is for a doctor to become fully engaged with the total human presence. For example, chest pain in a middle-aged man is a very common problem that invariably leads to an expensive and extensive workup. The doctor's response is stereotypic. After a cursory history, the patient is informed that tests are necessary to rule out angina pectoris, an indication of serious coronary heart disease. The patient is understandably eager to proceed immediately. After several anxiety-ridden weeks, during which a host of costly studies are carried out, the workup culminates in an invasive coronary angiogram. When the patient is finally informed that the angiogram is normal and the chest pain is unrelated to the heart, he is filled with high regard for the skill and thoroughness of the physician and enormously impressed with the magical powers of modern technology to probe inside his heart. The patient's grateful reaction affirms for the doctor that the right course had been pursued. Moreover, it reinforces the view that wrapping oneself in the ancient Greek robes of Cassandra and auguring the worst is both psychologically and financially rewarding for the physician.

But the whole rigmarole is unnecessary, an opinion based on my forty-five years' experience with many thousands of patients whose presenting complaint was chest pain. A diagnosis of angina pectoris could be ruled out in 90 percent of these cases in an unhurried interview. This was the opinion of Dr. William Heberden, who first gave a masterful description of angina pectoris more than two centuries ago, and no subsequent technological advances have contradicted his insight. In the large majority of cases, a careful history reveals that the chest pain is caused by arthritis, psychological stress, indigestion, or other common problems. Coronary disease is unlikely in the absence of gross lipid derangement, diabetes, or hypertension, especially if the family history is largely negative for heart disease and when the subject has neither smoked nor been subjected to undue psychological stress. This information can be derived from a history and a few simple laboratory tests. Being attentive at the outset spares the patient anxiety and saves society mammoth expenditures, in this instance a nearly fifty-fold difference in cost between the two medical approaches. We waste many billions of dollars annually in diagnostic overkill for chest pain alone. The fiscal crisis in medicine is ultimately a crisis in doctoring, as I will detail in the following chapters.

I imagine that at this point skeptical readers may be wondering why they should trust my opinion, which is contradictory to the glut of health information now deluging Americans. Who I am and the credibility of my witness is embedded in these pages, but I should probably outline briefly how I came to believe so strongly in what I am saying here.

I have accumulated medical vignettes over many years. At the end of a long day, I frequently make brief jottings on the patients I've seen. Reflecting on the insight they offered, I slowly came to realize how my early medical training led me to an interest in what makes each patient unique. When I entered Johns Hopkins Medical School in 1942, I was enchanted with psychiatry as a means of understanding a person's behavior, but I abandoned it because of its lack of scientific rigor and seeming medieval scholasticism. I craved order and yearned for the fine symmetries and predictabilities afforded by science. Psychiatry clearly was not for me. Youthful romanticism fostered the notion that science would soon demystify the human body and expose the essential processes underlying disease. I reveled in the scientific and technological breakthroughs of the day and wished passionately to contribute to the inexorable onrush of discovery.

Cardiology was then in the forefront of rapid advances in medicine. The introduction of cardiac catheterization by Nobel laureates André F. Cournand and Dickinson W. Richards, just as I graduated from medical school in 1945, opened wide vistas for new insights. For the first time heart chambers could be entered safely and explored minutely with remote sensing catheters. Diagnosis was instantly transformed from educated guesswork, based on generations of clinical observations, to exact scientific extrapolations from direct measurements. Innovative surgical techniques emerged for correcting congenital heart defects, repairing malfunctioning heart valves, and, eventually, bypass grafting of obstructed coronary arteries. The best and the brightest were propelled into cardiology.

When I entered medical practice, infectious diseases such as tuberculosis and poliomyelitis had been largely contained and heart disease was becoming the leading cause of death in industrially developed nations. In the United States someone died unexpectedly from heart disease every ninety seconds. The problems to be solved were numerous, complex, and challenging. New scientific insights were leading to innovative approaches and revolutionary devices, few diagnostic riddles proved elusive, and diseases that in the past were invariably fatal yielded to medical advances. Optimism was the currency of the day.

I came to Boston to take a fellowship with one of the great

clinical cardiologists of this century, Dr. Samuel A. Levine, a professor at the Harvard Medical School who was based at the Peter Bent Brigham Hospital, now known as the Brigham and Women's Hospital. My first research involved an ancient drug, digitalis, used for two centuries to combat heart failure. While a very effective remedy, it could cause serious derangements of heart rhythm as well as death. My investigative work demonstrated the critical role of potassium in determining the safe use of digitalis.

Discoveries followed one upon another, and at a young age I gained worldwide attention for my introduction of direct current for cardiac resuscitation and for the technique of cardioversion, which I invented for correcting various tachycardias, that is, runaway rapid heartbeats. These discoveries saved many thousands of lives and paved the way for coronary care units and for a surge in heart operations, including the bypass of obstructed coronary arteries. Our work also highlighted the horrendous problem of sudden cardiac death as we began to define methods for its prevention.

Another seminal figure in my life was Professor Fredrick Stare, who established the first Department of Nutrition at the Harvard School of Public Health and encouraged my early medical investigations. While managing a large research laboratory in his department, I never distanced myself from clinical practice. I saw patients weekly and participated in daily rounds at the hospital. My view of medicine therefore stems not only from the ivory tower of academe but also from the trenches of private clinical practice.

My philosophic outlook has been shaped by many elements: foreign birth, a Jewish heritage with a rabbinic tradition, a love of books, and above all, a continuing romance with medicine. My more than four decades of medical work have only increased my fascination with the magical art of healing as espoused by the great twelfth-century philosopher-physician Maimonides, who prayed, "May I never forget that the patient is a fellow creature in pain. May I never consider him merely a vessel of disease."

I feel extraordinarily privileged to be a physician. A doctor, after all, has a front-row seat for an unmatched theatrical performance. While art may imitate life, it never quite measures up to it. The doctor is a spectator to a sweeping panorama of events that constitutes a mirror of the social and cultural history of an era. I have often felt guilty about billing patients. Rarely is one permitted to gain such intimate insight. No pleasure is quite akin to the joy of helping other human beings secure and lengthen their hold on life. This book is a small recompense to my patients, ultimately my greatest teachers, who helped me to become a doctor.

I

Hearing the Patient:
The Art of Diagnosis

§

1

The Science of History-Taking and the Art of Listening

IN THIS AGE OF burgeoning technology, it is easy to forget that an essential element in medical care still derives from an art forged at the very dawn of human civilization. Twenty-five hundred years ago, Hippocrates counseled, "For where there is love of man, there is also love of the art. For some patients, though conscious that their position is perilous, recover their health simply through their contentment with the physician." In the sixteenth century, Paracelsus, the great German physician of his era, included among the basic qualifications of a physician "intuition which is necessary to understand the patient, his body, his disease. He must have the feel and touch which make it possible for him to be in sympathetic communication with the patient's spirit."

Principles like these have not lost any of their validity even in this age when scientific medicine reigns supreme. The style of practice I have adopted subscribes to this ancient legacy. My decision was neither heavenly ordained, nor influenced by a genetic endowment. Great teachers shaped my ideas of what doctoring is all about, foremost among them Dr. Samuel A. Levine, under whom I began a fellowship at Boston's Peter Bent Brigham Hospital in 1950. Although he was to become my mentor and role model, after two years under his tutelage, I let youthful arrogance get the better of me and I concluded that the old man had little more to offer. I was bored with his stories, which I had heard many times over, and attending hospital rounds with him every morning consumed several precious hours better devoted, I thought, to productive research.

For about six months I stopped rounding with Dr. Levine, working only in the cardiac outpatient clinic one session a week. It was soon difficult to avoid facing my ineptitude as a clinician. The contrast between the response of patients under Levine's care and those I managed was stark. He, with but little understanding of underlying pathophysiology, would prescribe an unproven potion and the patient improved, recovered, and prospered, while I, brimming with the latest discoveries hot out of the current revelations in the *New England Journal of Medicine*, had no such outcomes.

To allay my frustration, I resumed attending his rounds six mornings a week in the hope of mastering the art. I must have been a very slow learner, for it took me an additional eleven years with Levine to gain confidence as a clinician. But at last his art did rub off, enabling me to fathom rapidly each patient's uniqueness and to arrive at an individualized therapeutic prescription.

During these many years, my admiration for Levine's prodigious skill as a clinician grew. He recognized, with Dr. William Osler, that "medicine is the science of uncertainty, the art of probability." He believed that the bulk of relevant information could be obtained from a properly gathered history and meticulously executed physical examination. He taught that a battery of tests must not replace a mind willing to think, yet he gloried in scientific advances and maintained that the art of medicine consisted of bringing the science of medicine to the bedside. He had seen more than thirty thousand cardiac patients, and it seemed as though each had wrought a permanent niche in his memory. An uncanny capacity to recall precise detailed information about nearly every patient he had seen was the underpinning of his clinical acumen — a profound pattern of recognition that enabled him to distinguish the main lines from irrelevant decorative turns.

Levine instructed a generation of cardiologists about the uniqueness of the angina pectoris syndrome. Astounding as it may seem, I don't recall his ever being wrong when Levine diagnosed angina. He taught that in a patient presenting with chest discomfort there was generally no difficulty in determining whether the complaint stemmed from a diseased coronary circulation. This was especially true, he maintained, if the physician invested time in an unhurried interview, paying careful attention to numerous details derived from painstaking inquiry. Few modern doctors are equipped to recognize the subtle case of angina, largely because they are either ignorant of these details or unwilling to invest time in history-taking. At present, the diagnosis of coronary artery disease is largely made by means of noninvasive as well as invasive studies, including coronary angiography. Of the million coronary angiograms carried out in 1993, 200,000 revealed normal coronary arteries. Had Levine's teaching been heeded, few if any of the patients with normal coronaries would have been subjected to such a costly and invasive study.

Levine's approach permitted diagnosing angina pectoris correctly during the first encounter with a patient. Levine emphasized the art of misdirection, for example, asking the patient to "point with a finger" where "the pain" is located. Angina is not sensed as pain, nor can one point to it with a finger. If the patient nonetheless followed the instruction and pointed to a spot on the chest wall, one could forthwith dismiss the diagnosis of angina pectoris. If, however, instead of pointing, the patient clenched a fist or laid the flat of a hand on the midsternal area, angina generally was present. This was further confirmed if the patient, in describing the sensation, used such words as, "I find it hard to describe, it's really not a pain, it's more a tightness, or a heaviness, or a squeezing." Then the diagnosis was secure. Levine offered numerous other clues, so that the physician rarely had to be uncertain about the presence of angina, even before the initial interview was over.

While serving as a visiting professor in Los Angeles in the early 1960s, I heard Dr. M., a former Levine trainee, reminisce publicly about him. Dr. M. related that once they were presented with a healthy-appearing young man who complained of discomfort in his upper belly. After posing a few questions, Dr. Levine flatly ascribed the symptom to angina pectoris and wrote in the chart a single sentence, "This man has angina pectoris." The patient, only thirty-four, was without risk factors for coronary heart disease. A workup revealed an unusual finding in someone so young, a large hiatus hernia, which clearly accounted for the symptoms Levine ascribed to angina. According to Dr. M., "Levine showed that he was a cut above the run-of-the-mill doctors. He entered in the chart in bold letters, 'My diagnosis is wrong.' He easily could have fudged his error. This was not the way of good old SAL. There it was for all to see."

I had been making rounds with Dr. Levine after this episode occurred. As we were walking from the bedside, I innocently asked whether it was common to have this type of discomfort with hiatus hernia. I was taken aback by Levine's answer: "Of course not. I'm absolutely convinced this man has coronary artery disease and his complaint is due to angina."

"Then why did you write that note?"

"I am a teacher. It is therefore important to impress the house staff that no one is infallible." Then he said, with a chuckle, "Even the great Levine can be mistaken." And as an afterthought: "I did not want to appear like a small man to the young doctors who hang on to my every word."

The story had an ironic and tragic twist. About three years later, at the age of thirty-seven, this man sustained a massive heart attack. Clearly Levine's initial opinion was correct. In retrospect there must be a shudder of disquiet for Levine's failure to inform the patient of his condition. However, one must remember that this event occurred more than forty years ago, when nothing could have been done medically to change the outcome.

Levine communicated to students a process of clinical discovery in which tiny clues help weave an elegant diagnostic garment from threads readily at hand. First and foremost there must be a searching history that separates decisive clues from frothy irrelevancies. Then the physical examination must confirm or refute diagnostic hunches. The supreme tool, according to Levine, is the stethoscope through which the heart's mysteries are made audible. This simple, inexpensive device is invaluable for listening to heart sounds and heart murmurs. Levine maintained that after a thoroughgoing examination one is only occasionally left in doubt about the diagnosis. He hinted that frequent reliance on a so-called workup, engaging the heavy medical artillery of the day, such as X-ray or cardiac fluoroscopy, electrocardiography, phonocardiography, blood work, and urine analysis, is testimony to a lack of clinical skill.

Levine accumulated a veritable encyclopedia of small diagnostic clues that were generally related to curable conditions. For example, knowing that subacute bacterial endocarditis, an infection of diseased heart valves, is extremely rare in the absence of any cardiac murmur or in patients with preestablished chronic atrial fibrillation, the physician could spare the patient costly diagnostic procedures and the discomfort of numerous blood cultures. Levine had a genius for thinking up simple approaches for difficult problems, for example, his test to recognize coarctation of the aorta, a congenital constriction of the upper part of the aorta, the main conduit for blood from the heart to the body. This frequently unsuspected but curable entity causes high blood pressure that is restricted to the upper part of the body. Levine reasoned that if one compressed both big toe and thumb, then released the pressure, the blanching would last longer in the toe if coarctation was present. This turned out to be the case. The test can be performed in about ten seconds, requires no apparatus beyond a watch with a second hand, and costs nothing.

Levine was also extraordinarily astute in recognizing the cardiac condition from thyrotoxicosis, caused by an overactive thyroid gland. The disorder was commonly overlooked at the time, and he often made the correct diagnosis when no one else suspected it. The thyrocardiac patient presents many classic symptoms of heart disease and arrhythmia, yet the underlying problem is not the heart but an overactive thyroid gland, a completely curable condition. Levine would search for trivial signs, a slight tremor of fingers in the extended hand, a vigorous appetite without weight gain or even with weight loss, excessive but otherwise normal bowel movements, sweating in a cool room, preference for cold weather in an elderly person, a warm hand during a cold day, early graying of hair, a salmon-colored flush to the cheekbones. Finding any of the above, he would launch an intensive search for additional small clues. A smooth, warm, moist skin, a slight tremor to the tongue, hyperactivity of reflexes, and especially a bright, alert look, a barely detectable enlargement of the thyroid gland, or a quickness of movement helped secure the diagnosis.

I recall a time when Levine was asked by the hospital endocrinologist to consult on a woman suspected of having coronary artery disease. No sooner had we reached the bedside than Levine began to hop with unsuppressed excitement, and immediately after ausculting the heart he diagnosed thyrotoxicosis. He asked me what I thought of the first heart sound and I responded that it was snapping.

"How do you reconcile this with a long P-R interval* in the electrocardiogram?" he asked. "You know the only time a prolonged P-R interval is associated with a loud first heart sound is in pregnancy, mitral stenosis, arteriovenous fistula, Paget's disease, or severe anemia? Perchance, is this sixty-year-old woman pregnant, or does she have any of the other conditions?" I shook my head but protested that he was pinning a diagnosis on a thin reed of evidence. He then took a swipe at my lack of clinical acumen. "Bernie, you fail to observe the obvious," he concluded.

"What's so obvious?" I asked with irritation.

"Don't you see the unilateral stare of her left eye?"

I looked hard and of course, while it was not exactly obvious, there was an asymmetry of the two eyes, with the left upper lid being retracted a few millimeters. This is not an uncommon finding with thyrotoxicosis. Levine, now trium-

---

* P-R interval is the time required for an electrical impulse to traverse from the atrium to the ventricle, measured in hundredths of a second.

phant, rasped, "This clinches the diagnosis of a hyperactive thyroid even though I cannot palpate the enlarged thyroid goiter."

To the utter discomfiture of the endocrinologist, whose bread-and-butter practice was thyroid disease, the diagnosis was later proved.

Dr. Levine was impressed with the brightness and quickness of hyperthyroid patients. He admired them intensely and believed that the condition protected them against coronary artery disease. I later learned, when he became my patient, that he had taken three grains of thyroid daily for more than thirty years. He maintained that those with increased thyroid function had bright, sparkling eyes and appeared to be interesting people because personality is conveyed largely through the eyes. Levine suggested that the universal fascination with the Mona Lisa stems from her being hyperthyroid. He insisted that a slight stare makes viewers believe that she is focusing on them and is the basis for the attention this painting has received over the centuries. Levine once confided, "If you look carefully at the Mona Lisa's neck, you'll note that it is full due to a thyroid goiter."

Several times, while visiting the Louvre, I studied da Vinci's extraordinary damsel but could never spot the goiter. This is not meant to be dismissive of my mentor's diagnosis, for Levine frequently saw what others failed to observe. On reflection, why shouldn't teachers be permitted the same license for imaginative flights of fancy as poets?

Levine taught me the art of listening, the essence of the artistry of bedside medicine. Effective listening involves all the senses, not merely the ears. Practicing the art of medicine requires not only expert knowledge of disease but an appreciation of the intimate details of a patient's emotional life usually presumed to be within the province of the psychiatrist. The need for complex involvement with patients is never alluded to in medical texts or mentioned during medical training. To succeed in healing, a doctor must be trained, above all else, to listen. Attentive listening is itself therapeutic, for one encounters many fine tales. Few great books expose the human condition more clearly than a patient who has permitted one to look deeply into his or her eyes.

In the brief time available to take a history, the aim is to obtain, in addition to essential facts, insight into the human being. This seems easy, but listening is the most complex and difficult of all the tools in a doctor's repertory. One must be an active listener to hear an unspoken problem.

STARING AT THE CEILING

Chang Goyang, a Maryland scientist, was invariably accompanied to my office by his petite Chinese wife, who consistently stared straight ahead, penetrating me with a transfixing gaze. I was reminded of an emotionless, silent Buddha doll. Goyang had been my patient for a decade because of angina pectoris, the result of significant narrowing of his coronary arteries. He initially came to Boston for a consultation because his local doctors urged bypass surgery, which he dreaded. He returned for annual visits and his heart condition remained stable over the years.

On this particular visit, his story affirmed the stability of the coronary artery disease. He led me to believe that there had been no change in severity or frequency of anginal discomfort and that his exercise capacity was undiminished. He swam at least five times a week and walked unhampered by chest discomfort. To exercise without experiencing angina, he took a single prophylactic nitroglycerine under his tongue at the outset. I was pleased with the report.

During the physical examination, however, I could not shake a troubling perception. After a while what was bothering me became clear. Unlike the ten previous visits, something was different this year. Mrs. Goyang, who always stared at me, gazed consistently at the ceiling, never once looking at her husband or me. She had never behaved this way. Was it some sort of cue? Perhaps the two quarreled during their long auto drive here.

Perhaps she was bored. On the other hand, she may have been communicating something. If so, what?

"Nonsense, don't let your fancy get the better of you. Stop playing Hamlet," I muttered to myself. These thoughts grew obsessive and distracted me from examining Goyang properly. But why was I acting like an ancient ecclesiastic, trying to deduce from inadequate evidence, when I could easily ask Mrs. Goyang what this was all about?

The physical examination revealed nothing different from the past. I was reassured about his condition and about to send him forth for another year to follow the same program. But instead of having Mrs. Goyang join her husband in the consulting room for the final discussion, as is my usual practice, I met her privately. I asked how Mr. Goyang was doing. She responded that he had already given the story. "Has anything changed?" I asked. She stonewalled and gave me a runaround, repeating that her husband was the one I should question. For about five minutes we pirouetted fruitlessly. My irritation began to show, for it was clear that she was concealing something. My voice strident, I finally asked, "Don't you care what happens to your husband? A devoted wife would never refuse to provide important information to her husband's doctor."

This tough-minded, stolid-looking woman burst into tears. "Chinese wife not supposed to talk behind husband's back."

Switching from generalities, I gently questioned her about particulars. "Is Mr. Goyang taking more nitroglycerine?"

"Yes, he is popping them the whole day," she said between sobs.

"Does he exercise?"

"No, he has too much chest pain. He has not exercised for about a month."

"Does he swim?"

"No, he is afraid."

"Why the deception then?" I plunged on.

"He is deathly scared of a heart operation," she responded.

I promptly had Goyang exercise on a motorized treadmill,

which he had done many times without chest discomfort. In the past he was able to persevere for eleven minutes while adhering to a graded exercise protocol. Now he lasted only five minutes before severe chest pressure and profuse sweating caused him to stop. His blood pressure tumbled as he complained of dizziness. The electrocardiogram revealed profound changes and brief bursts of ventricular tachycardia, a potentially life-threatening disorder in the rhythm of the heartbeat. We took him by ambulance to Brigham and Women's Hospital, where a coronary angiogram showed critical narrowing of the left main coronary artery. This is the most dangerous type of obstruction because this artery is the feeder vessel to two of the three main coronary arteries. When this condition is identified, the consensus is that surgery is the only therapeutic option and should be undertaken immediately. He had an emergency coronary bypass operation, recovered uneventfully, and is doing exceptionally well.

Had his wife not accompanied him, and had I not "listened" with my eyes, I would have missed this profound change in Goyang's status. My patient probably would not have survived such an error.

Listening is not passive. A doctor's history-taking is a carefully structured interview that systematically reviews the present illness, family history, then covers past history comprehensively, going literally from head to toe. After preliminary introductions when encountering a new patient, the doctor is taught to focus on the chief complaint, namely, what brings the patient to the doctor. Unfortunately, the chief complaint may not be what bothers the patient most and may have little to do with the underlying problem. I learned this while still a student at Johns Hopkins Medical School.

More than fifty years after graduating, I remember few of my professors, but I vividly recall Dr. Leo Kanner, a pediatric psychiatrist, whose impact on me has grown with the years. It is hard for me to believe that I actually saw him only twice in my life — in 1943, my second year in medical school — when he presented cases.

THE CHIEF COMPLAINT

In one lecture, still securely etched in memory, Dr. Kanner told us of a woman he had seen several weeks earlier. Her chief complaint was that her eight-year-old boy, Dicky, was a behavior problem. On the third floor of the house, his parents had built for him a playroom equipped with everything F.A.O. Schwarz had to offer. But every morning, he came down to the living room and scattered comic books and the funnies from the daily newspaper over the Persian rug. No beseeching, bribing, or threatening made a particle of difference in the boy's behavior. The mother, thinking her son was seriously disturbed, sought Kanner's help.

That night Kanner attended a banquet to promote the sale of World War II bonds. Beside him sat a distinguished-looking middle-aged woman who, during dinner, told him, straining to maintain her composure, that her son Robert was a marine in the Pacific. She was overwhelmed with worry that he might have been killed while storming some distant Japanese-occupied islands. Then, quite unexpectedly, she posed a curious question: "Dr. Kanner, perhaps you as a psychiatrist can explain the strange psychological power of trivial events. When I think back, a most pleasurable memory is that of Sunday mornings when Bobby spread out the funnies on the living room floor."

Kanner explained that the first woman who complained about her son's behavior was deeply troubled. Her marriage was on the rocks and her husband was having an affair. She felt abandoned, desperate, and helpless. Her chief complaint was largely irrelevant to her problems. Her complaint, Kanner continued, was only the admission ticket to a theatrical performance. He asked us, "Suppose you are a theater critic. Could you write an intelligent essay merely from the admission ticket to a play you hadn't seen? All you could state is that a play with a certain title took place on such and such a night. You may know the author, but that is all you would know. The same with the chief complaint. It tells you that something is troubling enough for the patient to seek help. But that is all. The chief complaint frequently does not even identify the right organ."

Kanner urged us, as beginning medical students, never to prescribe for a chief complaint unless we had come to know the patient well and figured out what was truly troubling the person. A physician committed to healing could not and should not focus exclusively on a chief complaint, or even a diseased organ. If one was to help those who were sick, the stressful aspects of life had to be exposed. Regrettably, some doctors treated the chief complaint, but, the professor concluded, that was poor practice.

I have frequently heard a patient complain of a disabling discomfort, but after a thoroughgoing history identify a difficult social or family problem and dismiss the chief complaint. "Doctor, it's really not worth bothering about." Many times I find myself involved in domestic problems, work problems, psychological issues, family matters, even global problems. The most critical problems are invariably troubled family relations. Once these are identified, words rather than drugs are the efficacious remedy. I am persuaded that a majority of prescriptions intended to alleviate chief complaints are largely irrelevant. This may be a reason so many prescribed drugs prove ineffectual and is no doubt a major factor in medical costs. A patient with an unaddressed problem keeps searching for an answer and goes medicine-shopping. The many drugs prescribed for chief complaints often cause side effects. In desperation, patients acquiesce to costly and invasive procedures.

Doctors focus on the chief complaint primarily because medical schools do not train students in the art of listening. Obtaining a careful history, while emphasized, is not actually taught. A cynical aphorism is popular among doctors: "If everything else fails, talk to the patient." Another contributing factor is that probing beyond the chief complaint requires time, and time is money. Furthermore, the history provides soft data while a doctor craves solid facts. Yet the penchant to pursue technology is not solely driven by the hunger for certainty. To my mind, another factor is that technology is regarded as an effective substitute for time.

Limiting history-taking to the chief complaint often initiates fruitless pursuit of irrelevant matters that are quite tangential to the main problems. What happens when the main issue is sidestepped by focusing on the chief complaint is shown by an encounter that took place early in my career.

A FATHER'S BAD HEART

Saying, "My father has a bad heart," a woman in her forties introduced me to her father. She was wringing a handkerchief and appeared quite agitated. The old man, very withdrawn, looked off into remote space, clearly uneager to be involved in the conversation. He was not senile, for he responded lucidly and precisely to questions. Yet he conveyed a sense of hopelessness.

When I asked the patient what was bothering him, the daughter responded that he was too sick to answer. She stated categorically that he suffered from severe angina pectoris. She talked as though he was not present; he paid no attention to what she said. Her father's days were numbered, she implied. I asked him whether he experienced any chest discomfort. Disconsolately he nodded his head. Then he contradicted himself by assuring me that there was nothing physically wrong with him.

"Daddy, how can you deny what is so obvious to everyone?" the daughter cried.

I was stymied. No matter how hard I tried, the daughter, like a first-rate football tackle, ran interference. The father looked sick, emaciated, indifferent, and much older than his seventy-five years. A physical examination revealed a small and healthy heart, low blood pressure, and no sign of cardiac disease.

When I hurried in to share the good tidings with his daughter, her response dismayed me. "Oh, *no, no, no!*" she shrieked, breaking into convulsive crying. I finally quieted her down. "You don't believe Daddy has a serious heart condition?" she asked incredulously.

I finally coaxed the facts from her as she continued to sob uncontrollably, punctuated by the repetitive "What am I to do?"

The father owned a successful drugstore in which her husband was one of several pharmacists. When her mother had died, five years earlier, she and her husband persuaded the old man to move in with them. They furnished the third floor and converted it into a self-contained apartment. After about a year, the father was persuaded to turn over the pharmacy to his son-in-law.

During the last few years her father had begun to grate on her husband, who insisted that his father-in-law not eat with them. Even her father's simply walking around the apartment got on her husband's nerves. Her father was aware of the agitation and was afraid to move out of his chair when his son-in-law was home. Eating sparingly, he lost massive amounts of weight. He became increasingly reclusive. The daughter, beside herself with remorse and guilt, dreaded crossing her ill-tempered husband. A few months earlier, he had issued an ultimatum — either the father went or the husband departed. This was the point at which she became convinced that her father was dying from a serious heart condition.

This was a human tragedy concealed by a chief complaint. The imagined problem had nothing to do with the reality affecting this sick family.

THE HIDDEN CLUE

I am convinced that listening beyond the chief complaint is the most effective, quickest, and least costly way to get to the bottom of most medical problems. A British study showed that 75 percent of the information leading to a correct diagnosis comes from a detailed history, 10 percent from the physical examination, 5 percent from simple routine tests, 5 percent from all the costly invasive tests; in 5 percent, no answer is forthcoming.

This result is not surprising. After all, the patient is the bank, the only place where the money is deposited. To get to the money one must deal credibly with the bank. Some of the most challenging medical problems I have encountered could be solved only through information provided by the patient.

The time invested in obtaining a meticulous history is never ill spent. Careful history-taking actually saves time. The history provides the road map; without it the journey is merely a shopping around at numerous garages for technological fixes. When detailed historical data are lacking, a doctor may be paralyzed into inaction or resort to improper therapeutic options.

Before the days of ambulatory electrocardiographic monitoring, I was standing by the bed of a patient who had intractable arrhythmia. The man was disabled by rapid heart arrhythmia several times daily, but having been hospitalized for a week, exposed not a hint of the disorder. Rounding with house staff, I commented with frustration, "If we could only precipitate the arrhythmia, the problem would quickly be solved." The patient, who was listening, looked puzzled and said, "Doc, I know how to bring it on."

"How so?" I asked with embarrassment.

"By standing up straight and bending over to tie my left shoe."

The answer sounded outlandish, so I humored him and encouraged a demonstration. He bent over, and lo and behold, precipitated the tachycardia we had helplessly been awaiting.

Frequently a patient not only tells what is wrong but provides information suggesting how best to manage the problem. A college president consulted doctors over a decade for ventricular tachycardia, a very serious heart-rhythm disorder. He had been hospitalized in many of this country's leading centers and more than a dozen different medications had been tried, all to no avail. On his first visit, I asked at what time of day the arrhythmia occurred. He responded that it was almost consistently in the morning, before he raced off to work. When questioned further, he stated that it happened between about 7:30 and 8:30 A.M.

After gathering more information, I told the patient that his problem would be solved if he set an alarm clock to 5:30 A.M., and as soon as he awoke, took a double dose of an anti-arrhythmic medication before going back to sleep. I advised that he take no more of this medication during the day. Following this counsel for the next eight years, he was totally free of arrhythmia.

It is astonishing that no doctor had tried to identify the precise time the arrhythmia occurred. Taking a much larger total dose of the same drug at intervals around the clock, as he had been told to do, provoked many adverse symptoms without containing the arrhythmia. The reason for the failure was straightforward. His evening dose had dissipated by early morning. The morning dose was taken too close to the onset of the disordered heart rhythm for the drug to have reached an effective therapeutic blood level. Furthermore, he needed a higher dose at that time to prevent the arrhythmia from breaking through. No amount of technical wizardry could have resolved his difficult problem. The solution would never have been unearthed without the information the patient provided.

WORDS OF WIVES

History-taking is always improved when another member of the family, especially a spouse, is present. Most doctors prefer to see patients alone, explaining that it is easier to focus on essentials and retain control. Another justification is that a patient alone is less inhibited. Intimate problems can be addressed which would otherwise remain undiscovered.

I don't agree. Of course, I first ask the patient if he or she wishes the spouse to be present during the interview. The reply is invariably in the affirmative. I am convinced that such a presence speeds rather than impedes the flow of important information and shortens the time required to get to know the patient. Without the spouse, vital information is often forgotten; embarrassing issues are evaded. Most important, a couple provides insight about family dynamics not readily conveyed with words. By listening to the patient's responses and watching the spouse, one is immediately alerted to areas of potential trouble. Is the marriage successful or are they at each other's throats? Is there a skeleton in a family closet? Are there conflicts with children, in-laws, or other family members? Is the patient's job too frustrating — a no-exit situation — or too painful to discuss? These and many more problems are quickly brought to light when husband and wife are together.

Many of the examples I cite demonstrate the importance of a wife in focusing on the essential issues that bring a patient to a doctor or in conveying more truthfully what is transpiring. I say "wife" rather than "husband" for several reasons. Women generally are more knowledgeable and informative about a husband's health than the other way around. In addition, coronary disease, which makes up a good part of my practice, is far more prevalent among men. Also, a husband is often unwilling or unable to take time from work to accompany his wife. A woman invariably finds the time to be with her husband.

At times, lesser matters than Mrs. Goyang's staring at the ceiling come to light only when the wife is present. When I questioned one man about sex, he promptly responded, "Sex no problem."

At each yearly visit, we went through the same exchange.

"Sex?" I would ask.

"Sex no problem," he replied instantly.

After he had been my patient for about five years his wife came along for the first time. During interval history-taking, when I posed the same old question about sex, he gave the same answer. His wife appeared startled and looked quizzically at him.

I asked, "How, exactly, do you punctuate that sentence?"

He answered with some embarrassment, "Sex *no*. Problem!" He defended himself by saying, "For five years I have been giving the same answer, but you were not paying attention."

I am aware that with aging a doctor's listening becomes transformed. Facts and data slip by more rapidly, making me wonder why time is spent in acquiring these gossamers. However, losses are compensated by gains. I focus more on the interstices between words, on meanings imbedded in pauses, on inflections, on words that emerge haltingly. Silence usually communicates essence. One learns to decipher an unspoken subtext. Intuition is sharpened, enabling one to grasp a new order of complexity, to absorb the subliminal and integrate it almost instantly into a gestalt embodying the true other. The pity is that it takes a lifetime to gain the clinical wisdom that enables a doctor to comprehend the essential medical problem with an economy of discourse.

CHEST PAIN FROM HEARTACHE

A Californian in his mid-seventies came to me for a second opinion about his needing a bypass coronary grafting heart operation. For the past two months Mr. A. had been suffering from chest pressure that afflicted him in late afternoon and lasted until bedtime, sometimes marring sleep. The doctor in La Jolla, where he lived, had surged ahead with technology while neglecting to obtain a comprehensive history. A thallium stress test showed several areas of reperfusion, a sign of threatened mischief from impaired coronary artery blockages. While Mr. A. had coronary artery disease, the chest pain was definitely not from angina. It occurred while he was at rest, not with exercise, and was especially disabling in the evenings; lasting for many hours, it was not alleviated by nitroglycerine. These factors argued forcefully against angina. But it was not enough to know what it wasn't. One must be able to give a patient an explanation that not only makes sense but is acceptable and contributes to coping with the symptoms.

Two years earlier I had seen Mrs. A. during a single visit. She was badly crippled with a serious heart problem, but even more threatening was the end-stage emphysema she was suffering. She was a lady in the true sense, exuding an abundance of dignity and charm. Although in a wheelchair, with every breath an effort, she had radiated a joie de vivre that left me breathless with admiration and respect.

"Every day is a joy when I wake up and see the sunshine. I count my blessings, which are many. Above all is having a companion for nearly fifty years whom I continue to love." She stated this with a smile, as though she was savoring this delectable fact at the very moment.

All this came to mind as I listened to Mr. A.'s complaint of chest pain. I also recalled quite vividly, as though she had just told me, that the smog and pollen-filled air in Texas, where they had been living at the time, made her health problems much worse, and they were planning to move to California.

I asked Mr. A. when they had moved to California. "January twenty-eighth," he replied — exactly two months earlier, the very time he began to have the chest pains. I stored this little fact away for later use, and my history-taking turned to family and friends. Their children were still in Texas, as were most of their friends.

I started to sense an aura of depression. When I inquired about sleep, Mr. A. stated that out of concern for his wife, he seldom slept through the night. Frequently he rubbed her back to help her breathe. He made it clear that they were completely homebound, but he did not mind because it was quite a hassle for them to go out. She was bedridden and wheelchair-bound. Social engagements frequently had to be canceled when Mrs. A. had a bad spell of breathlessness and became completely oxygen-dependent.

An exercise test on a motorized treadmill did not provoke any chest discomfort. Surprisingly, Mr. A. persevered a little more than ten minutes before being halted by fatigue. This was an exceptional performance, even for a man several decades his junior. It reflected the two hours of intense exercise that he performed daily "to keep my mental balance."

When we met in the consultation room for a summary, with his son present, I began with the facts. "You have a remarkably sound cardiovascular apparatus; the coronary artery disease demonstrated several years ago by the angiogram has remained absolutely stable. You do not have angina pectoris. The chest discomfort is unrelated to your heart, but I am surprised that it is so mild." He looked puzzled as I continued. "Given the impossible bind you are in, I admire enormously how soundly, calmly, and humanely you are handling your difficult plight. You moved to California for your wife's sake. You are now bereft of any support system. Your duty begins before sunrise and does not end until after sunset. You doctor around the clock. Even a hardy young intern many years your junior would find it hard to take such a grueling, unending ordeal. The heaviness in the chest coming late in the afternoon is the body language summarizing the stress you are being subjected to. It is worse at night because all of us feel more helpless in the dark."

As I spoke, Mr. A. turned away from me as his shoulders convulsed; the son unashamedly wiped his own eyes. I went on to make some concrete suggestions on how to enlarge the circle of responsibility. As he was leaving, Mr. A. indicated that he would shorten the interval between visits. When next he returned, he was entirely free of chest discomfort.

Attentive history-taking does more than add details. It is the most important aspect of doctoring. While obtaining a history takes time, no time is more productively spent. Ultimately it lays the foundation for a human relationship between patient and doctor based on mutual respect. The time invested is but a small sacrifice for curing as well as healing.

2

Listening through Touching

LEWIS THOMAS, in *The Youngest Science*, comments wisely that touching is the oldest and most effective tool in doctoring.* This statement rings true for me. I am persuaded that touching a patient provides advantages to the internist, as compared with the psychiatrist who sits removed and merely listens. Touching is a means for gaining significant insights. Frequently the conversation at a first interview is impersonal. The relationship with the patient often alters dramatically after the physical examination. The remoteness dissipates, supplanted by comfortable easy-flowing conversation. Material that was neither divulged nor suspected emerges without much probing. Questioning is no longer resented. A stranger a few minutes earlier opens up with intimacies usually earned only through long and trusting friendship.

Doctors in the middle ages placed an ear against a patient's abdomen or chest wall to listen to bowel sounds or heart rhythms. Some grew adept at detecting loud murmurs. One could hardly come closer to the patient. The ear riveted to the chest wall was a display of human affinity. "It is hard to imagine a friendlier human gesture, a more intimate human signal of personal concern and affection, than these close bowed heads affixed to the skin," Thomas wrote, deeming this to be one of the great advances in the history of medicine.

* Lewis Thomas, *The Youngest Science: Notes of a Medicine-Watcher* (New York: Viking, 1983).

The first touch, when doctor meets patient, should be the handshake — a greeting of welcome, a gesture of hospitality, and a signal of readiness to accept someone as a fellow human being. For the doctor it is a veritable treasure trove of information. In the first place, the entire transaction is a cameo depiction of character and psychological state, providing important information: Is the hand extended with gusto, held out tremulously with diffidence, or advanced reticently, only in reluctant response to the doctor's outstretched hand? The firm handshake of a person who is in control contrasts with the slippery, barely touching fingers of an uncertain or troubled patient.

A treatise could be written on the diagnostic value of a handshake. For example, a sixty-five-year-old man came to see me in midwinter because of troubling heart palpitations. On shaking hands I was intrigued by his warm, slightly sweating palm. It was blustery cold outside and I commented that he must have nice warm sheepskin gloves. He replied that he rarely wore gloves. I immediately suspected an overactive thyroid, which was later confirmed by appropriate laboratory tests. When the thyroid is overactive the metabolism of every organ is increased, the skin, receiving more blood flow, is warm and flushed, while the heart, beating rapidly, is predisposed to arrhythmias.

As Thomas pointed out, the doctor's oldest skill was the laying-on of hands. Until this century relatively little else could be done in most cases. With the passage of time, this simple act of compassion was transformed into an art. Eventually it grew into a scientific skill, and the hand became an important diagnostic instrument. The pulse was felt for heart rate and heart rhythm — the leading physician in Roman times, the Greek Galen, was the first to analyze heart rhythm by feeling the pulse. Palpating the chest wall could reveal the size of the heart or the existence of an aneurysm, the neck an enlarged thyroid gland or the presence of abnormalities of the aortic valve. The belly furnished an abundance of information for sensitive fingertips — an enlarged spleen or liver, a dilated aorta; the presence of an inflamed appendix and tumor could first be detected by a palpating hand.

While I have never mastered the art of listening with my ear against a belly or chest, I have been rewarded on many occasions by carefully palpating a chest wall. My claim that one may at times detect an ongoing heart attack is generally greeted with disbelief by colleagues. However, about thirty-five years ago, on a hot July day, I did just that. When two new postdoctoral fellows had arrived on my service at the Peter Bent Brigham Hospital, the first patient we visited was a robust, middle-aged athlete, a former quarterback from Salt Lake City. He'd had his gallbladder removed that day, and ours was a routine postoperative visit. Vital signs were intact, but on laying my hand on the man's thick chest, I detected a paradoxic heave of the upper outer left chest wall that normally is devoid of any movement. I whispered to my staff that we should immediately order an emergency electrocardiogram, since a heart attack might be in progress. The fellows looked at each other dumbfounded. The more cynical and brash of the two let go with a low-pitched guffaw, suggesting I was putting them on.

We proceeded with rounds. About twenty minutes later there was a code on the ward we had just visited and we learned that the man we had just seen had had a cardiac arrest. He did not respond to resuscitation and a postmortem showed a massive heart attack. The two fellows, cowed and puzzled, regarded me with inordinate awe, at least for a few days.

Another method of touch is percussion, introduced by the eighteenth-century physician Leopold von Auenbrugger, to further probe the body's mysteries. Young Leopold watched his father, a wine merchant, tap barrels to determine how much wine remained in them. When he became a doctor, he applied the same tapping to body cavities. Percussion helps detect consolidation of lung tissue (such as occurs in pneumonia) and fluid in the chest and abdominal cavities, and provides an approximation of heart size. Further helping to connect doctor and patient, it was a confidence-promoting measure.

TOUCHING DEEP SECRETS

I am reminded of two patients in whom careful history-taking divulged little that was relevant. However, during the physical examination, an act of communion through touching, a flood tide of shocking information emerged.

The first, an eighty-five-year-old woman, presented complaints of multiple aches. The history was completely unrevealing and matter-of-fact, but she appeared introspective and shrouded by overwhelming sadness. During the physical examination, in a leap of wild imagining as I was gently squeezing her forearm, I asked, "If you want me to help, why are you so secretive?" As the words slipped out, I regretted being so brazen and intrusive. Her body shivered, she looked like cornered prey; head moving from side to side in a softly articulated, barely audible murmur, she said, "*No*, oh no." After an interminable pause, she half asked and half affirmed: "You know, then?" I remained silent, not aware of what I was supposed to know and not prepared for what was coming. Looking straight ahead, focused on some remote point of grief, she related a tale suppressed over many years.

Reared in a proper, well-to-do Boston family, she consorted, at age nineteen, with an older man in his mid-thirties. Her parents, vehemently opposed to this relationship, warned that she would come to a bad end. When she realized that she was pregnant she obtained a job on a Vermont farm. There she delivered the baby by herself, then dropped the newborn down an old well. She remained a gentle, ghostly spinster, never revealing, until that moment, that she had murdered her own baby.

The other patient was a Brazilian woman from Rio de Janeiro, petite, very intense, attractive, who appeared to be in her late forties but was actually sixty-one. She consulted me because of numerous episodes of paroxysmal atrial tachycardias. Her demeanor indicated high society, and she was obviously a woman who had been accustomed to having her own way from birth. She commanded adherence to her whims and was not to be crossed. When she told me that she had been receiving psychotherapy in New York, commuting there several times a year for this purpose, I asked, "And why not in Rio?"

"Oh, it is too small a community; gossip is our major industry."

I tried to discover the roots of her emotional turmoil through painstaking history-taking, but to no avail. She indicated that she was devoutly Catholic and had one child, a married son. When I reached the aspect of history dealing with her marital life and sex, she deflected the questions by stating categorically that these issues had nothing to do with the heart. Furthermore, this was the province of her psychiatrist.

I offered a long exposition of our research work on the connection between brain and heart and how treatment is frequently unsuccessful when these relationships are ignored. She listened detachedly and did not respond. But after a thorough physical examination something changed. No longer aloof, she was eager to talk as I led her to be fluoroscoped. In those days fluoroscopy was carried out in a pitch-black room; to adapt to the dark, one wore red goggles. She was standing against the cold slab while I moved the fluorescent screen over her chest. I was sitting very close and our bodies were nearly touching. As I turned on the fluoroscope, there, lying over her heart, was a large crucifix that she had not removed. At that instant she asked, "Doctor, can you get an abnormal heart rhythm from masturbation?"

I shut off the fluoroscope but did not switch on the light. In the utter darkness, sounds were amplified. I spoke in a whisper. "A very interesting question. Why do you ask?"

Low-keyed and matter-of-fact, she began to talk.

Madly in love, she had married forty-three years earlier. The wedding was one of the most spectacular in Rio, but after the ceremony her husband disappeared, leaving to visit his mistress on their wedding day! As she told me this, her voice betrayed emotion for the first time. She learned about her husband's betrayal the following week and swore never to have sexual relations with him again. Instead, she masturbated frequently. An orthodox Catholic, she would not consider divorce.

"Have you discussed this with your psychiatrist?" I asked.

"No, I haven't told it to anyone else," she answered. "This cross I must bear alone. It is my fate."

Touching has become perfunctory as the physical examination has grown increasingly cursory. The distancing began 176 years ago, when the French physician René Laënnec introduced a rolled cardboard tube that evolved into the stethoscope. While it vastly enhanced listening power, it broke a bond of intimate contact. The journey of medicine as a science has taken us far and most of it is positive. It would be nonsensical to crave a return to the bowed head with ear tuned to body noises for deducing malfunctions in the heart or lung. But scientific progress and technological innovations do not mandate jettisoning those qualities which enhance intimacy and promote caring. "Medicine is no longer the laying on of hands, it is more like reading signals from machines," Lewis Thomas wrote. What must be deplored is the loss of the close bond between doctor and patient.

3

Mind and Heart

IF LISTENING is so important, what is it that the doctor is listening for? Fundamentally, the aim is to understand the medical problem as well as the person behind the symptoms. The latter is what usually needs clarification. During history-taking, the doctor begins to know the patient as a human being. This means not only learning the basic facts about family, education, work, and the like, but also comprehending character, namely, "what makes Sammy run." The focus is on inordinate emotional stresses and psychological coping behaviors.

From the dawn of medicine, physicians have been aware that emotions can predispose a person to disease as well as affect its outcome. Cardiologists have learned that psychological stresses can influence the most intimate aspects of heart function. Behavioral stresses may speed the heart rate, raise blood pressure, reduce coronary artery blood flow, enhance the electrical irritability of the heart, and change the contractile properties of the myocardium, the muscle that pumps the blood. In fact, a perturbed mind can disrupt heart rhythm, predispose to angina pectoris, precipitate a heart attack, and provoke sudden cardiac death.

Thus, history-taking involves not merely learning about a disease, but grasping what is agitating a patient's mind. Nowadays we hear much about the mind, as though it were a new discovery, but in the history of science the mind long antedates the physical brain. Until the late nineteenth century, the mind was regarded as inseparable from the body, but as science gained dominance, dualism began to pervade medical thinking. The mind was sundered from the body and seemed a thing apart, a spiritual rather than a scientific entity. The body, as an object for scientific inquiry, can be probed, studied, penetrated, dissected, and objectified. Its fluids and secretions can be sampled and chemically analyzed. A pathological process can be identified, its progression predicted, the response to treatment assessed and quantified. All this is within the domain of science. This is not the case with the mind, for its tonalities are perceived and imagined rather than measured. To date there is no methodology that objectifies perturbed inner states expressed by feelings of anxiety, tension, inadequacy, and depression. These emotional states are risk factors for illness, shaping the presentation of sickness, determining its progression and the speed of recovery.

When psychological problems dominate an illness, as is commonly the case, the general physician often diagnoses psychoneurosis, a wastebasket term to which are consigned a host of conditions lacking scientific explanations. The patient is seriously shortchanged by this dismissal of the psychological aspects of illness, and ignoring the emotional dimension lessens a doctor's capacity to ameliorate a chronic disease. Drugs may improve some of the presenting symptoms for a time, but the underlying illness is not healed. Inattention to the psychological domain fractures medicine at its heart by divorcing curing from healing. This common practice has injured the image of physicians and considerably diminished their standing in society.

My preoccupation with psychology antedates my interest in medicine. As a high school student I devoured Freud and became absorbed in psychoanalysis, which I regarded as a key scientific advance of this century. As previously noted, I intended to become a psychiatrist, but soon after I entered medical school, psychiatry lost its luster for me. I was shocked to discover how subjective it was and disenchantment foolishly pushed me to another extreme. On graduating from medical school, I spent a miserable year dissecting dead bodies at the

Grace New Haven Hospital as an intern in pathology. However, though overtly discarding the formal discipline of psychiatry, I did not lose my fascination with the mind-brain relationship, the core of what makes us human.

After becoming established in academic cardiology, I returned to my early scientific infatuation. It is strange how life's cycles and epicycles lead one back to youthful fixations. Although I quickly abandoned my initial interest in psychiatry, my life's work has culminated in a preoccupation with the psychological aspects of illness. While this was neither deliberate nor consciously planned, my research work over three decades has increasingly focused on exploring connections between mind and heart. No doubt what one does is largely the result of who one is. I have returned to my early beginnings as though mandated by unswerving fate.

My interest in the psychological was constantly rearoused by clinical observations and by studying the encyclopedic literature. A report in an Indian medical periodical, "Killed by the Imagination,"* left an indelible impression early in my career.

A Hindu physician was authorized by prison authorities to conduct an astonishing experiment on a criminal condemned to death by hanging. The doctor persuaded the prisoner to permit himself to be exsanguinated — bled to death — assuring him that death, though gradual, would be painless. The convict, on agreeing, was strapped to a bed and blindfolded. Vessels filled with water were hung at each of the four bedposts and set up to drip into basins on the floor. The skin on his four extremities was scratched, and the water began to drip into the containers, initially fast, then progressively slowing. By degrees the prisoner grew weaker, a condition reinforced by the physician's intoning in a lower and lower voice. Finally the silence was absolute as the dripping of water ceased. Although the prisoner was a healthy young man, at the completion of the experiment, when the water flow stopped, he appeared to have

* N. S. Yagwer, "Emotions as a Cause of Rapid and Sudden Death," *Archives of Neurology and Psychiatry* 36 (1936): 875.

fainted. On examination, however, he was found to be dead despite not having lost a single drop of blood.

Over the centuries, a wealth of similar anecdotes has been amassed. The medical profession has long known that nervous activity influences every part of the body. Nearly 350 years ago, William Harvey, discoverer of the circulation of the blood, stated: "Every affection of the mind that is attended with either pain or pleasure, hope or fear, is the cause of an agitation whose influence extends to the heart."

During my professional career, I have also been concerned with the problem of sudden cardiac death, an important cause of fatality in the United States. It was therefore quite natural to combine my two preoccupations by investigating whether psychological stresses were triggers for instantaneous cardiac death. Long before doctors focused on this association, the folklore of diverse societies and cultures concluded that stressful emotions can cause sudden death. Ordinary language is freighted with such expressions as "he died of a broken heart," a "weight on the heart," the "heart was full to bursting," each alluding to unbearable emotional stress. In contemporary times, press reports have associated sudden death with intense emotions. However, the medical profession had been at a loss whether to ascribe these beliefs to folklore or folk wisdom and remained deeply skeptical despite a wealth of epidemiological data implicating emotions in cardiovascular death.

At the beginning of this century, Karl Pierson, the father of modern biostatistics, studied the death dates of spouses on cemetery headstones in Britain, Holland, and Germany and noted that husbands and wives tended to die within a year of one another. This seeming coincidence has since been steadily corroborated. Those suffering the loss of a spouse or a close family member are at higher risk for cardiac death. Since Pierson's day, numerous epidemiological investigations have shown diverse social stresses to be associated with increased coronary artery disease and death. One carefully documented study reported on the changes in cardiovascular morbidity and mortality of Japanese who moved to Hawaii and then to the San

Francisco Bay area. In Japan, coronary artery disease is infrequent. It increased among those who settled in Hawaii and equaled the high American prevalence rate for Japanese-Americans residing on the West Coast. The usual explanation is that the Japanese succumb to unhealthy American habits like a high-fat diet, increased tobacco consumption, and sedentary lifestyles. The striking fact, however, is that West Coast Japanese who resist assimilation, even when they match American cholesterol, blood pressure, and smoking levels, have a low prevalence of heart disease and cardiac death. If maintaining Japanese culture defends against the ravages of heart disease, psychological processes must play a key role in the immunization.

Similar data on the impact of stress, in this case related to employment, have been generated in surveys among London civil servants. Executive and administrative personnel enjoy the highest life expectancy, while those who engage in menial blue-collar jobs have an astounding fourfold rate of cardiovascular mortality. Correction for known risk factors, assuming that lower economic classes indulge in unhealthy lifestyles, does not alter these striking statistical disparities. Again the implication is that psychological factors associated with unsatisfying low-paying jobs constitute risk factors for heart disease. This is also true in the United States.

In addition to occupation, level of education is an effective predictor of life expectancy. College graduates live longer on average than those who have only completed elementary school. And if a stressful job is a risk factor for cardiac disease and death, so is the lack of a job. In the United States, each percentage point of unemployment increases coronary artery deaths by six thousand annually. On the positive side, heart disease exacts a lower toll among those who are happily married, have broad-based social networks, live in close-knit families, have interesting hobbies, and harbor a diversity of interests. Among those who live alone, pet ownership lessens risk. A heart attack is likely to have a far better outcome for people with social connections. For example, those who live with a spouse, family member, or friend have, within six months of a heart attack, half the recurrence rate of those who live alone. Indeed, among patients with coronary heart disease, living alone carries the same risk as having congestive heart failure, one of the most serious complications of a heart attack. These facts argue strongly for the power of mind to affect heart disease and its outcome.

Other supporting data come from natural disasters and wars, which impose profound psychological stresses, with a resulting increase in cardiac morbidity as well as mortality. For example, the severe 1981 earthquake in Greece was followed within twenty-four to forty-eight hours by a trebling of cardiovascular deaths. The Iraqi missile attack on Israeli cities provoked an increase in cardiac mortality. The day the first Scud missiles landed saw a remarkable peaking in heart disease deaths, which increased by 58 percent, women being twice as vulnerable to dying as men.

While negative life events predispose to cardiac morbidity and fatality, positive and meaningful events may postpone death. Two San Francisco psychologists, D. P. Phillips and E. W. King, have suggested that those who are about to die may enter a "bargaining" phase in which they ask God to postpone their death until the arrival of an important occasion, such as a birth, wedding, anniversary, religious holiday, and the like. If some people are indeed able to postpone death, there should be a dip in the fatality record before a meaningful psychosocial event and a peak just afterward. Phillips and King investigated the distribution of deaths among Jews and non-Jews around the time of Passover, an important Jewish holiday. They found that elderly Jewish males are much less likely to die the week before Passover. This observation was consistently noted every spring over a nineteen-year period for which data were available.

Like Passover for Jews, the Harvest Moon Festival each fall is a joyous occasion for elderly Chinese women, who experience a postponement of death during the week preceding the holiday. This was followed by a surge in deaths the week after the holiday.

As I commented earlier, people appreciate the critical relationship between stress and the heart. When I ask someone which day of the week one is most likely to drop dead, the answer is invariably Monday. Because a majority deem work an unpleasant chore, the first day of the week is perceived as the most stressful. This public impression has been corroborated in a large Canadian study that followed more than fifteen hundred males for more than forty years.* While cancer deaths were distributed equally throughout the week, this was not true of sudden cardiac death: Monday saw twice as high an incidence as any other day of the week.

Clarifying the role of psychological factors in sudden cardiac death (SCD) was a daunting challenge. Even the lesser task of objectively defining stress is quite elusive. What is stressful to one person may be pleasurable to another. Psychological descriptors of stress or personality characteristics are largely verbal and subjective. Another obstacle in researching mind-brain relations is that medical thinking is dominated by mechanistic models in which cause and effect are viewed as being linked either spatially or temporally. This is true in the macrophysical domain where stresses and their consequent strains are measurable. But in the case of the complex psychological-brain domain that I refer to as higher nervous activity, a stimulus, whether innocuous or stressful, does not exist as an absolute divorced from the qualities imparted by its perception. For example, if we are worried about a child's being out late at night, a telephone ring may provoke an ominous premonition of an accident; suddenly the heart is racing, blood pressure is up, and we are in a sweat. Yet at most other times the telephone ring does not promote psychological arousal.

Whether a particular event proves emotionally stimulating and anxiety provoking is determined by a host of factors including genetic predisposition, early childhood experience, and lifelong processes of conditioning, as well as an array of social

* S. W. Rabkin et al., "The Electrocardiogram in Apparently Healthy Men and the Risk of Sudden Death," *British Health Journal* 47 (1982): 546–552.

and cultural forces. All these shape that unique and highly individual psychological prism that refracts daily events. Furthermore, an aversive stimulus is rarely singular, overt, and substantial. More frequently it is chronic, intermittent, and seemingly insignificant. In addition, psychological responses may be long delayed, thereby obscuring our ability to detect the causal connections.

In the investigation of the complex issue of the role of stress in sudden death, a first step was to determine whether electrical stimulation of particular brain centers predisposed experimental animals to ventricular fibrillation (VF), the electrically deranged heart rhythm that is the cause of SCD. Working with anesthetized animals and probing with special electrodes, we stimulated the small pea-size brain center that controls heart rate. The underlying hypothesis was that electrically stimulating such critical brain centers would overwhelm an already injured heart and provoke VF.

I entrusted this task to Dr. Jonathan Satinsky, a postdoctoral clinical fellow. His relative inexperience was an asset, since he was unfazed by this daunting project that more knowledgeable fellows had rejected. Tooling up and familiarizing himself with the complex anatomy of the brain required a year of arduous work. Fortunately, this proved to be time well spent, for the results were far more convincing than we had expected.

In an anesthetized animal, VF consistently follows the abrupt closure of a large coronary artery. We selected a small coronary vessel which when occluded rarely resulted in VF. In control animals, the coronary vessel was closed off without brain stimulation, though the brain electrode was properly positioned. Only 6 percent of these control animals developed VF as a result of the coronary artery occlusion. However, when the two events were simultaneous, namely, the brain was electrically stimulated while the artery was being narrowed and then totally occluded, the incidence of VF was 60 percent, a tenfold increase.

We soon learned that one does not have to stimulate central-brain structures to predispose the heart to VF. The noxious stimuli from the perturbed brain are transmitted via nerves in the sympathetic limb of the autonomic nervous system. Stimulating these nerves en route to the heart resulted in a similar outcome without the need to probe blindly the mazelike network of neurons in the brain.

As the site for stimulation, we selected the stellate ganglion, the transformer-type way station in sympathetic nerve traffic from brain to heart, located accessibly in the neck. Dr. Richard Verrier, a physiologist, directed this research in my laboratory. When the heart was deprived of blood flow by the slow constricting of a coronary vessel, heart rhythm remained intact. But when the constriction was accompanied by stellate ganglion stimulation, VF consistently resulted. To be certain that the outcome was the direct consequence of sympathetic neural activity, we had to prevent other effects of the stimulation such as the invariable rises in heart rate and blood pressure. When these changes were precluded, stellate ganglion stimulation still enhanced cardiac vulnerability for VF. Further experiments proved that the malignant arrhythmia resulted from action of noradrenaline directly on heart muscle. Noradrenaline is the sympathetic neurotransmitter, the chemical substance released in minute amounts by nerve terminals that stimulate an electric pulse and serve as the basis for neural information transfer.

The awesome power of sympathetic nervous activity, the system that informs body organs about stressful emotions, was brought home to me in an experiment in which the coronary circulation was completely intact, yet merely stimulating the sympathetic nerves to the heart could precipitate ventricular fibrillation. There is a discrete time in the cardiac cycle when an electrical stimulus of sufficient strength can provoke VF, which is referred to as the ventricular vulnerable period (see Chapter 13). In this experiment we found that sequential weak electrical stimuli, too weak to perturb the heart even when delivered in the ventricular vulnerable period, consistently induced VF when coupled with sympathetic nerve stimulation via the stellate ganglion. Each form of stimulation by itself was completely innocuous, yet the combination of simultaneous electric stimulation of sympathetic nerves and heart muscle caused arrhythmic death.

Having found that higher nervous activity was able to provoke potentially fatal disorders of the heartbeat, we were ready to tackle a much more difficult problem, the question of whether behavioral and psychological factors can do the same. We faced two methodological problems, one related to VF, the target arrhythmia of our experimentation, and the other to selecting an appropriate psychological stress for dogs, our experimental model. To study their psychological factors, animals have to be awake and unsedated. Here we faced a seemingly insuperable problem. It seemed logical to expect that in order to study ventricular fibrillation, we had to induce it. However, inducing VF is extraordinarily traumatic, particularly when accompanied by painful resuscitative maneuvers; it would not only be inhumane, but the pain and agitation of the animal would preclude meaningful investigation of psychological variables.

How then is one to track for susceptibility for VF? I concluded that it was necessary to devise an appropriate end point that could serve as a surrogate for vulnerability to VF without ever overstepping the bounds by provoking VF itself, the object of our experimentation. I was finally guided to a solution by the clinical understanding gained while developing the direct current defibrillator (see Chapter 13). In patients who die suddenly from VF, the malignant arrhythmia does not usually spring forth unannounced. It is preceded by oft-recurring lesser arrhythmias, showers of repeating sequences of closely coupled extrasystoles. Could these harbingers of VF serve as substitute targets for VF? Instead of aiming for VF, could we derive as much information by trying to provoke these premonitory arrhythmias? We found this to be the case under diverse psychologic and physiologic conditions, and the experimental animals remained unaware of these arrhythmias.

For the psychological stress, we initially used classic aversive conditioning. Dogs were exposed to two different environments, a cage in which an animal was left undisturbed and a Pavlovian sling in which an animal was suspended with the paws just off the ground. On three successive days, while they were in slings, the dogs received a single small electrical shock. These animals were never again shocked. Several days later, the dogs were retested in these two environments for ease of induction of arrhythmias premonitory of VF.

The animals in the sling were restless, heart rates were rapid, and blood pressures were raised. The animals in the cage appeared relaxed. It seemed incredible that merely transferring animals from the noninvasive cage to the stressful sling lowered substantially the ease of induction of arrhythmias premonitory of VF. Many weeks or even months had elapsed since the animals had been shocked, yet the memory of the minor trauma was deeply imbedded in the brain and profoundly changed cardiac reactivity. These findings demonstrated for the first time that psychological stress can substantially increase the cardiac susceptibility to potentially malignant cardiac arrhythmias.

Arrhythmias including ventricular fibrillation were provoked in animals with narrowed coronary arteries by their being placed in a formerly aversive environment. The type of psychological stress was not critical; thus, results were the same when animals were trained to push a lever in order to avoid a small electric shock. Further investigations proved that the response to stress was mediated by the sympathetic nervous system, one of the two limbs of the autonomic nervous system. This was deduced from the fact that pharmacologically blocking sympathetic neural activity protected animals from psychological-stress-induced VF.

Another piece in this jigsaw puzzle was the role of the other limb, the parasympathetic nervous system. These nerves reign in sympathetic neural activity during psychological and physical stresses. As stated earlier, the sympathetic system excites heart and blood vessels, tuning the organism to anticipate and respond to danger, what the great Harvard physiologist Walter B. Cannon termed fight-or-flight reactions. The parasympathetic system, on the other hand, has an opposite effect; the heart is slowed, blood pressure is lowered, and heart muscle grows less irritable.

The vagus nerve is the parasympathetic system's prime conduit from brain to heart. Increased vagal activity is therefore desirable and can be augmented by exercise training. The healthy, vagally conditioned cardiovascular system is marked by a slow pulse, a low blood pressure, and a more efficient heart contraction that requires less oxygen. So it was important to define the role of vagal input during psychological stress. Unraveling this complex maze of neural relationships occupied us for more than five years. One can summarize the work in a single sentence: vagus activity diminishes or entirely annuls sympathetic, neurally mediated emotional arousal, thereby protecting against sudden cardiac death.

Through animal experiments and clinical studies, we came to the conclusion that SCD is an electrical accident in a heart starved for oxygen that occurs in those with severe coronary artery disease. The triggering event, or transient risk factor, may derive from emotional and behavioral stresses. These act episodically and momentarily and are unlike the familiar chronic risk factors such as high cholesterol, hypertension, obesity, lack of exercise, and diabetes, which act continuously, occasionally over a lifetime, to predispose to coronary artery disease. The operation of transient risk factors, many originating in higher nervous activity, account for the puzzling paradox wherein someone dies suddenly but without the telltale marks of an acutely closed off major coronary artery.

The validity of the concept of transient risk factors was brought home to me by an unusual clinical experience. Mr. Jones, a thirty-nine-year-old educator, appeared to be the very embodiment of good health; he was strappingly robust in physique, never having had a sick day in his life. The year was 1974, when my clinic was a center for patients with life-threatening arrhythmias. Jones was referred from a small community hospital in Connecticut with the admission diagnosis of sudden cardiac arrest caused by a heart attack that presumably resulted from closure of a coronary artery. The diagnosis of coronary artery disease was surprising, as his cholesterol was only 160 mg/dl, he had never smoked, his blood pressure was within a low normal range, and both his parents were alive and free of heart disease.

The day of the cardiac arrest was in no way exceptional. For unclear reasons, he decided to return home early in the afternoon. While playing with his teenage daughters, he collapsed, turned blue, gasped stertorously, and then stopped breathing. Jones was given cardiopulmonary resuscitation by family members and rushed to a nearby hospital, where he was promptly defibrillated. Within twelve hours he regained consciousness and was free of neurologic deficits. Serial electrocardiograms showed none of the telltale indicators of a heart attack. Specific cardiac enzymes were also normal. He did show numerous ventricular extrasystoles for which various antiarrhythmic drugs proved largely ineffective. After twenty days in the community hospital, he was transferred to my service at the Peter Bent Brigham Hospital.

A comprehensive workup including cardiac catheterization and a coronary angiogram demonstrated a perfectly normal heart and widely patent coronary vessels. Monitoring of heart rhythm, however, showed frequent extrasystoles and short paroxysms of ventricular tachycardia, a rapid burst of abnormal beats that may be prodromal of VF.

The heart stoppage was completely mystifying. Psychiatric interviews did not point to a serious emotional derangement but did reveal considerable stress in his life. Having grown up in an impoverished working-class family, Jones was the first member to attend college. A prodigious worker, he burgeoned with intense and momentary enthusiasms and was fiercely energetic, plunging into every project with zeal. However, he was often disappointed by the failings of his associates and as a result constantly seethed with rage at real and imagined betrayals. The high titer of anger was dissipated by vigorous solitary exercise. He frequently had erotically charged violent dreams, which he disowned as not being part of his true self. From his childhood in a fundamentalist religious family, he was imbued with strong moral sensibilities focused especially on the sinfulness of sex. He denied any sexual attractions other than to his wife, admitting, however, that many of his women coworkers had made advances. He feared violent sexual behavior and loss of control. Managing aggression was the pervasive theme in his life.

A first career setback, jeopardizing his job during a downturn in the economy, occurred six months before the near-fatal episode. Filled with emotional turmoil, he found little support from his wife, who was preoccupied with her aging sick parents, or his children, who were increasingly out of the house with friends. Just before the episode of ventricular fibrillation, Jones was, in his word, "roughhousing" with his teenage daughters. Involving much sexually provocative play, it was interrupted by a neighbor's ringing the doorbell. The instant one of the daughters opened the door, he slumped to the floor saying, "I'm sorry."

During his psychiatric interviews he appeared completely at ease, but when the psychiatrist entered the room, Jones's heart rhythm was agitated by surging arrhythmias. The change was striking and readily quantifiable; the extrasystoles increased at least fourfold during the psychiatric interviews compared with the rest of the day. Complex arrhythmias that had been controlled with antiarrhythmic drugs recurred during the psychiatric sessions.

Careful monitoring of his heart rhythm over many days showed an unusual pattern. The major incidence of extrasystoles came during early morning hours, when Jones seemed to be sleeping peacefully. This was further confirmed in a sleep study that recorded brain waves, eye movements, and muscle tone, enabling the identification of rapid eye movement (REM) sleep, the stage associated with dreaming. During REM sleep, Jones had a higher frequency and more complex forms of extrasystoles than when he was awake. Generally, ventricular extrasystoles diminish and advanced forms largely disappear during sleep. That these extrasystoles were harbingers for life-threatening arrhythmias was startlingly brought home when he had a second cardiac arrest coinciding exactly with the time of REM sleep.

When again resuscitated, Jones was panicked by fear, imploring me not to let it happen again. For the first time he was ready to divulge the content of a dream, specifically the one he had had immediately preceding the VF arrest. He had dreamt he was in an automobile with a completely nude woman. The motor was running and the car was perilously perched on the crest of a cliff. As passions mounted, his behavior grew violent. Suddenly he froze, noticing in the rearview mirror an approaching policeman. Horrified at what he was doing, he stepped on the accelerator, the car plunged, and everything went black.

The critical role of higher nervous activity in the genesis of his arrhythmias was also demonstrated by the measures that eliminated them. Meditation reduced the frequency of extrasystoles, and three drugs successfully employed as antiarrhythmics, each operating differently, modified neural traffic to the heart. One drug worked directly on the brain to prevent Jones's unheralded storms of rage, which simulated epileptic fits, the second blocked sympathetic nervous activity, and the third enhanced parasympathetic vagus nerve activity. When these three drugs were combined, all arrhythmias were abolished and could not be induced by visits from the psychiatrist. To ensure against dangerous recurrences, Jones was counseled to meditate whenever his degree of tension became unbearable. A consistent exercise-conditioning program was initiated as well. More than twenty years later, he leads a full and productive life. Though he has been through a number of stressful life events, these have never again catapulted his heart into a disordered rhythm.

The unique case of Mr. Jones illustrates the profound role of the mind-brain in provoking death. The extraordinary fact was that despite intensive investigation, we were unable to discover any structural abnormalities in his heart. Never before, to my knowledge, had there been such a connection made between deep psychiatric problems and deranged beating of the heart. Jones had continually been struggling to control erotic and aggressive behavior. The two episodes of cardiac arrest were triggered by symbolic expressions of sexuality and violence. His heart rhythm was surfeited with complex advanced grades of ventricular extrasystole, harbingers and perhaps progenitors of VF. The arrhythmia could be precipitated by psychological stresses, increased during REM stage sleep, reduced by meditation, and ultimately abolished with drugs that diminish the effect of nerve traffic from the brain to the heart. Rarely does one encounter a patient who provides such extraordinary insights into a complex process that had long eluded scientific elucidation. But is Jones an exceptional case with scant relevance to the general human condition? I don't think so. I believe that his problem is a hyperbolic caricature of the pervading reality.

Stimulated by the experience with Jones, we examined the role of psychological stress in a larger group of patients who had been resuscitated from cardiac arrest or had had near-fatal ventricular arrhythmias. We reasoned that if psychological factors could indeed provoke sudden death, one should find an increased incidence of intense emotional states in the twenty-four hours preceding the onset of the life-threatening cardiac arrhythmia.

Working with Dr. Peter Reich, then director of psychiatry at the Brigham and Women's Hospital, we found that one fifth of this group of 117 patients had experienced acute psychological disturbances in the twenty-four hours preceding the cardiac event, most often less than an hour before. Among the situations leading to the psychological stress were interpersonal conflict, public humiliation, threat of or actual marital separation, bereavement, business failure, and in several instances, a nightmare. The predominant affect associated with the psychological disturbance was helpless anger. Other leading affective states included acute depression, fear, anticipatory excitement, and grief.

The fact that we were unable to identify psychological triggers in most patients does not mean that they were not present. The psychological techniques we employed were subjective and too imprecise to expose latent emotional perturbations. Nonetheless, we did show for the first time that psychological stimuli were implicated in 21 percent of patients who experienced a potential cardiac arrest.

Many people suffer deep-seated stresses that are not detected by physicians or appreciated by close family members but nonetheless are veritable cancers eroding psychological well-being. Over an extended time, harmful stressful emotions exact a biologic price in illness and premature death. How are deleterious chronic stress states to be detected objectively? This challenge is less daunting than the question of how to alleviate such stresses once exposed. It would be far better to prevent the noxious stresses in the first place, but life rarely permits this option.

One can arbitrarily pigeonhole these psychological tensions into two distinct categories: those caused by objective conditions and those that are self-generated and related to deeply ingrained, partly genetic behavior patterns. With maturing clinical experience, I have grown more disconsolate about how to ameliorate innate maladaptive behavior, be it expressed as alcoholism, cigarette or drug addiction, obesity, absence of self-esteem, obsessive work habits, or simply a lack of joy in living.

The issue demands less hubris. At this stage of inadequate psychological knowledge, perhaps we should be satisfied with reducing Prometheus's anguish rather than futilely trying to free his binding coils. The question for the cardiologist, put simply, is how to lessen potentially adverse brain nerve traffic to the heart even while the noxious stress exists, be it self-induced or outwardly provoked. A new possibility was provided by the innovative investigations of Professor Richard Wurtman and his colleagues at the Massachusetts Institute of Technology Neuroscience Division. They discovered that the synthesis of brain neurotransmitters, such as serotonin and others, can be modified by dietary means. Neurotransmitters, the chemical message units between nerves, are manufactured in nerve endings from blood-borne amino acid precursors derived from the daily diet. Therefore the concentration of brain neurotransmitters depends in part on what we eat.

We focused initially on the neurotransmitter serotonin, since it appeared to modulate nerve traffic in the sympathetic nervous system. It was unknown whether an increase in brain serotonin concentration would substantially reduce cardiac sympathetic neural activity, but when we gave animals the amino acid precursors of serotonin, we found that nerve traffic from brain to the heart was strikingly diminished. For example, it protected the heart against lethal arrhythmias that follow the abrupt occlusion of a large coronary artery. These findings have opened a new avenue for probing central neural modulation of cardiac activity, one that awaits testing in human beings.

Why have the effects of the brain and mind on the cardiovascular system been so long ignored? One reason is the difficulty in finding suitable methodologies to address the daunting complexities. The human brain is estimated to have 20 billion or more nerve cells. Each resident neuron is able to communicate with more than 10,000 neighbors. These interchanges generate up to 100 messages per second. The chatter can grow into a potentially maddening cacophony, since there are more than a thousand trillion possible connections.

Moreover, the brain is not isolated; it is showered by a flood of sensory inputs. Adding to the complexity is the fact that the brain, which defines us, may not be an adequate instrument to determine its own nature. The paradox is that if the brain were simple enough in its organization for us to understand it, we might be far too simple to do so.

In the night-bound world of insensate circumstance, we confront other impediments in comprehending mind-brain activity. The great medieval Jewish philosopher Baruch Spinoza maintained that "everything in life is a cause from which flow some effects." Poets, as well as modern chaos theory, capture this essence in the thought that a falling leaf causes a distant star to twinkle. What I label as the Spinoza effect makes interpretation of scientific data consistently problematic. In the realm of mind-brain, it becomes a veritable quagmire of obscurity. A report in the journal *Science* by Sigwart Ulrich deepened my understanding of this dimension. The question he addressed was whether there was a difference in postoperative recovery from gallbladder surgery if the window in the room in which patients convalesced faced a parking lot or a wooded area. At first blush Ulrich's question seemed fatuous, but on reflection its implications are overwhelming. He demonstrated a Spinoza effect by finding that patients recovered more quickly in rooms with a window facing a tree. These patients required a lesser dose of narcotics, healed faster, and were discharged from the hospital earlier than those randomly assigned to a room facing a desolate parking lot.

These complexities, some stated but many as yet undefined, make the climb toward the light steeper than I had imagined in my younger days. I remain persuaded that the quest, though appearing Sisyphean, must be pursued. The ancient rabbi Tarfon, writing in the Talmud, urged, "Do not flinch from a task which by its very nature cannot be completed." My conviction is undiminished that the mind-brain connection is the most challenging problem we confront in medicine.

4

Münchausen's Syndrome

LISTENING IS the quintessential first step in reaching a correct diagnosis, but as we have seen, it is not merely verbal. One must be attentive to the unspoken word, to the facial grimace that contradicts what is being said, to the inappropriate nervous twitch, to the clasping of hands, to body language generally. Comprehensive listening, always rewarding, is indispensable with patients who deliberately aim to deceive. The numerous and sundry reasons for deception may relate to drug addiction, alcoholism, or schemes to gain compensation for faked injuries or illness. The most difficult or deceptive patients are psychologically deranged people who challenge a doctor's wits to the limit. Detecting a charade behind plaintive words is an acid test of a physician's clinical skill and imagination.

These patients provide a sobering realization of how little the medical profession understands the human condition. After practicing for several decades, doctors believe that they have seen every type of behavioral vagary and eccentricity. They are in for a surprise, however, when they encounter patients with Münchausen's syndrome. This peculiar entity is named after a German soldier of fortune who, in the eighteenth century, wrote a series of far-fetched tales of phony exploits. Those with the condition go to extraordinary lengths to feign a serious medical disease. Their behavior appears to be bizarrely motivated and at times beyond the victims' control, though the symptoms and medical findings are produced intentionally. Many of these patients are consummately gifted in weaving a skein of deception. Some are drug addicts out for an easy fix, others hysterics, sociopaths, or people stressed by wrenching life situations without seeming escape except through pretending illness.

No less gullible than the lay public, doctors are almost invariably taken in. Judging by the success of Münchausen patients in peddling their fake illnesses, one might conclude that the medical profession is especially susceptible to con artists. Perhaps this is inherent in the doctor's work ethic, which trusts patients to be truthful when reporting their illness, by virtue of self-interest. Seeing through the sham of an experienced faker is never easy, but at times a doctor is fooled through want of inquisitiveness, common sense, or sheer obtuseness. The aberrant behavior is often grotesque and lacking ready explanation. An encounter with a Münchausen patient is consistently chastening and disconcerting, leaving the deluded physician troubled about the workings of the human mind.

I met my first case of Münchausen's syndrome while I was still an intern. The patient, a young woman who was only twenty, had just delivered her third child. Her husband, a merchant seaman, was out at sea. As her mother had to stay with the two older children, she had no visitors from whom we could gain insight into her home situation. She was kept hospitalized by a postpartum fever. We presumed that she had a uterine infection but could find no corroborative telltale signs. Hard as we tried, we failed to identify a cause for her rising temperatures.

Wraithlike, thin, pale, and given to ready tears, she appeared to be barely a teenager. Possessing a mellow disposition, she was the embodiment of innocence and the favorite of doctors and nurses in a large medical ward. Nearly every afternoon she spiked a high fever, invariably above 102 degrees Fahrenheit, and readily acquiesced to many invasive studies that turned up nothing.

Eventually, someone raised the question of factitious fever, that is, an artificially high temperature resulting from the patient's somehow manipulating the thermometer. No one really believed that this sweet thing could be manufacturing a steep temperature rise. For the sake of thoroughness, however, we moved her bed away from an adjoining radiator, switched to rectal temperatures, and had a nurse stand by while the temperature was being recorded. She continued to have episodic fevers.

Doctors experience intense discomfort when forced to admit that they don't know what is going on. A common ploy is to designate a condition with a meaningless diagnosis promoting the thought that they know exactly what is the matter. Following this tradition we labeled her problem FUO, fever of unknown origin.

Once a month we presented our difficult cases to an attending physician. Dr. L., a seasoned diabetologist and astute clinician, listened carefully and seemed perplexed that in a month we had not come up with an answer. When he arrived at the young woman's bedside, he asked only a few questions, then transformed himself into an angry, demonic ogre as he thundered, "Tell the doctors how you fake your temperature." She cowered, pulling the blanket to hide all but her frightened green eyes. She was soon sobbing, pleading, "Oh, don't force me to go home. I can't go home. I will kill my babies and myself." The agonized human outpouring was hard to take.

As we moved away from her bedside, I asked Dr. L. how he knew that the patient was able to raise her temperature. He explained that it is unlikely for anyone to have such high temperatures without other signs of infection such as a rapid heartbeat, an increased white blood count, and the appearance of being sick. She had none of these. Furthermore, he continued, this had been ongoing for several months, yet she had maintained her appetite and weight. It had to be faked; he concluded that the only way she could raise her temperature with a nurse watching must have been by massaging the thermometer with her rectal sphincter. As outlandish as this sounded, the patient later confirmed that this was the way she heated up the thermometer. She was transferred to a psychiatric ward and made much progress.

The second patient, Sam, was a twenty-seven-year-old man with festering leg sores, ulcers of the foot, and bad phlebitis, which was the source of recurrent blood clots that propagated to the lungs, endangering his life. I ministered to him as a medical junior resident at the Montefiore Hospital in New York. Sam, so young, so bright, so cultured, so humane, yet so afflicted, tore at my vitals. His left leg looked as if he had stepped on a land mine. After weeks of soaks and local and intravenous antibiotics, healthy-looking granulation tissue covered the sores. No sooner did the leg heal than it would mysteriously break open again, streaming with smelly pus. During such recurrences he had a high fever, sharp rises in blood count, and shaking chills. Sam would then scream as though tortured, calming down only after receiving large doses of morphine to which he had grown addicted. This went on for months.

Having spent many leisure moments talking with him and cheering him on, I had a good relationship with Sam. At last, sometime in February, he began making good progress. For the first time, the leg looked almost completely healed. We were congratulating ourselves and planning a party to celebrate Sam's hospital discharge scheduled for the following day. I was off duty that night. When I got to the medical ward the next morning, Sam again looked sick; he was covered with blankets, experiencing a shaking chill. He looked at me accusingly, as if I had failed him. The leg looked worse than ever.

One of the night nurses pulled me out of earshot. She said that before I commiserated too much with this wretched man, she had something important to tell me. She had difficulty containing her rage as she spoke.

"Last night, during the blizzard, I couldn't find Sam. The john was unoccupied. Since the curtain on the doorway leading to the open outside walkway was ajar, I looked there but could see nothing in the darkness. All I could make out was a light snowfall until I turned off the lights in the ward. Then I could make out the shadow of a person dressed in white. I grabbed a coat and raced out. On coming closer, I heard painful moans and recognized Sam, who was bent over and doing something. He sounded as though he was being tortured. He did not hear me coming. Then I saw the most horrible sight I had ever seen in all my nursing days. Sam was hitting his leg with a board that had a huge rusted spike at one end and ripping out part of his own leg. I screamed and he dropped the board and raced back to his bed."

"I find it hard to believe," I muttered. "Follow me," she said.

From the door to the middle of the walkway was a trail of blood in the freshly fallen snow and at the end of the trail lay the brutal instrument itself. Sam was moved to a mental hospital that very day.

Many years later, at the Peter Bent Brigham Hospital in Boston, I encountered my third Münchausen's syndrome patient. The man, in his mid-to-late forties, a former merchant marine with numerous tattoos on each arm, arrived in the coronary intensive care unit with excruciating chest pain. He was sweating but did not look very sick. His temperature was normal, blood pressure was maintained, heart rate was not rapid, and white count was in a normal range. Over a short period, he required a surprisingly high dose of morphine to relieve his discomfort. No one suspected anything fishy because he showed the early electrocardiographic changes of a possible heart attack.

When I entered the room, he was lying in bed with his eyes closed, moaning and writhing despite the narcotics. He sat up facing me, and we talked about Jack London sea stories, which interested him. The discussion may have continued for about ten minutes. Suddenly something odd dawned on me. This man had no pain at all. As our exchange grew animated, the grimacing had ceased; he was completely at ease and smiling readily. This was not the patient I had encountered on entering the room. At that very moment he seemed to have read my mind, for he instantly plunged back on the bed and once again began to moan and groan histrionically.

I told the nurses to give him a placebo, namely, a large slug of intramuscular salt water. By this time his blood enzymes had returned to normal. I suspected that he was a drug addict and decided to confront the issue directly. As I walked in, he jumped out of bed and packed his overnight bag with his few meager belongings.

I asked, "What's the rush? Let's talk. We're eager to help you."

He appeared amused and sat down. "I give you credit. You're a lot brighter than the other docs."

"What do you mean?"

"Chest pain was good for three thousand hospitalizations so far. Porphyria was even better."

"I don't understand," I said.

"It all began fifteen years ago in Seattle. I was addicted to narcotics and came into the University of Washington Hospital with severe belly cramps. The intern examined me carefully, then loaded me with Demerol. The next morning he rushed in excitedly. 'I have the diagnosis, I have the diagnosis! You have porphyria. We proved it. Your urine is dark and positive.'

"I never heard of the condition before. What do you think he did next? This idiot brings me Harrison's textbook of medicine as well as several articles on porphyria. Within a day I am an authority on this bizarre condition. The entire medical service is in a state of excitement. No one had seen an honest to goodness case of porphyria. I was even presented at grand rounds. I stayed at the hospital for two weeks and was a celebrity. The intern kept bringing new articles. So I really became sharp on porphyria. It was good for more than two thousand hospitalizations."

This claim and his others like it were outlandishly impossible, but I was not about to challenge the patient. I was more interested in hearing his intriguing replies to further questions. "But what about the urine? How could you make it positive for porphyrin pigment?" I asked.

"I was also puzzled," he responded. "But then I recalled that for a few days before my hospital admission, I had been drinking moonshine. The night before I wanted to go in the hospital, I would load up on the poison and my urine turned positive."

Eventually he had been hospitalized in nearly every hospital in the Northwest and West. He proudly said that his case had been written up in several leading medical journals. But after five to six years his ploy was discovered and porphyria was no longer a salable diagnosis, so he switched to chest pain.

About eight years later, I was covering the Brigham emergency ward for a cardiology colleague when a resident asked whether I would mind assessing a middle-aged man with a heart attack. Worried that despite large doses of narcotics, the patient was still in pain and the hospital coronary care unit was full, the resident wanted my opinion before sending the man to a medical ward.

I hastened over to find a man in his mid-fifties who looked familiar, but I couldn't place him. He presented a medical record of a recent admission to a hospital in Brooklyn. The discharge diagnosis was unstable angina, a condition resulting from severe coronary artery narrowing that augured an impending heart attack. Judging from his hospital record, he seemed to have driven doctors to distraction with uncontrollable chest pain and changing electrocardiographic patterns, but little else to go on. Reading the chart, I had a strong feeling of déjà vu. As I peeled back the blanket to examine him, the tattoos on his arms brought instant recognition. "Baron Münchausen himself!" I blurted.

He jumped off the examining cot and began to dress. "I still maintain that cardiologists are stupid," he said with disgust, "but in every barrel there's one rotten apple and it's my luck to meet up with him."

"What has happened since we last met?" I probed.

"Chest pain is far better than porphyria as an admission ticket, and I don't have to drink any rotgut."

"What do you mean?"

"I've had more hospital stays with unstable angina than with any other complaint in my life. All I have to do is give the Levine sign," he said, clenching a fist over his lower breastbone, "and it's good for several weeks. But I have to avoid being catheterized."

"You didn't succeed at the Maimonides Hospital. You had an angiogram. Wasn't that a risk?"

"My medical reading made me certain I could only be a winner. I figured for someone like me, a middle-aged male with an elevated cholesterol, the chances were probably better than eighty percent that I would have one blocked coronary. If it was negative I wouldn't go back to Maimonides, but if it was positive, what a bonanza. It was guaranteed admission to every hospital in the good old U.S.A."

He was becoming impatient with my interrogation.

"One final question," I said. "What do you do to switch your electrocardiographic T-waves around?"

"That's a trade secret." Then he added, with a chuckle, "What the shit. I hyperventilate." (Doctors have long been aware that with sustained deep breathing, one could alter a normal electrocardiogram to make it appear there was inadequate coronary circulation.) He then stalked out of the emergency ward to the surprise of a staff who had minutes before judged him to be critically ill.

The fourth and last Münchausen patient I met was the most bizarre of the lot. The patient had been transferred by ambulance to the Brigham coronary care unit from a Rhode Island hospital, where he had been admitted for blackout spells. The following morning at rounds, when I asked what brought him to the hospital, the answer was not fainting spells.

"I have mercury in my heart."

"How did the mercury get into your heart?"

"By eating doughnuts."

"Eating doughnuts?" I stuttered incredulously.

"Yes, eating doughnuts," he said quietly.

"Tell me the story."

"Well, we bought some doughnuts. My wife and son ate

them and suddenly one doughnut fell to the ground and mercury spilled out on the floor."

"How did you know it was mercury?"

"I work with it. I'm a hospital technician working with Van Slyke apparatus determining blood oxygen. We constantly use mercury. My wife and son are now critically ill with kidney failure. We're suing the bakery."

I was dumbfounded and wondered if I was dealing with a schizophrenic. As though reading my thoughts, he said, "If you don't believe me, all you have to do is take an X ray of my heart and you'll see the mercury."

I decided to humor him and took him down for cardiac fluoroscopy. When the fluoroscope was turned on, I saw to my utter astonishment a large, heavy glob of black material dancing around helter-skelter, like beads in a kaleidoscope, in his right ventricle.

There is absolutely no way for a heavy nonabsorbable metal like mercury to get into the heart. If eaten it would pass through the gut without being absorbed and end in the feces. Of course, it could get there by injection into a vein, but that would be insane. And wife and child also afflicted — no, it was impossible. I called the Providence hospital where he said his wife and child were being treated, and indeed, people with those names were patients there. The mystery deepened.

I alerted the nurses to keep a close eye on the patient, and a day later, they told me that the patient had had cardiac arrest alarms several times. His electrocardiographic trace on the monitoring oscilloscope suddenly went flat line, that is, no heart action whatever. They discovered, however, that the patient had disconnected one of the leads, for they had observed him doing it several times. After he was told that the alarms were caused by a disconnected electrode, the alarms stopped.

Believing the man to be a psychopath, we requested a psychiatric consult, but the psychiatrist, incredible as it may sound, bought the story. He told us that the patient, who was stable and without psychopathology, had complained that we mistrusted him and believed his story was faked. The psychiatrist accused me of unprofessional conduct. "After all, you proved that mercury was present in his heart."

At the next bedside medical round, I asked the nurses to collect the patient's urine, indicating that the mercury would undoubtedly be excreted from the body by the kidneys. He listened with great interest as I fabricated this cockamamy story for the staff. When we were outside the room, I explained to the nursing staff that there was absolutely no way for mercury to be excreted by the kidneys and asked them to keep count of thermometers. The following day his urine contained globs of mercury — and a vigilant nurse discovered broken thermometers wrapped in newspapers in his wastebasket.

His job as a hospital technician was to measure the oxygen content of blood by equilibrating blood with a mercury column. The patient therefore had a ready supply of mercury as well as syringes and needles. So he had the means to inject mercury into a vein, the only way it could reach the right side of the heart, where it was lodged. He must have done the same to his wife and child. Having reached this conclusion, I tried to obtain corroboration from the patient. But when I began to address the issue, he appeared hurt and shocked, and my resolve weakened. My questioning was inept and led nowhere.

The next day his bed was empty. I was informed that he had left in a huff, saying that he was shocked by the absence of professionalism in this so-called famous hospital. I called his referring physician in Providence and shared my suspicion with him. The doctor was outraged. He said he knew the patient well and that a sizable suit against a bakery accused of mixing mercury in its doughnuts was in the courts. Having been rebuffed in trying to learn more about this mysterious case, I never followed it further. I still wonder about the outcome.

The encounters with Münchausen led me to search the medical literature, where I rapidly learned of even weirder cases. A National Institutes of Health report told of a patient who surreptitiously injected herself with adrenaline, resulting in malignant hypertension and rapid heart action that simulated an adrenal tumor. Both her adrenal glands were surgically removed in a desperate attempt to save her life. Eventually her bedside table exposed the syringes, needles, and vials of adrenaline, but the damage had already been irretrievably done by the physicians who were trying to treat a difficult and insoluble problem.

Far worse are the cases of Münchausen by proxy, in which small children are victimized with a simulated illness by a parent. In one such case, a mother brought a small baby to a hospital with the complaint of excessive drowsiness and fecal vomiting. An extensive examination found the baby to be normal; sleuthing revealed that the mother was feeding the baby sedatives and its own feces.

Perhaps it is a credit to medical practitioners that they are so often fooled by those with Münchausen's syndrome, for the doctor should trust a patient's tale, just as the law assumes a person is innocent until guilt is established beyond a reasonable doubt. Understandably, this can lead an unsuspecting well-trained physician to be caught in a web of incredible deception. As the art of listening atrophies, as medicine becomes increasingly beholden to technology that cannot possibly detect the warped workings of the human mind, Münchausen patients will become more successful than in the past.

II

Healing the Patient:
The Art of Doctoring

§

5

Words That Maim

HISTORY-TAKING is the most important aspect of doctoring. The time required is a small investment in curing and healing, and a proper history is therapeutic in itself. Words are the most powerful tool a doctor possesses, but words, like a two-edged sword, can maim as well as heal.

I first witnessed the catastrophic power of words early in my medical career, shortly after I had begun fellowship training in cardiology at the Peter Bent Brigham with Dr. Samuel Levine, who, one morning a week, conducted an outpatient cardiology clinic. After an apprentice physician examined a patient, Levine would appear with an entourage of visiting doctors to assess the problem and provide guidance in diagnosis and management. Intolerant of long-winded discourse, he demanded a capsular sketch of the highlights. With one or two crisply phrased questions, Levine pinpointed the essential problem. Unlike the circuitous responses they gave to my queries, patients answered him with remarkable brevity and exactitude. The interaction, often spellbinding, was always instructive. His physical examination seemed cursory, a quick palpation of the apex of the heart, a percussing tap over the lower back of the chest, a short auscultation with his stethoscope, then a Platonic dialogue leading to a proper diagnosis. After a few encouraging words to the patient, he would move on to the next cubicle. Each session with Levine was highly charged, rarely lasted more than five minutes, yet I always learned something important.

*   *   *

It was a hot July day, before the days of air conditioning. The patient that morning, a woman in her early forties, had been a clinic patient for more than thirty years. Levine had cared for her when a childhood bout of acute rheumatic fever left her with a badly scarred and narrowed tricuspid valve. This valve is positioned on the right side of the heart, and when it is constricted, blood backs up to the liver, to the abdomen, and to the extremities, but the lungs are unaffected. Patients with tricuspid valve stenosis experience bloating rather than breathlessness and frequently develop swollen bellies simulating an advanced stage of pregnancy.

Mrs. S., while limited by fatigue when exerting, did not experience shortness of breath and slept in bed without being propped up by pillows. Although her legs and abdomen were consistently swollen with fluid, she continued to work as a librarian. She revered Levine as he admired her fortitude and stoical demeanor. The feelings of mutual high regard and affection were quite evident. I heard Levine mutter, "She is a decent and brave woman." This was as much of a compliment as Levine ever permitted himself. Mrs. S., who similarly did not gush, acknowledged that she carried on largely because of his encouragement.

On the particular day the drama unfolded, Mrs. S. was experiencing a good deal of congestion that proved resistant to diuretic injections. The water pills no longer induced the kidneys to rid her body of excess fluid. Her weight remained stable, a deceptive finding, since she was losing tissue because of a poor appetite and replacing it with fluid.

As usual she was full of optimism and expected Levine to pull a trick from his magician's hat as he had on many previous occasions. That morning Levine was overwhelmed with visitors and clearly harassed. His visit was more hurried than usual and his examination quite perfunctory. Adding to the unpleasant atmosphere were the many physicians crowding around to catch the old teacher's pearls. Levine barked out that this was a case of TS, medical jargon for tricuspid stenosis. As many doctors loitered after he left to auscult for the murmur, this usually taciturn woman grew increasingly anxious and visibly agitated. Finally, when we were left alone she murmured, "This is the end."

After I probed the reason for her disquiet, she responded, with terror on her face, "Dr. Levine said that I have TS."

"Yes, of course you have TS," I affirmed.

She began to cry quietly, as though bereft of any hope.

"What do you think TS means?" I inquired.

I almost burst out laughing at her answer. "It means terminal situation."

I told her that Dr. Levine used the term TS as an abbreviation for tricuspid stenosis, but she was no longer listening. All my attempts at reassurance were unavailing. I noticed with alarm that her breathing was becoming labored and rapid. For the first time ever she was unable to lie back, the breathlessness forcing her to sit bolt upright.

Reexamining her, I was dismayed to detect moist rales one third of the way up her chest, denoting severe congestion of the lungs. Only minutes earlier her lungs had been completely clear. A chest X ray confirmed lungs flooded with fluid, and she was promptly admitted to a medical ward. None of the usual measures, such as oxygen, morphine, or diuretics made much difference. I mustered the courage to call Levine at his private office, but after I told him what happened, it was clear from his doubting voice that my story sounded outlandish. He commented that people with tricuspid stenosis do not behave this way clinically. Levine promised to see her around 7:00 P.M., after finishing with his private patients, but before he arrived to remove the seeming hex, she was overwhelmed with pulmonary edema and died. Patients with tricuspid stenosis waste away and die slowly, not with frothing congestion of the lungs. Such congestion is invariably the result of a failing left ventricle, but her left ventricle was not diseased. As she died, I stood transfixed, helpless, and aghast.

Throughout my medical life I have encountered many similar though less dramatic reactions to a doctor's words. While still in training as a postdoctoral fellow in cardiology, I was rounding with an attending physician who was treating a man with a recent heart attack. It was early November, and the patient asked whether he would be home for Thanksgiving. The doctor responded flippantly that he would be lucky to be home by Christmas. No sooner were these words uttered than the patient lost consciousness from a sudden onset of very rapid heart action. He was resuscitated with difficulty from a near cardiac arrest.

In a large hospital it is next to impossible to insulate a patient from the words of the inexperienced or the thoughtless. Improper words can maim as readily as a physical assault. I recall visiting a patient who was recovering uneventfully from a heart attack. He appeared dispirited, his pulse was racing, and he was developing evidence of cardiac congestion. As there was no objective reason for this turn of events, I imagined that he had received some bad family tidings.

"Mr. Jackson, why so glum and depressed?" I inquired.

"Anyone would be, if told what I heard this morning," he responded.

"What is that?"

"The intern tells me that I had a heart attack, the junior assistant resident speaks of an acute myocardial infarction, the senior resident calls it a coronary thrombosis, while the attending physician indicates that I had suffered an acute ischemic episode. How in God's name, can anyone survive when there is so much wrong with his heart? Worse still," he continued, "when I ask the nurse what is happening, she tells me that I better not ask."

All those terms are different verbiage for a single condition. A patient can be driven to morbid despair, imagining the worst, after overhearing an inappropriate phrase or an ill-chosen word.

Physicians should never instill a patient with uncertainty and dread, but regrettably, they commonly do. As a cardiovascular consultant, I see many patients who seek second opinions about the advisability of coronary bypass or heart valve operations. They frequently appear anxious and filled with morbid apprehension, and I have learned with dismay that these emotions are largely iatrogenic — resulting from the language doctors use. Over the past few years I have jotted down many frightening remarks patients have recalled from an initial medical opinion. As it is my practice to see husband and wife together, I have recorded only those expressions repeated by each independently. By now I have accumulated several hundred of these maladroit sentences. The following are among the most common.

> You are living on borrowed time.
> You are going downhill fast.
> The next heartbeat may be your last.
> You can have a heart attack or worse any minute.
> The *Malach amoveth* (angel of death) is shadowing you.

I have heard numerous variations of the phrases "You have a time bomb in your chest" and "You are a walking time bomb." A cardiology consultant pointed to an obstructed artery on a coronary angiogram and informed a patient's wife, "This narrowed blood vessel is a widow maker." Another patient recalled his doctor saying, "I'm frightened just thinking about your anatomy."

A patient who had experienced a heart attack and resisted undergoing bypass operation reported, "The doctor said he couldn't guarantee that the next heart attack wouldn't be my last." The urgency of operation was conveyed to another patient by "Surgery should be done immediately, preferably yesterday."

A patient having a heart attack arrived in an emergency room with ventricular tachycardia, a rapid and serious disturbance of the heartbeat, and recalled, as the most frightening aspect of the ensuing ordeal, a resident shouting, "We're losing him! We're losing him!"

This is only a small sample, and I find it disquieting that I am encountering such maiming words with increased frequency. At times they can be readily dismissed, but occasionally they cause unending grief.

NO SECOND OPINION POSSIBLE

Mr. Glimp, not quite seventy, lived in Florida. A bald head fringed with white did not jibe with his wrinkle-free youthful countenance and smiling blue eyes, but there was a helpless sadness as he turned to his still handsome wife. "You tell him," he said after groping unsuccessfully for the proper words. His right arm was bent motionless at the elbow, the aftermath of a recent stroke. The essentials were crystal clear. But why did he wish to close the barn door after the horse had been stolen? Why had he traveled to Boston to seek my medical opinion? He had already had his bypass operation.

"Never had a sick day in my life," he stated.

"But you did have angina" — the symptom that most commonly leads to coronary artery surgery — "and that is why you had the operation?"

"What is that?" he responded.

"Chest pressure or tightness with exertion." I swept a flat hand across my breastbone, the usual locus for anginal discomfort.

"No, never," he said emphatically, his speech fractured by the stroke.

"What symptoms led to the operation?"

"Doc, let me explain. I have been healthy all my life, rarely took an aspirin. I decided to have an annual checkup. A famous clinic with a very good reputation moved in close by. I went merely for a checkup. It was Friday morning. The doctor thought I needed an exercise test for thoroughness' sake. After that he indicated some trouble and advised a thallium stress test. The clinic is very efficient, moved you from test to test without any waiting. After the thallium, he tells me that I am in big trouble. He urges that a cath should not be delayed. The doctor explains that a cath will provide a picture of my coronary arteries. I trust him because he is a very simpatico doctor. Basically he indicates that I have little choice, the cath is merely a benign test and everyone regards it as the gold standard. He did not think it was wise to delay, because a fatal heart attack could strike at any time. What choice do I have?"

All this was said haltingly, punctuated by many pauses, the words spat out with a low hiss and a fine mist of saliva.

His wife continued the tale. "By late Friday afternoon I am worried why Harold is delayed so long. After all, he went only for a routine checkup. My worry grew frantic when Dr. P. called and urged that I come right over as Harold is in 'big trouble.' I reach the clinic more dead than alive. The doctor was waiting to show me the film of Harold's coronaries. What do I know about coronaries? They looked like squirmy white worms. The doctor indicated that all the major arteries had blockages. It blew my mind when the doctor said that Harold was a walking dead man. According to the doctor we could not afford to wait. 'He could die any moment.'

"I asked, 'Where do I sign?' 'You don't have to sign, Harold already did.' I felt God was watching over us. Whew, what a close call! Now we were in good safe hands. The doctor indicated that we were in luck; there was an opening in the operating schedule the very next day, which was Saturday. While on the operating table, Harold had a massive heart attack. The doctors didn't know whether he would make it. His bad luck hadn't run out. Two days later, on a Monday, he had a stroke. Did he need the operation? The doctor was so convincing. After what happened he was very upset. He is a very nice man, not at all like a salesman, but like a real doctor. I trusted him and felt that every moment we delayed might cost Harold's life."

Mrs. Glimp appeared full of confusion and anger. Before the operation, her husband had been even-tempered, imperturbable, always upbeat. Now he moped and cried readily.

But what did these people expect from me? The damage was done. Nothing I could do would restore his injured brain or mend the badly damaged heart muscle. I asked why they did not seek a second opinion before the operation. Both looked surprised at what must have seemed like an inane question. "It was a matter of life or death to delay. And where do we go for a second opinion and why would we want it? 'He had three blockages,' the doctor said. 'It can't be worse.'"

The wife was irate. "When your house is on fire, do you ask for a second opinion? You call the fire department. That is what we thought we were doing. The doctor assured us that since Harold's heart muscle was in great shape, he would breeze through the operation."

This man had normal heart muscle function and was asymptomatic. Such patients invariably do not require operation. An operation is advised to prevent sudden death or a heart attack. However, when the heart muscle is intact, life is neither prolonged nor is a heart attack delayed by grafting the coronary arteries. It was the maiming words that had both husband and wife terrified and ready to do anything the cardiologist advised. With few exceptions, when a doctor describes a medical situation as life threatening, most people, irrespective of how little they trust the medical profession, think twice before questioning the doctor's advice.

Here are a couple of simple rules of thumb. First, when a patient is largely asymptomatic or experiences a rare episode of angina, there is rarely an urgent need for cardiac surgery. In fact, one has ample time to obtain a second opinion. Second, the more a doctor resorts to scare tactics, uses frightening terminology, and renders a dismal prognosis if some prescribed intervention is not pursued, the less credibility one should attach to his or her advice. A doctor who hangs out black crepe is either a salesperson or a charlatan who has never outgrown the infantile wish to play God. When obtaining a second opinion, indicate up front that whatever invasive procedures are counseled will be performed in another hospital. The physician who provides consultation must have no financial incentive whatsoever in the course of action being prescribed.

* * *

Doctors and their families are not immune from assaults with maiming words. Dr. S.N., a midwestern psychiatrist, had recurrent bouts of a serious arrhythmia, known as ventricular tachycardia. His physician told him that this might be fatal and urged the implantation of an electric device in his chest to reverse instantly the life-threatening rhythm whenever it occurred. The procedure was costly and not without complications and Mrs. N., wife, who had read about these implantable devices, was vehemently opposed. After a long marriage, Dr. N. valued his wife's uncanny intuition. On the other hand, he trusted his experienced cardiologist. He therefore came to Boston for a second opinion.

Through his history I learned that the attacks were short-lived and never caused him to faint or even grow dizzy. He merely experienced palpitation. Furthermore, the interval between the three paroxysms he had experienced were four or more years. I identified consistent precipitating factors that could be readily avoided, and therefore advised against the implantable device. The doctor was delighted, but his wife remained apprehensive.

When I talked to Mrs. N. alone, she told me that the cardiologist back home, in disgust over her not following his advice, asked, "Could you live with yourself when one day you wake up and your husband is lying quietly by your side, stone dead, knowing that this device would have saved his life?" She must have wondered whether a doctor would say something like that if there was not a kernel of truth in it. How could she trust my judgment, or for that matter any fallible human prognostication? I could do little to reassure her, and she left my office still fearful and anguished.

KNOCKING OTHER DOCTORS

As medicine becomes big business, as competition grows fiercer by the day, it is not uncommon to hear doctors or hospitals knocking one another in an effort to recruit patients. Criticizing a patient's doctor is extraordinarily undermining. Doctors need to be charitable to one another. Even an exceptional physician commits serious errors. Furthermore, hearing from a patient about the misdeeds of a colleague is but one side of a story. Many people maintain, quite rightly, that doctors have for too long been overly protective of one another, rarely blowing the whistle even when they are aware of malpractice or witness gouging or corruption by colleagues. This type of reprehensible behavior must never be condoned, yet one must be careful about condemning before learning both sides of a story.

Far too often I hear doctors bad-mouthing colleagues simply because they do not agree with their particular approach to a medical problem. Hearing a doctor disparage a colleague can be devastatingly demoralizing to a patient. It can also boomerang, undermining trust in the intemperate doctor, and diminishing confidence in a profession that, more than most, requires trust to be effective. Ultimately it subverts a doctor's capacity to heal.

A number of my patients have told me that their doctors reacted hostilely to their obtaining a second opinion. One New York cardiologist said, "You don't need a second opinion. I'll send you to him, but there are better ways to spend your money. Contribute to a charity."

Once I received a panicked call from a Philadelphia patient whom I had seen three months earlier. He had a difficult heart problem that was not improving. After I altered his medical program and added a new drug he was able to return to work and resume normal living.

"What happened?" I asked somewhat uneasily.

"Nothing has changed. I was feeling very well until I saw my cardiologist today. I'll repeat his exact words: 'I am rather surprised that Lown put you on this drug, which for you is a poison. Sooner rather than later you will have a major complication.'"

Though the new medical program had worked well, the patient was undermined, and it was a long haul to regain trust.

THE PERMANENCE OF HURT

Doctors don't generally recognize the persistent power of discomfiting expressions in exacting pain and contributing to illness. While I was at Johns Hopkins Medical School, there was on the faculty a maverick psychophysiologist, Dr. Horsley Gant, who was the only American student of the great Russian physiologist Ivan Petrovich Pavlov. Gant had conditioned dogs, so that their pulse accelerated and their blood pressure rose, by delivering a small electric shock to a dog's hind leg shortly after a bell was rung. After several repetitions, the mere ringing of the bell raised the heart rate and blood pressure even when the electric shock was no longer applied. This cardiovascular response to the bell did not attenuate over time. After many months, heart rate and blood pressure surged whenever the bell was rung.

Invariably, a response to a nonpainful conditioned stimulus fades with time, then extinguishes entirely if not reinforced. According to Gant, noxious-stimuli cardiac responses may be permanently evokable. He suggested that the heart acquired a memory that didn't wash with time, labeling the phenomenon "schizokinesis," a condition I have encountered in many patients.

Such reflex responses become permanently fixated in the nervous system. Unlike most neutral events, which vaporize without a trace, painful, threatening, and fearful experiences seem to be hardwired in the brain almost as though genetically programmed. Sadly, pleasurable memories vanish while distressing ones endure. Over millions of years, pain has been a major teacher, warning of danger. The neurophysiologic response repertoire to pain persists because it affords survival value. For contemporary human beings, it may have less adaptive function, though by no means has it lost the power to educate. However, memory traces of pain can misshape normal physiologic responses and be a source of morbid fixations that can undermine health.

* * *

After a long absence, Mrs. Z. had returned to the clinic for a recheck. Her dark blond hair and startlingly blue eyes graced a simple, pretty face. Her skin had the translucent pallor seen in medieval paintings of the Madonna. At forty-six she still had a sweet, girlish playfulness, perhaps because of her years as a schoolteacher. Several years earlier her doctor had found that she had frequent ventricular extrasystoles, or heart skips, and told her that, in view of her mitral valve prolapse condition, she might die suddenly at any time. Terrified, she submitted to numerous drugs, tolerating none.

When I saw Mrs. Z. for the first time, she was introspective, answering questions as though roused from a deep sleep. She trembled a good deal and at times was incoherent. She was receiving two drugs that caused lethargy, weakness, dizziness, ulcer pains, and insomnia. Despite the incapacitation, she was too frightened to discontinue the medications.

A careful evaluation revealed a completely normal heart except for mild mitral valve prolapse that was completely innocuous. Her skipped beats were best ignored and forgotten. I stopped all drugs and urged her to resume normal living and go back to schoolteaching. She woke from a nightmare. Over subsequent annual visits her personality was completely transformed. She was full of gaiety and given to easy laughter.

Five years had now elapsed. Mrs. Z. was first seen by my cardiology fellow, who described her as completely recovered. As I walked in with the fellow to reexamine her, she was reading a book about teaching English literature to high school students. We talked for several minutes about the difficulty of teaching when many youngsters consider reading passé. I continued to think about this subject and without reflection commented, "You certainly have a problem."

She sat straight up, fear written on her lovely face, her neck a livid crimson, and began to tremble as she had the first time I saw her. "What do you mean? What do you mean, Doctor?" It was more a plea of despair than a question. Within an instant this easygoing woman had been transfixed with dread.

In such instances, I have learned that one is more persuasive in addressing a fellow health worker. Instead of offering reassuring words by speaking to her directly, I turned to face my fellow, ignoring her entirely and commented on what had just transpired.

"I was referring to the problems that English teachers have in this country, and this poor woman thinks I'm referring to her heart. I thought I had convinced her that there is nothing the matter with her heart, but a hurt once inflicted lives on like an unextinguished coal. It can burst into flame any moment." She interrupted. "Oh, thank God! I'm so relieved. I thought you were talking about my heart."

WHY DO DOCTORS USE SUCH WORDS?

Why do many doctors paint dire scenarios for their patients? Elementary psychology teaches that fear is an improper way to motivate constructive behavior. Instead of mobilizing patients' inner resources, such talk dissipates hope. When fear predominates, intelligent decision making is undermined. Worse still, intense negative emotions aggravate symptoms, adversely affect healing, and impair a patient's prognosis. Sickness humbles and corrodes the sense of self, rendering patients especially vulnerable to the words of a doctor on whom they depend for healing and for staying alive.

There is no ready answer to why doctors resort to such hype. Certainly the doomsday forecasting seems to be imbedded within the social marrow of our culture. Weather is reported with anxiety-provoking bombast, and the presumption that to be heard one must be strident is becoming as pervasive in medical prognostication as in weather prediction. The bleakest possible diagnostic scenario is presented in the belief that the truth must not be blemished with equivocation. The end result is that doctors, in the words of Reinhold Niebuhr, mean well, do ill, and justify their ill-doing by their well-meaning.

Another possible explanation is that in a litigious age doctors feel compelled by legal imperatives to tell a patient the unvarnished truth. Confronted by strangers who are potential sources of malpractice suits, many doctors are persuaded that presenting the worst-case scenario insulates against later blame. In fact, such cold-blooded treatment only sows the seeds of future litigation (see Chapter 10). When a physician does not cushion a dire prediction with kindly words, the patient infers an absence of compassion. The physician thus deprofessionalizes a relationship which, to be effective, needs to be bonded by respect and trust. It is the absence of trust that paves the litigious road.

How is the physician to advise a course that involves discomfort and risk? Clearly, any problem, as Norman Cousins emphasized, can be presented as a soluble challenge or as a proverbial death sentence. Why choose the latter?

The denaturing of human values begins in medical school. In my mind it is a grievous error to start the study of medicine with dissection of a cadaver in anatomy class. To overcome the dread of this engagement, one prefers to view the repulsive formaldehyded body being dissected as an inanimate object, forgetting that it was once a fellow human being. This is the beginning of a four-year intensive indoctrination aimed at instilling scientific competence, with little time or effort being devoted to honing skills in interpersonal relations or in the cultivation of caring. The young physician is therefore neither interested nor trained in the art of listening. Later, powerful economic factors undermine a readiness to listen. Presenting a grim scenario fosters acquiescence and avoids time-consuming explanations.

I believe an additional factor operates. Physicians are rarely sure of their ground. When facing the possibility of a major intervention, it is natural for a patient to explore options. Searching questions may expose the thin veneer of medical knowledge relating to the prognosis. Based on epidemiological studies that define probability for a large group, a well-educated physician can offer precise predictions for short- or long-range outcomes. The patient, however, is not a statistic and may care little what happens in general, hungering instead for a sense of certainty about his or her own case. The doctor learns quickly that dogmatically phrased, grim formulations limit inquiry; in fact, they may shut off questioning entirely.

Dire predictions can also be a form of merchandising. The utilization of mammoth technology, some of dubious merit, requires acceptance by the consumer. Inspiring fear for one's life and limb guarantees expeditious melting of sales resistance and transforms patients into pliant customers.

What I am saying would anger many doctors who argue that they do not practice surgery, they do not split fees, nor do they themselves carry out lucrative invasive procedures. They are, of course, right. The disquieting aspect of all this is that many doctors are barely aware that they have become docile health care merchants. Doctors have been trained since medical school days to romance with technology. Their education emphasizes that the most effective way to help a patient is by means of a comprehensive workup beginning with and guided by history. Invariably history-taking is given short shrift as the patient is shuttled to a multiplicity of specialists and subjected to a gamut of procedures. This type of medical practice is nearly universally accepted as the highest scientific and moral standard.

A hospital, where physicians acquire most of their practical knowledge and form their enduring medical habits, brims with technology and expertise. On a number of occasions I have had run-ins with house staff who wish to discharge one of my patients prematurely. When I protest, I receive the same stock response from either intern or resident: Why occupy a much needed bed when the necessary testing is complete and no surgery is needed? It matters little that the clinical condition remains undefined, or that a management program for prolonged chronic care has not been worked out, or that the patient, living alone, is still too woefully disabled to care for him- or herself.

Another factor shaping the practice of medicine is the belief by both patients and physicians that anything broken must be fixed. Elderly patients often present numerous symptoms that would prove tolerable if they were reassured of their harmlessness. Aches and pains, fatigue, forgetfulness, and occasional insomnia are part of living. The chase to diagnose the incurable, to treat the untreatable, to prognosticate the unpredictable, not only is a form of hubris but opens a Pandora's box with dangerous consequences. What about the risks involved in dismissing a sign or symptom that may be an initial manifestation of an illness? One may argue that a so-called diagnostic exploration is a small price to pay for identifying a potentially curable but life-threatening illness. The answer is straightforward. In the overwhelming majority of cases, a careful history, a thorough physical examination, and a few simple laboratory tests provide a doctor with certainty that nothing major is brewing. Most illnesses are not catastrophic, and time itself provides a powerful test of whether a condition warrants further investigation.

There is an additional consideration. Doctors are as much a product of a technological consumer culture as anyone, and their tendencies to rely on technology are further enhanced by the distorted emphasis on making diagnosis a treasure hunt for the outlandish and the esoteric. In this type of gamesmanship, status accrues to the clinician who correctly suspects some odd ailment. To win the competition requires subjecting patients to a bevy of tests and procedures. Medical schools and hospitals brim with doctors who are engaged in intense competition to mount the academic ladder, which requires publication. Extensive data are required for articles to be accepted in peer-reviewed journals. How else to accumulate data except by turning patients into involuntary guinea pigs subjected to multiple bleedings and probings? The doctor-in-training incorporates these practices as the gold standard defining scientific medicine.

I return to a fundamental fact. Whatever the stimulus for extensive procedures, whether greed or an eagerness to learn, shrill language helps ensure patients' compliance. Although an individual patient may profit only minimally from the torments of a so-called extensive workup, the rhetoric has to be convincing, and nothing works better than insinuating that the patient's well-being and survival depend on the results of the proposed studies or procedures. Even the most intelligent and skeptical patient readily succumbs to such a persuasive argument.

In a doctor's efforts to sate a huge medical industrial complex, patients are frequently willing accomplices. The patient, filled with foreboding and grasping for reassurance, readily gives in to endless laboratory tests and a deluge of specialists. On many occasions I have had family members urge that no stone be left unturned to learn what is wrong and that everything possible be done to effect a cure. While patients complain of a doctor's aloofness, callous and frightening language, this seeming inhumanity is regarded as the inevitable price for scientific medicine.

At times I grow disheartened when, after spending a long time obtaining a detailed history that tells me precisely what is going on, the patient remains unimpressed. But when I take the patient into my examining room, where in a corner there stands an ancient mammoth image-intensifier fluoroscope, a machine with an instrument panel worthy of an airliner, the patient is impressed, and I can imagine the thought: "Am I glad to be here in an office with the latest instruments" or "Are you going to use this wonderful machine on me?" The childish faith in the magic of technology is one reason the American public has tolerated inhumane doctoring.

Whatever the explanation, there is absolutely no justification for assaulting patients with language that cows and disempowers. A patient must never be compelled by fear into difficult choices. If there is to be a partnership in medicine, the senior partner has to be the patient, who must not be deflected from having the decisive word.

6

Words That Heal

ALTHOUGH a doctor's words can injure, they have a far greater potential for healing. The healing process demands more than science; it requires mobilizing patients' positive expectations and stimulating faith in physicians' ministrations. I know of few remedies more powerful than a carefully chosen word. Patients crave caring, which is dispensed largely with words. Talk, which can be therapeutic, is one of the underrated tools in a physician's armamentarium. Medical experience provides constant reminders of the healing power of words.

I attempt to discover a silver lining in the cloudiest situation. This has little to do with truth or falsehood. It flows from the deepest intent of doctoring, to help a patient cope when a condition is hopeless and to recover whenever it is remotely possible.

I use two approaches, one for patients with a heart problem and one for healthy patients. Once the examination of a patient with significant coronary artery disease is over, I have both patient and spouse come into my consulting room for a detailed summary of the findings. I outline explicitly the possible complications and outcomes of coronary artery disease, including the possibility of sudden death. For many doctors this is a taboo subject. Yet I can't imagine that an intelligent patient with coronary disease is unaware of this possibility. Even if the doctor does not talk about it, the patient will surely brood about this awesome threat. Frequently each of us awakens from a deep sleep, overwhelmed with angst, contemplating some symptom as a harbinger of cancer or another fatal illness. For the coronary patient, even a trivial symptom, especially in the dark of night, may be regarded as an omen of sudden death. The terror and helplessness is magnified by the fact that these morbid fears cannot be shared with family or friends.

My talk of sudden death invariably is accompanied by a tense silence, patient and spouse looking as though they wished they were elsewhere. Rarely do they interrupt with questions. After detailing the threat, I conclude with something like the following: "I raise this issue because there is absolutely no chance at all of your dying suddenly in the next few years. This conclusion is based on the present examination. I have never had a patient die suddenly who, like you, is entirely free of heart irregularities on twenty-four-hour monitoring, has a normally contracting left ventricle, and is able to exercise on a treadmill for more than nine minutes with a wholesome rise in heart rate and blood pressure. These very happy findings are the basis for my confidence in predicting your good prognosis."
When this is not the case, and I cannot be categorically reassuring, I do not raise the subject of sudden death.

As the patient with whom I have spoken about dying suddenly leaves the consultation, there is a palpable easing of tensions. Several years ago I had a young and very bright secretary, who, after one such patient visit, burst out as though the matter had long troubled her. "Dr. Lown, do you give your patients pot?"

"What!" I exclaimed, completely astonished.

"Marijuana, pot?" she repeated.

Taken aback, I asked why she had posed this odd question.

"They walk out of your office looking stoned, high, floating on air. When they're from out of town, they ask for the name of the best restaurant in Boston, because they want to celebrate."

I frequently wonder at the source of my buoyant clinical optimism. Certainly much derives from my great teacher Dr. Samuel A. Levine, who remains a lifelong role model. While he was an exceptional diagnostician, his skills in managing the very sick were even more prodigious. He brought a buoyant spirit and incorrigible optimism to the bedside, yet he always planted it in a solid foundation of realistic appraisal. Levine stressed the importance of constructive worry on behalf of the patient. "When a physician offers a grave prognosis or, worse still, when he indicates that the patient is going to die — and miscalculates — the entire medical profession suffers greatly. It is generally best to leave the door a little ajar, even under the darkest circumstances."

A number of the theories Levine propounded have since been proved to be erroneous, many of the drugs he prescribed have since been found to be wanting and have been replaced by far more effective agents. Yet the approach to patients that he preached remains true, having even greater relevance now, in an age of impersonal technology. Several times I heard Levine worry that the golden age of medicine was about to pass, as concern for a patient was being displaced by preoccupation with disease.

As soon as he approached a patient, optimism permeated his every word. When SAL, as we called him, finished with a consultation and was about to leave the bedside, he would invariably place his hand gently on the patient's shoulder and quietly confide, "You'll be all right."

When Levine became terminally ill, I inherited some of his practice. One was a cardiac patient, A.B., whom I have doctored for more than thirty years. During a visit not too long ago, he reminisced about being admitted, in 1960, to the Peter Bent Brigham Hospital, critically ill with a high spiking fever. Levine diagnosed subacute bacterial endocarditis, a potentially lethal infection on a damaged heart valve. Before the days of antibiotics, it was nearly 100 percent fatal, and even now it is a grave illness. "Levine told me, 'You are seriously ill, but you need not worry. I know what is wrong with you. I know how to treat you. I know how to make you well. You will recover completely.' Despite the fact that I was very sick, I did not worry and am still around."

As much as I learned from Levine, my greatest teachers were patients who provided me with a rich clinical experience, who showed me the complexity of the response to a doctor's words, how frequently an innocuous word is a source of encouragement and of hope. The first time I became fully mindful of the extraordinary power of words to heal, I was quite unaware of what had happened until the patient later told me. Even though I used a word with an adverse connotation, the patient's positive spin on what had been said proved decisive. It had to do with a heart sound called a gallop.

A WHOLESOME GALLOP

The patient, a sixty-year-old man, looked critically ill. Two weeks after the heart attack, he was still in coronary intensive care. It had been a tough struggle. We encountered nearly every complication in the book. Now the problem was easy to define: nearly half his heart muscle was destroyed. He was in congestive heart failure. Because of inadequate contraction of the left ventricle, blood was backing up and engorging his lungs, making every breath an effort. At the same time, inadequate pumping of blood into the circulation caused low blood pressure, and sitting up induced dizziness and near fainting. Breathless and weak, he had no energy to eat; worse still, he had absolutely no appetite, as the smell of food nauseated him. Lack of oxygen made him restless, disrupting his sleep. The end appeared to be very near; wan and pasty, lips purplish blue from insufficient oxygen in the blood, he periodically gasped for air as though drowning.

Each morning at rounds, my staff and I entered his hospital room like a morose-looking bunch of undertakers. We had exhausted all the reassuring platitudes we knew, and in any case believed any reassurance would insult his intelligence and further undermine his trust. We tried to speed up the round so we wouldn't have to face his questioning stare for too long. Every day the situation deteriorated. After consulting with his family, I wrote a "do not resuscitate" order in his chart.

One morning he looked better, claimed to feel better, and indeed, vital signs were improved. I could not account for the change and was still unpersuaded that he would survive. The prognosis was grim despite the temporary improvement. Believing that a change of environment would be less stressful for him and at least allow him to sleep, I had him moved to a step-down-care unit; within a week he was discharged, and I lost track of him.

Six months later he showed up at my office, looking to be in remarkably good health. While his heart was badly damaged, he was free of congestion and largely asymptomatic. I was filled with disbelief. "A miracle, a miracle!" I exclaimed.

"Hell no, this ain't no miracle," he responded.

I was rather taken aback by his certainty that divine intervention was not responsible for the miraculous recovery. "What do you mean?" I asked sheepishly.

"I know the exact moment when this so-called miracle happened," he stated without hesitation.

He told me that he was aware that we were at our wits' end, blundering and confused, and did not seem to know what to do for him. While he was feeling punk, we were slowly persuading him that he was a dying man and he was obliging. He thought we had given up hope and his goose was cooked. Then he said, quite emphatically, "On Thursday morning, April twenty-fifth, you came in with your gang, surrounded the bed, and looked as though I was already in a casket. You put your stethoscope on my chest and urged everyone to listen to the 'wholesome gallop.' I figured that if my heart was still capable of a healthy gallop, I couldn't be dying, and I got well. So you see, doc, it was no miracle. It was mind over matter."

The patient was unaware that a gallop was a bad sign, namely, a sound generated by an overstretched and failing left ventricle straining ineffectively to pump blood. A wholesome gallop is an oxymoron.

My most remarkable experience in prolonging life was also a sheer accident, as well as an act of pretentious bravado. It started innocently enough when I was attending a dying middle-aged man, but I was soon playing God with tongue in cheek.

THE HAPPIEST DAYS OF MY LIFE

With a shock of white hair above a swarthy Italian face, bedridden, he looked like a tamed lion about to roar. However, Tony was silent, and when he spoke it was in monosyllables. His brooding, large, handsome brown eyes and dark, drooping lids betrayed past passion and romance, but he was awaiting death from a failing heart badly damaged by coronary artery disease. The only subject that roused him from a state of torpor was pigeons. He bred them, raced them, loved them, and when the subject was broached, he livened up and related that one of his birds flew eight hundred miles.

He was referred to my hospital service with end-stage cardiomyopathy, a severe heart muscle disease. Now it had progressed to congestive heart failure involving both pumping chambers, the right and left ventricles. He could not be cheered. He slept a lot, which was a blessing, but his sleep was not restful, and he woke even more tired than when he went to sleep. Long spells of apnea were intermittently interrupted by convulsive movements accompanied by loud stertorous gasping. These periods without breathing were unnerving. Each one seemed to announce the end.

A beautiful young woman, his daughter I assumed, sat by his bedside day and night. She was already there when I began rounds at eight in the morning, and when I dropped by in late evening, I always found her hovering at his bedside, trying to make him comfortable. Rarely had I witnessed such filial devotion. She appeared to be in her mid-twenties, poised, and like Tony, silent. Although she watched everything carefully, she rarely questioned the doctors or nurses, but concentrated instead on anticipating Tony's every need, whether for a swallow of liquid or a urinal.

She was one of those women who is so attractive that one wishes to inhale her, and I kept casting furtive glances to assure myself of her gossamer reality. It was hard to concentrate on sickness and impending death in the presence of such life-affirming youth. She was always there, very quiet, trying but failing to be unobtrusive, sometimes crying quietly, clearly harboring great affection for this dying patriarch.

One day, I said to Tony, "You are lucky to have such a devoted daughter; she never leaves your bedside."

"She's not my daughter, Doc, she's my mistress," he responded matter-of-factly.

I was shaken by a possibility that never entered my mind.

Some days later I said to Tony teasingly, "You should marry her."

He looked quizzically and even dreamily at me. "No, Doc, I don't want to leave a widow immediately after the wedding."

"Who says that you will?"

"Well, Doc, I'm ready to make a deal. Lisa is eager to marry, and if you guarantee in writing that I'll be around for five years, I'm ready to follow your advice."

So then and there I drafted a statement guaranteeing, without equivocation, that Tony would live for five years. He improved in the ensuing days and was soon well enough to be discharged from the hospital. A few days later I received a postcard from the honeymooning couple. I did not see Tony for several years and frequently worried about my impulsive and not very rational suggestion. Was it fair to encourage a marriage between a woman in the prime of life and an intractably incapacitated and dying man?

One day Tony showed up looking none the worse for the passage of several years and said, "The five years are up, Doc. I need a new contract." It didn't seem possible that five years had passed so rapidly. But on glancing at his chart, I saw that Tony was indeed right. In another month it would be the fifth anniversary of the guarantee. So once again I drafted the same type of contract. Lisa, more beautiful than ever, was blooming and clearly deeply in love.

Five more years elapsed without my seeing Tony, and I started to look at the calendar expectantly, aware that the tenth anniversary was fast approaching. On the very date Tony appeared, miserably sick, struggling to breathe, burdened with edema, which distended his abdomen to the size of a large pillow. But he was calm, uncomplaining, emanating a quiet dignity. I expected him to ask for renewal of the guarantee, but he didn't. In the past he had demanded the impossible, but he was wise enough not to ask a fellow human to accomplish the miraculous.

I admitted him to the Peter Bent Brigham. We tinkered without hope, leached out some of the edema, eased his breathing, and made him comfortable. He lived two more years.

Shortly after his death, Lisa appeared in my office. She was then a woman in her mid-thirties and had reached a state of mature womanly perfection. She was eager to talk, beginning with great emotion laced with serenity. "Doctor, you have given me the happiest days of my life. I expect no other such fulfillment." Her speech was correct and carefully nuanced.

"What will you do with your life? You are still a very young woman," I said.

"I desperately want to be educated, I want to go to college. You see, when Tony picked me up I was a teenage prostitute. I came from the South. My parents abandoned me at age fourteen. When I met Tony, I had no hope for the future. He hired me to be a cocktail waitress in his bar. Tony was involved with numbers, and God knows what else. He could be tough and mean, but to me he was always the gentle lover. He taught me more than books could. He educated me to be human. Tony wanted me to give you this envelope to help with your heart research. It's anonymous."

She got up abruptly and left. The envelope contained one hundred freshly minted hundred-dollar bills. That was twenty-five years ago — and I have never seen her since.

These are far from exceptional experiences, further examples of elderly Jewish males' and elderly Chinese females' seeming ability to postpone death during important religious holidays. Such delays were brief, lasting only a few days, but I am persuaded the phenomenon is valid. Quite conceivably, dying can be postponed for much longer periods. Many patients have told me that they had been diagnosed with a fatal disease, given only months to live, then recovered and survived for many years. Such seemingly miraculous recoveries are frequently claimed at religious shrines the world over.

Faith and optimism have life-giving qualities. Hippocrates, the father of medicine, said, "For some patients, though conscious that their position is perilous, recover their health simply through their contentment with the physician." That comes from trust, which a doctor promotes by conveying optimism. Certainly promoting optimism is critical to good doctoring and is a significant aspect of the art of healing. I have never tried to frighten a patient or paint a grim scenario. Even when the condition is serious, I focus on the encouraging elements without indulging in Pollyannish cant.

Early in my practice, when fluoroscoping patients, I placed a mirror opposite the translucent imaging screen. My wife had made a small window shade that could be pulled up or down. Patients could face the mirror and see their own heartbeat. When the heart looked good, I would raise the shade and point happily to the wholesome cardiac silhouette and the healthy pulsing beat. When the image was poor, with a weak, barely visible contraction, and there was nothing good to say about it, I would leave the shade drawn over the mirror and remain silent.

I find that optimism also plays a critical role in dealing with a young or middle-aged patient who is free of heart disease but has been entrapped in the coils of the medical industrial complex. Trivial deviations from the normal have been exaggerated, leading them to an endless pursuit of doctoring. Persuading people that nothing ails them is at times a thankless task, if not a losing proposition. For some the secondary gains of illness, such as eliciting sympathy from an indifferent spouse or absenting oneself from an unpleasant job, may exceed the pain and disability of pretending sickness. Others are morbidly anxious about dying. Mere words of assurance may not reassure.

Doctors who attempt to encourage them often hedge when patients demand an unequivocal answer that nothing is wrong.

One approach that I find useful is to discourage patients from revisiting soon when there is no evidence of heart disease. At the end of an interview, when a patient asks about scheduling the next appointment, I say, "Yes, I would like to see you in about ten years."

The patient chuckles nervously. "You really mean it, Doctor? Do you think I'll live that long?"

To which I give various replies: "You'd better. I depend on your fee for a living" or "I'm more concerned about whether I'll be around. I have no doubt about you." There is usually a satisfied laugh, and those with a sense of humor may ask whether they can make the appointment immediately. Invariably, the patient leaves feeling happy and encouraged.

For patients with stable minor heart conditions who have been seen by their doctors monthly, receiving unnecessary procedures and medications with adverse side effects, I suggest another visit in two to five years. The value of this approach is illustrated by the story of a man who called my secretary one day, insisting that I had asked to see him on Wednesday of the following week. I could not recall having made such an appointment or even remember the patient.

When questioned by the secretary, the man refused to say what was wrong, though he insisted it was an emergency. Fortunately we had an opening. When he arrived, something clicked in my memory, but hard as I tried, I could not dredge up any details to fill in the empty space in my brain. He asked whether I knew the significance of this day. When I said I didn't, he looked surprised and hurt.

"Don't you remember? Today is exactly twenty years since you last saw me."

His father, he explained, had been under my care at the Peter Bent Brigham Hospital with a heart attack two decades earlier. Although he himself was only twenty-three at the time, he began to develop severe chest pain and was convinced that the symptoms were similar to his father's and that he was about to have a heart attack. Terrified that he might drop dead at any moment, he sought my counsel. The examination revealed a perfectly normal cardiovascular system, but when I reassured him that there was nothing wrong with his heart, he asked if I could see him again in a month. I refused, suggesting instead that he return in twenty years.

"You said 'precisely twenty years,'" he reminded me. Until a month ago, he had never had another cardiac symptom, but now was experiencing frequent bothersome palpitations accompanied by dizziness. Overcome once more with dread of impending doom, he realized that the time for a reappointment was close at hand.

"I had an appointment with you or an appointment in Samara," he said with utmost seriousness.

A careful history and physical examination still divulged no abnormalities. Most likely the symptoms were brought on by a resurgence of old anxieties. After much reassurance, I suggested that he revisit in ten years, explaining that while he was as healthy as ever, I was getting on in years.

Some years ago I asked a Soviet physician from Siberia what the essence of doctoring was. She responded simply: "Every time a doctor sees a patient, the patient should feel better as a result." This was a wise insight, and in my experience the improvement is invariably wrought with positive words. It is now fashionable and even chic to indulge in pessimism, thereby pretending philosophic depth. Human life is regarded as mere animal existence, nothing more than the indifferent unwinding of a dismal biologic clock. Notwithstanding intellectual pretensions, there is little substance to pessimism. It tears at the social connective tissue and contributes to alienation. Instead of reaching out, it compels an individual to search for a full measure of life within the narrow confines of the self. In the process, life is degraded and the promise of tomorrow is jeopardized.

Thomas Mann counseled that we must behave as though the

world was created for human beings. Optimism, although a subjective emotion, becomes an objective factor essential for unleashing the energy needed to shape one's health. Optimism is a Kantian moral imperative and, for the physician whose role is to affirm life, a medical imperative. Even when the outlook is doubtful, affirmative words promote well-being if not always recovery.

7

Hearts of Darkness,
Words of Light

A PHYSICIAN committed to healing cannot focus exclusively on a patient's chief complaint and diseased organs but must attend to the stressful aspects of the patient's life as well. This alerts the patient that the doctor is interested in him or her as a person, not just in the immediate problem. The patient is then more willing to share intimate and painful matters, and the doctor is better able to assess how healing is to be accomplished. As I noted in Chapter 3, "History-taking involves not merely learning about a disease, but grasping what is agitating a patient's mind."

The stresses that may be operating are as numerous and diverse as life itself. Generally the most critical areas arise from work or family conflicts. If these are ignored, a chronic disease cannot be effectively addressed, whatever its anatomic location. While treatment with drugs alone may be temporarily effective, an entirely new symptom frequently fixates on a different bodily part. The chase to cure the patient is seemingly endless and ultimately frustrating to both patient and doctor.

The following four vignettes share a leitmotif despite the cultural differences between the patients: two Indians, a Madras Christian and a Bombay Hindu, and two orthodox Jews, one from the Midwest and one from New Jersey. Although they were worlds apart in upbringing and values, their medical problems were not dissimilar, and in each case the illness was a manifestation of a troubling family conflict. Addressing the painful family misunderstandings began a process of healing.

ON BEING A GURU

After a lapse of two decades, Mrs. V. came to see me again. She was slight and dark with delicately chiseled features and large brown eyes that conveyed subdued intelligence and resignation. Her movement was gossamery; she floated gracefully into the room, her feet seemingly never touching the floor, as though she was defying gravity. A dark brown sari pirouetted around a girlish figure. Like her husband, she had a heart condition, but hers was the result of childhood rheumatic fever. Her presence stirred the embers of ancient memories.

Rajiv V., her husband, had been a visiting scholar at a Boston university. He spoke impeccable English, accented by Harvard and Oxford exposures, with a rhythmic lilt, conveying the fluidity of his Indian antecedents. When he was only thirty-eight, he had been admitted to my service at the Peter Bent Brigham Hospital, critically ill with an acute myocardial infarction. I was puzzled at such a massive heart attack in someone so young, especially as he lacked risk factors for precocious coronary artery disease. As a matter of fact, his cholesterol was unusually low, as was his blood pressure. He had never smoked and for the past several years had jogged three miles daily. I was also baffled by his fatalistic acceptance of this near-tragic event. Unlike most American patients, he never questioned why it had happened despite his intelligence and medical knowledge.

Nearly a decade later, although I had come to know him intimately, there still was no clue to what had triggered the attack that nearly claimed his life. His parents were long-lived and he was by no means tense or hard driving. If anything, I judged him to be a laid-back type B personality, exhibiting little sense of time pressure or undue ambition. Numerous times I had asked whether he was at all tense. His response was always "No, Doctor, my life is without any stress whatsoever."

One day I asked Mrs. V., in his presence, why she thought her husband had had a heart attack. Without a moment of hesitation she responded that it was caused by stress. He promptly and completely dismissed this suggestion. Then, after long reflection, he commented, "I have no stress except for my damnable brother-in-law."

Rajiv looked ill at ease, as though regretting the admission. While normally placid and soft-spoken, he grew animated, his voice rising to a slightly higher pitch, the words coming at a faster clip. Apparently his brother-in-law, his sister's husband, had been eager to come to the United States but needed family sponsorship to be able to immigrate to this country. The brother-in-law had no money, and Rajiv had worked hard over several years to bring the couple and their children over, borrowing $5,000 from a bank, which he loaned to this brother-in-law interest free. When the family arrived in America, Rajiv found an apartment for them and an engineering job for his brother-in-law. "I spared no effort for my beloved sister," he explained. Rajiv spoke more fondly of this sister than of his wife. The two families lived near each other and their children enjoyed close cousinly attachments. The relationship between the two men, however, deteriorated rapidly.

Throughout the long conversation, Rajiv never mentioned his sister's husband by name; as he spat "brother-in-law," he always prefixed it with the word "damnable." It emerged that the brother-in-law refused to pay back or even acknowledge the loan. And to his dismay, Rajiv learned that this "damnable" brother-in-law had alienated the affection of Rajiv's revered mother, spreading rumors about Rajiv that enraged his mother back in India. Several weeks before the heart attack, Rajiv had learned that his mother had disinherited him. The upshot was that Rajiv and his sister severed all contacts. He spoke with pain of how much grief his sister was experiencing. He added that he knew how she felt, "but what can the poor creature do, married as she is to a scoundrel who fathered her three lovely children?"

As I listened to the outburst of seething rage, it appeared likely that this was the critical factor in the heart attack. It also seemed likely that unless the abscess was lanced, another and perhaps fatal attack was in the offing. Rajiv kept intoning sadly that what was most painful was the loss of his revered mother's affection. He would say over and over, in a soft tormented voice, "Doctor, how is it possible that my mother rejects me?"

Sitting there, almost touching the palpable pain that had just been exposed, I was at a total loss as to what to do next. Rajiv's distress was well outside the province of my cardiologic expertise, but was it outside my domain as a doctor? What medicine should one prescribe? What advice would help untie this Gordian knot? I grew hot and sweaty, my tie was suddenly too tight, my buttocks itched. I had stuck my hand in and stirred up an emotional hornet's nest. This was a problem beyond my ken.

I listened with amazement to the flow of advice I found myself offering with the certainty of a revelation. "You must invite your brother-in-law and his family to dinner as though nothing happened," I suggested. Before I could finish the sentence, he angrily exclaimed, "Never, never!" His face suddenly was suffused and he was brimming with anger as he continued. "I would rather die than have this despicable rogue ever again enter my home. I would not expose my children so that they, may God forgive me, are influenced by this damnable scoundrel. I am not the Mahatma ready to turn the other cheek. Though a Christian, I am not about to forgive and forget." The torrent of words gushed as though a dam had been breached.

I was not a judge adjudicating the rights and wrongs of a complex case. In my role as doctor I gently coaxed. "Your deep anger and feeling of betrayal are justified. Forgiving in this case is not a religious act. You will not be inviting your damnable brother-in-law in order to immolate yourself before him. On the contrary, this will be a most powerful act of revenge as well as an act of education for your children, a testament of your personal decency. It will demonstrate who is human and who is a savage. It is meant to rescue your beloved sister from her torments of hell. As you just said, she is but an innocent victim."

Rajiv suddenly grew very attentive, urging me on, while his wife sat like a wooden Buddha without even a spark of emotion.

"Can you imagine his guilt and consternation when you

invite him and his family for an evening together?" I continued with great gusto, sensing Rajiv's mounting excitement. "He would be at a loss what to do. Since you will mention it to your sister as well, he can't keep it secret from her. He would be worried that you are indulging in a vile stratagem. But he would not be able to resolve the conundrum. All the time your sister will remind him of your commitment to let bygones be bygones. Think of the sleepless nights he will have! Don't set the date for the get-together soon, maybe wait three weeks, so he can stew in the juices of uncertainty and indecision."

Rajiv, his face now aglow, was clearly intrigued but not yet persuaded.

I continued. "His children will be puzzled as you entertain them in your home with care and affection. No doubt he must have told them that you are an evil person who severed ties between the two families over trivial money issues. I am certain that the greater your friendship, the more difficult it will be for him to deny his financial obligation to you. Sooner rather than later he will pay back his debt."

Rajiv listened with rapt attention while mopping a perspiring brow, though the office was comfortably cool. But it was clear that he remained unconvinced.

Now my trump card. "If you follow through with my suggestion, I will write a letter to your beloved mother and detail how you had a major heart attack from which you nearly died. Wishing to spare her the anxiety, you never wrote her about it. I would emphasize in this letter that rarely have I encountered a man so devoted to his mother. I will urge her to send words of support during your difficult travail. I will also speak of your noble character and how you made peace with your brother-in-law for the sake of your sister's, her daughter's, peace of mind."

He no longer hesitated. He leaned forward, his body arched for action, like one of Kipling's brigadiers eager for battle. "I will do it, I will do it!" he shouted.

His wife unexpectedly stirred from her Buddha-like trance and began to talk in a low voice. I strained to catch her words. "You are not a doctor, but a great guru."

Some fifteen years before this incident, I had spent a month rounding in the coronary care unit at the Brigham with an attentive young Ethiopian doctor. On the very last day of his visit he burst out, "Dr. Lown, you are like our old Ethiopian witch doctors." There was an embarrassed shuffling among the staff, and the Ethiopian doctor later came to apologize. I assured him this was one of the very greatest compliments I had ever received.

Being designated a guru was equally complimentary. Six months elapsed, and I awaited Rajiv's next visit with subdued excitement. Did Rajiv go through with the plan? Did his brother-in-law accept the invitation? Was there peace between the families? Was all forgiven? As promised, I had written to his mother, but had he heard from her?

When he arrived, Rajiv did not mention our last conversation. "How is your brother-in-law?" I finally asked.

"He is quite okay, not a bad chap and very good to my beloved sister."

"You have made up then?"

"We never really had a rift."

"And your mother?"

"At her insistence, I will soon visit my revered mother in India."

I should have been elated, but instead discovered a weakness in my character. His matter-of-fact tone, denying me the credit due, troubled me. Still, I was deeply satisfied with what I thought was a successful act of healing. Ultimately, however, this was marred by a tragedy. Rajiv accepted a most prestigious job in India; unlike his relaxed, tenured academic position in Boston, the new job was akin to entering the vortex of a tornado, with conflicting ethnic and political forces tearing the place apart. Recalling the heart attack which nearly claimed his life was brought on by psychologic stress, I counseled Rajiv against going back to India. He would not hear of it, maintaining that this job had been the aspiration of his life. After only a year in India, Rajiv succumbed to a sudden cardiac arrest.

* * *

Rajiv's wife had returned to the United States to live with a son. Once a year Mrs. V. arrives in Boston for a medical visit. On each occasion, we momentarily recall Rajiv and that fateful office visit of more than thirty years ago when she anointed me a guru.

Far too frequently, the family psychopathology is so deep-seated that a cure is impossible. Healing, though, is never impossible. Even in insoluble cases, a doctor's caring helps mitigate the misery and makes life more tolerable.

A MOTHER'S CURSE

Professor B.K. was an intense Hindu scientist at one of Boston's medical schools. He came to the United States at the age of thirty-five and within six months sustained an acute myocardial infarction. He was in the hospital coronary step-down unit and we were trying to determine whether he had had a heart attack. Reading the chart, I found it odd that he should have been admitted, since tingling in shoulders and chest is not a symptom emanating from the heart and is certainly not due to angina pectoris. Coronary beds were at a premium, and furthermore, it was the end of May and the medical house staff that handles admissions had had nearly a year of intense experience; they should have known better. The mystery resolved on my encountering Professor K. Rarely had I met anyone more suffused with anxiety. He looked as though he wanted to jump out of his own skin. His panic no doubt made the young house staff suspect an impending cardiac event.

After a few questions establishing indubitably that his symptoms were unrelated to the heart, I asked whether he was sleeping well. He said that he had slept only fitfully since a successful coronary artery bypass operation ten months earlier. Nightly, unable to sleep, he left the bedroom and watched television until, drained with fatigue, he finally fell off to sleep at two or three in the morning. He was up again at 6:30 A.M. to take his children to school. Some nights, tossing restlessly, he got no sleep at all, and since the operation he had had no sexual relations with his wife. Sleep deprived, he barely dragged himself through the day. His wife was distraught and didn't know where to turn.

I spoke with the categorical certainty of a parent assuring a frightened child. "Your pain is not anginal! You are not going to die either slowly or suddenly. If you wish to punish yourself for something, don't disrupt your sleep. Do something else." He looked startled, as though I had read his mind, and said, "Yes, Doctor, I believe you." The rest of the day I kept puzzling about why he should have had such acute sleep disturbance after a successful bypass operation.

Several months later I again saw Professor K. in the hospital. This time he had been admitted not for a cardiac problem, but for a lower right abdominal quadrant mass. This had been festering with low-grade fever for some weeks. He looked delighted to see me.

"How is your chest pain?"

"It is all gone."

"What about your sleep?"

"I am back sleeping in my own bed."

I expressed gratification at this happy outcome.

"Without a doubt you cured me."

"How so? I saw you for only about ten minutes and before that you had been disabled for ten months."

"Dr. Lown, I hope you won't be insulted, but you are like the old Hindu doctors of the last century. They did not equivocate. They did not say rule out this or that. They knew their patients. Now I do not mean disrespect to science and scientists, but uncertainty is their professional style. They can say on the one hand and on the other. A doctor must go beyond science. Patients have to be addressed with certainty if they are to be helped."

With the new authority vested me, I was emboldened to search for more fundamental causes for the heart problems. I asked him how he accounted for a heart attack in someone only thirty-five who is free of any of the classical risk factors for coronary disease. After all, his cholesterol was only 160 mg, his blood pressure low, he had never smoked, was free of diabetes, and hailed from a long-lived family. He interrupted me impatiently. "I know exactly what caused it. My tyrannical, feudal mother. She dominated my life totally. When I had this unique opportunity to go to America with an appointment at a Boston medical school, fulfilling my wildest dreams, she utterly forbade it. When I nonetheless left India, she cursed and disowned me."

He continued with the soft liquid tone of the Indian language grafted on the harsher English. "When I came here, every night my dreams were one continuous nightmare. There was my mother, veritably choking me to death, night after night without respite. I dreaded sleep and confronting my vengeful mother. During the day I ate four to five eggs, was too tired to exercise, yet worked feverishly to prove myself. The nightmares abruptly stopped with my heart attack." Ruefully and reflectively, he added, "I have now paid my dues."

But he had not quite paid his dues. I saw him again after another six months; although largely asymptomatic, he was still preoccupied. He dreaded returning to India, explaining that medical care was poor there. Conversation brought out a deeper reason: dread of his mother was once again suffocating his life. I urged him to confront his mother.

The last time I saw him he told me that he had phoned his mother and said, "I fall on my knees and kiss your feet, Mother. I have suffered much. I had a heart attack and needed a heart operation. I had to be operated again on my belly. I have been punished more than any human being deserves. Please forgive me."

She responded, "Yes, I forgive you now."

"You should be pleased."

"She didn't mean it."

"Why do you say that?"

"Her tone of voice, which I know well. My younger brother is now her favorite."

One could anticipate more rapid progression of his heart

disease on his return to India. I was at a loss how to heal this deeply troubled man; our cultural divide was far too great.

SOME CHUTZPAH

Treating differs from healing. The former deals with a malfunctioning organ system, the latter with a distressed human being. The story of something that happened more than twenty years ago illustrates the difference. It left an indelible impression and still makes me squirm.

Mr. S.D. was a burly, heavyset man from the Midwest. He was a self-made man, comfortable, kindly, and affable, whose only activity outside work, besides golf, was the synagogue of which he was president. He was seeking medical advice for recurrent atrial fibrillation, a disorder of the heartbeat in which the pulse is rapid and irregular. Though the palpitation may be unnerving, the condition is largely benign. For Mr. D., however, the paroxysms of arrhythmia were proving increasingly disabling.

His wife, Rachel, accompanied him each time, a largely speechless witness. She must have been a beauty at one time, with her raven black hair, now touched with a dab of dye, nicely chiseled features, high cheekbones, deep-set olive eyes austere and sad, always looking away as though more than momentary eye contact might provide insight into a cavern better left unexposed. Scrawny, she was tensely coiled like a tight steel spring, with a cigarette defacing a voluptuous lipsticked mouth. She extended a limp, cold, moist hand that refused to grip or make human contact. She never talked but deferred to her husband. He weighed about two hundred and fifty pounds and she would not have tipped the scale at one hundred. Despite their differences, they had been together for thirty-five years, had three devoted children in college, and I could feel the warmth in their relationship.

A careful history divulged no psychological problems. Although in retrospect I remember her wincing when Mr. D. discussed the family, it did not register at the time. Various antiarrhythmic drugs successfully controlled his problem, but only temporarily. Over the years I came to know the couple well and respect their unpretentious, small-town dignity, but each visit left a tingle of discomfort that hidden somewhere was a burning hot coal. Attempts to identify the source of the heat were consistently rebuffed.

One day, as I once again implored Mrs. D. to stop smoking, she insisted that it was impossible, adding impassively, "You should know we have four children, not three." I sat bolt upright in my swivel chair, my voice tinged with excitement and irritation. "Tell me about it. How come you waited so long?"

"My husband made me swear never to mention her name. For him she is dead. Many nights I cry myself to sleep."

"I don't understand, your daughter died?"

"No, she is very much alive."

"Do you see her?"

"No, even when she writes to me, I hide her letters."

This was not an easy-flowing conversation. Every word was clearly painful for her.

When Mr. D. returned from having an electrocardiogram, she stopped talking, displaying a guilty, furtive, fearful look. I resisted the urge to pursue the subject of the lost daughter until the next visit six months later.

This time, I made it a point to see Mrs. D. alone. She again beseeched me not to mention the daughter to her husband. She feared his having a stroke or harming her for divulging the family secret, which could certainly be no secret as everyone in their community must have known about it. Apparently, this daughter had been her husband's favorite. Bright, quick, temperamental, opinionated, she twisted her father around her little finger. She began to date a gentile boy in high school, and when she graduated, they eloped and settled in Cleveland. Mr. D., on learning of this event, sat shivah (the Jewish mourning period for the dead) for a week, had a nervous breakdown, and after recovering, ordered that any scintilla of remembrance of his daughter be removed from their home. When he discovered a letter from his daughter he had a violent temper tantrum. I suspect he may even have hit Rachel, although she was evasive about that.

One time, in exasperation, I made a more frontal assault on Mr. D. After all, we were now friends. "I can't help you unless you are aboveboard with me. I sense something is troubling you deeply, yet you are ashamed to talk to me. If a doctor is denied the facts, he has a fool for a patient."

He thereupon told me the story his wife had sketched out earlier, but with much more anger and emotion. His daughter had married to spite him. It was a deliberate rejection of her Jewishness. With Israel threatened and the Holocaust still an open wound, how could he allow this? If his daughter rejected being a Jew, then she was not his child. At each subsequent visit we discussed the problem, but without progress.

His medical situation deteriorated. He did not adhere to the anticoagulant medication and experienced a small stroke. We were getting into a crisis situation. I had the feeling that his life was becoming unbearable and he was committing a slow self-immolation that everyone seemed helpless to prevent, including the victim, who was walking in his sleep toward a precipice.

One visit took place on a late, drizzly autumn afternoon, gray and dismal. I was swiveling restlessly in front of a large picture window, extending from floor to ceiling, overlooking a parking lot six stories down, and amplifying the drab melancholy outside. Rocking to and fro, I was frustrated, angry at the whole world for my inept helplessness.

Then out of the blue, without seeming provocation, I began to shout at him. "I don't know why I am wasting my time with a miserable human being like yourself. You make me sick with your self-pity, but more so with what you have done to your daughter, to her family, to your wife, to your other children, and to yourself. You are ruining everyone's life. It is mind-boggling what a selfish man you are. According to the Jewish religion the Lord can forgive sins committed against Him, not sins committed against other human beings."

I quavered with apprehension. Who was this maniac talking through my mouth, a veritable biblical Balaam's ass? Mr. D.

lurched forward like a bull about to charge a matador, eyes bulging, breathing stertorously, his neck veins corded. I could visualize myself being shoved backward, shattering the plate glass and plunging down to the asphalt parking lot. Mrs. D. began to weep hysterically, limbs flailing, shrieking as if being exorcised. I was drenched with perspiration, anguish, and remorse at my idiotic outburst.

It was improper of me and yet, like a wind-up toy, my spring was so tightly coiled I couldn't stop myself. "If you had any decency, you'd drive directly to Cleveland, right now, knock on your daughter's back door — you do not deserve the front entrance. On bended knee, ask her forgiveness. Only she can relieve you of the burden of sin, not God."

Had I gone psychotic, pretending to be some Jeremiah, the ancient prophet of the strong word? Is there no balm in Gilead? I heard a loud suppressed sob, and saw Mr. D.'s huge body convulsing. He rose slowly, suddenly weighed down with grief and age, and left the room. His wife, looking even more shriveled, followed him. I was consumed with guilt, yet another motif was welling up, a thought was nudging, "It's okay. This is what healing is all about — it sometimes takes pain to lessen pain."

When the next appointment rolled around, I was astonished when Mr. D. actually showed up, chastened but more relaxed. He had done exactly as I had urged. He went to Cleveland and begged his daughter's forgiveness. The festivities were unending and he did not stop exuding excitement. The two families were now inseparable and he couldn't stop talking about his little grandson. He looked back on the past few years as a mad aberration that he would rather forget. Incidentally, the atrial fibrillation had ceased to be a problem. The same medicine that previously failed to control his heart rate was now keeping it well in check.

Reflecting on Mr. D. more than two decades later, I am not as proud as I was at the time. The fact that the outcome was favorable does not convince me that the means were proper. Poor means are never sanctioned by good intentions or justified by good results. Was this the only way to have reconciled Mr. D. with his daughter? Would gentle persuasion over time have achieved a similar outcome? Provoking such a storm of emotion could have done him great harm, physically as well as psychologically. What truly happened is that I lost control, acting as though I was possessed. This is absolutely no justification for improper behavior. It is a costly part of nearly every doctor's education. Patients are our unwitting guinea pigs. I never again lost my cool with a patient. In a similar situation some years later, I had learned from experience.

THE IMPERMISSIBLE MAY BE MANDATORY

Mr. G., a sixty-year-old New Jersey businessman, owned a successful machine shop and was happily married to a caring, intelligent wife. But why the premature coronary artery disease? His cholesterol level was normal, as was his blood pressure, and he never smoked. Though he was the tense and worrying type, his occupation was not overly stressful. His coronary disease, though, was intractable and progressive. He had had three operations — two coronary artery bypasses and one balloon angioplasty — yet the angina waxed and waned on a substantially hefty medical program.

I saw him many times over a number of years and felt utterly at a loss regarding his treatment, constantly tinkering with various antianginal drugs such as nitrates, and beta blocking and calcium channel blocking agents. At this particular visit he appeared more depressed than usual. Nothing emerged from a careful interim history, but after the physical examination, when he and his wife were in my consulting office, I began to feel that I was missing something. His wife seemed bursting to talk about some matter but wouldn't say what it was.

I returned to the subject of their children, somehow believing that was where the skeleton in the closet might be hidden. The couple had two daughters and a son, the middle child. Among orthodox Jews, a son is central in the family hierarchy and I suspected that was where the problem resided.

"Do you have any problems with your children?" I asked blandly.

At this point Mrs. G. chimed in. "For God's sake, tell him about Richard!"

He told her to shut up. "Richard has nothing to do with my angina."

"Do you get along with your son?" I asked.

"No," he answered abruptly.

"Why not?"

"Because Richard is a homosexual and I would rather he was dying of cancer," he said, clearly angry at me for prying.

Gently, coaxingly, I replied, "You surprise me. For a decent man whom I have come to respect, your behavior is irrational and even mean." I implored, in a low tone, "Does it make sense to shorten your wife's life, ruin your son's life, and kill yourself in the bargain, all because you have made a narrow-minded judgment?"

I went on to talk about homosexuality as a biological and genetic issue — not a behavioral problem — one that should not cause anyone feelings of guilt. While I insisted that a father has no right to condemn his own son to incarceration in hell, I expressed great sympathy for his shame and suffering, however misguided. The conversation was long and intense, and many tears were shed. I urged family counseling, but when they left I was uncertain whether they would follow my advice.

What seems a happy resolution in the consulting room may evaporate after the patient leaves and begins to reflect on the doctor's invasion of the most intimate aspect of his or her life. I was uncertain whether Mr. G. would show up the following year, whether he would have addressed the problem, tried to resolve it, whether it could ever be resolved or would continue to aggravate the already serious coronary artery disease.

He did return, and I could see instantly that he was a different person. The surly demeanor was gone. He did not avoid looking me in the eyes. For the first time, a smile played across his broad face.

"What's the good news?" I inquired.

"We just had a Passover Seder and both Richard and Gilbert were there, and they both read the Haggadah. Gilbert, his friend, is a lovely man, you can't find any better. They've been living together for several years. Both are very successful, earn more than a hundred thousand dollars each year. The Seder was a beautiful affair. Richard was a little jealous that I was paying so much attention to Gilbert. My wife and I are now active in gay rights. We even marched in the last parade." This hitherto taciturn man poured out words without letup. He talked with ease and pride and didn't want to stop sharing the unbelievable story of what had happened to him in the past year. Combatting bias against homosexuality had become Mr. and Mrs. G.'s major social preoccupation, and his angina had at last ceased to be a major problem.

8

The Power of Certainty

IN THE CASE OF Professor B.K., the panicked Hindu scientist, I chastised the house staff for putting him into a coronary unit when his real problem was clearly anxiety. After all, it is a common clinical fact that tingling in the hands is a manifestation of hyperventilation, the rapid shallow breathing that accompanies an anxiety attack. The staff assured me that they had told the patient several times that the tingling was not a cardiac symptom. So why did he not believe them? And why did he instantly accept my words as gospel truth? Investigating this matter, I learned that the intern as well as the medical resident were indeed quite reassuring, but they planted doubt at the same time by attaching B.K. to a monitor in a coronary step-down unit. Owing to inexperience, they lacked certainty and sent the patient a mixed message. I was authoritative and completely rejected the notion that his symptoms had anything to do with the heart. The professor needed certainty, not equivocation.

A clinician rapidly learns that patients crave a firm hand to help them overcome the anxiety-provoking uncertainty that sickness brings in its wake. A doctor's words need a ring of authority without being dogmatic. There is a fine line separating the two. The words must be carefully chosen to fit the particular personality of each patient.

A significant reason why doctors equivocate is that they have been indoctrinated to regard medicine as a scientific discipline.

The science of medicine teaches that symptoms may have a variety of causes. A medical student learns more than fifty causes for an enlarged spleen, but a patient derives no benefit from such academic thoroughness. On the contrary, the possibilities may translate into probabilities, which if communicated to the patient fuel unease and induce a further panoply of symptoms. The Indian professor hit the nail on the head when he stated that uncertainty is the professional style of science and scientists.

A doctor owes it to a patient to be precise and affirmative. This is not difficult when the clinical condition is unambiguous or when symptoms are trivial. It is more problematic when the doctor is less certain, for example, when a serious condition is remotely likely but not completely out of the realm of possibility. At times it invites stretching certainty to nearly absurd limits and coming close to the domain of shamanism or charlatanry. Yet a doctor who appreciates the power of the word is aware that in some cases certainty may just tip the scale and relieve a patient's pain or other symptoms when all else has failed.

Is it then ethical to assure a patient of something that, strictly on scientific grounds, may not be plausible? In an age frothing with deception, medical ethicists constantly emphasize a doctor's being truthful with patients. But more than fifty-five years ago, the great medical scientist L. J. Henderson argued, "The idea that the truth, the whole truth, and nothing but the truth can be conveyed to the patient is an example of false abstraction, of the fallacy called by Whitehead 'the fallacy of misplaced concreteness.'"*

At times I have gone so far as to guarantee recovery when the scientific basis for a cure was tenuous or nonexistent. What is at stake in promising a cure that does not follow? The doctor may be proved wrong and possibly lose the patient's confidence or invite a malpractice suit (see Chapter 10). However, my many

* L. J. Henderson, "Physician and Patient as a Social System," *New England Journal of Medicine* 212 (1935): 819–823.

years of medical practice have convinced me that if a patient perceives that the doctor is motivated exclusively by concern for his or her well-being, the patient's trust is rarely diminished, even when the doctor turns out to have been wrong. On a number of occasions when I promised a cure that did not come about, the patients were almost apologetic, as though they had failed me by not living up to my expectations. When I was heartbroken for the family of a patient who died on the operating table, they comforted me. I have often heard, "We know that you tried your best." In a long life in medicine, I have never been tried in a malpractice suit.

When I am proved wrong, as happens, alas, far too frequently, I parade it, announce it to colleagues, especially to my young students. I take to heart the words of the poet Yevtushenko:

> And all mistakes, sins that have been secreted
> Pound themselves like epileptics,
> Saying: "That which is not expressed will be forgotten,
> And what is forgotten will happen again."*

Acknowledged mistakes provide potent learning experiences. Admitting them helps ensure that they will not be repeated. The humbling avowal of error prevents doctors from confusing their mission with a divine one. We possess no omniscient powers, only intuition, experience, and a patina of knowledge. These are most effective when one is constantly probing to advance the interest of an ailing human being.

HEALING A BACKACHE

I was making morning rounds on Ward B at the Peter Bent Brigham Hospital, accompanied by Jim, a postdoctoral clinical fellow who arrived with good credentials as a scientist but

---

* Yevgeny Yevtushenko, "The Unexpressed," in *Almost at the End,* trans. Antonina W. Bouis, Albert C. Todd, and Yevgeny Yevtushenko (New York: H. Holt, 1987).

rapidly proved lacking in common sense. He was opinionated, arrogant, and lacked a sense of humor.

We visited a patient who was to be electrically reverted (cardioversion; see Chapter 12) from atrial fibrillation, a cardiac rhythm irregularity that had occurred as a result of a recent mitral valve operation. In cardioversion, an electrical discharge delivered across the chest wall eliminates the abnormal rhythm. Mrs. H., a robust woman in her late forties who hailed from Maine, was utterly uninterested in our plans and cared little about her deranged heart rhythm. She was writhing with lower back pain, unable to find a comfortable position as she twisted and turned this way and that, grimacing and grunting. The prescribed narcotics added to her grief by provoking nausea, dizziness, and constipation. She was quite vehement. "I don't want to undergo this cockamamy what-you-call-it unless it helps my back pain. I want a straight answer. Will the electric treatment cure my back?"

I replied without hesitation, "Of course it will!"

Jim, who had his foot on the frame of her bed, slapped his thigh with mirth and burst out with "This is asinine. Pray explain how cardioversion can help sciatica." I twirled as though on a spit over a hot fire, flushing with discomfort and embarrassment. Mrs. H., looking puzzled and angry, asked, "Who is this character?" I responded that he was a novice who had much to learn.

When we left her room, my boiling anger stifled my voice and I remained mum. Next morning, we cardioverted Mrs. H., restoring a normal heart rhythm without mishap. Later that day I visited her by myself to inquire about the back pain. She indicated that the treatment was a miracle; the pain was completely gone. She asked for Jim, because this farm lady believed in direct action and was ready to punch him in the nose. I counseled against violence and suggested instead that she give him a piece of her mind.

The next morning at nine, the Ward B nursing station was buzzing, a veritable beehive of activity crowded with doctors, nurses, ambulating patients, and orderlies. Jim and I were examining charts when Mrs. H. suddenly stalked in. Red-faced, she had worked herself into a lather, and in a stentorian voice she demanded quiet. When everyone was silent she bellowed: "I want to tell you something. Dr. Lown's fellow here, whose name I don't know and don't care to know, is pretending to be a doctor. He is more stupid than a chicken, and you should be ashamed to have him around." She then related in pungent prose what happened, ending with a string of angry expletives. Jim turned red initially, then white, until he looked quite apoplectic. What educational impact this had, I do not know, for Jim did not elect to stay with us for the full two-year term.

If a medical student were to ask me whether cardioversion could relieve back pain, I would have to answer categorically in the negative. Jim would have been fully justified in disagreeing with me privately, but in front of a patient in pain, it is an unpardonable sin to remove any vestige of hope that a procedure might lessen the pain.

This case raises several issues. First, of course, is it ethical to offer a patient assurances about something that is unlikely to happen? Certainly there is no anatomic connection between the back and the heart, and it would have been outlandish for me to volunteer that cardioversion would relieve a severe backache. I did not initiate this chain of thought; the patient did. She was grasping at straws, wanting to believe that this procedure, in fact any procedure, would lessen her misery. Why should a doctor remove the straw that a desperate patient is clutching at? What higher laws are being upheld by such categorical ethicism?

How could one be sure that cardioversion would not help? The electric shock may overload nerve circuits, block neural traffic to the muscle, and thereby interrupt a cybernetic loop, in which muscle spasm stimulates pain nerve fibers that provoke discomfort which in turn promote more spasm. After all, the Chinese, for several thousand years, have cured all sorts of chronic aches and pains by inserting acupuncture needles at sites remote from pain or applying small electrical currents through such needles. It is even possible that the transient anesthesia prior to the cardioversion may prove salutary. If a patient anticipates more than is likely from a clinically justified procedure, is the doctor obligated to convey that uncertainty? Shouldn't the patient's well-being be the primary, if not the exclusive objective of doctoring?

To instill confidence a doctor must possess confidence. Above all this means that the doctor should not worry about being proved overly optimistic. Possessing confidence can save a patient from endless doctoring, growing hypochondriasis, and ultimate invalidism.

The following vignette shows how unequivocal reassurance can break a cycle of illness as decisively as a surgical scalpel can lance a boil.

THE WOMAN WITH SWEATY PALMS

A thin and fragile waif rested in a small ward holding four patients, although there was barely enough space for two. She looked like a forlorn bird perched on a leafless tree in mid-winter. Her voice was choked as she sobbed continually. Her knuckles were white and bony, her fingers laced tautly around knees pulled close to her chin. When I held out my hand, she hesitated and appeared flustered. The handshake was quick, perfunctory, our palms barely touching, and she quickly jerked her sweating, limp hand back.

She and her husband had been married two years, had a lovely year-old boy, but were barely eking out a living. In her early twenties, she was in good health until the onset of a bothersome heart palpitation. Finally she got up the money and courage to see a doctor. The past few months, following the first medical visit, had been an unspeakable nightmare.

The doctor she saw initially diagnosed a potentially life-threatening heart rhythm disturbance and told her that her numerous extrasystoles could be harbingers of instant death. Terrified, she had seen the doctor weekly, although she could ill afford the visits. Each week, in addition to the cost of the electrocardiograms and the doctor's high fees she had to pay a baby-sitter. Her medical diagnosis was mitral valve prolapse, and she articulated these mysterious words as though they were a fatal hex. Worst of all, the doctor had told her that it was unsafe for her to be left alone with the baby. As the prescribed antiarrhythmic drugs made her nauseated and dizzy, she was growing increasingly unable to care for her child. The doctor had urged her to have a baby-sitter around throughout the day in case of an unexpected collapse.

As they could not afford to pay anyone, her mother-in-law, with whom she got along poorly, had moved in and completely displaced her as mother and wife. She was beginning to feel like a stranger in her own home. At the age of twenty-four, she felt her life was over. Her heartrending sobs welled up from helpless anguish.

Examining her, I found her heart entirely normal except for an innocuous murmur and a few extra heartbeats that had no adverse prognostic significance. I explained carefully that her heart was entirely normal, that she could take care of her child without any danger, that her mother-in-law could move back to her own home. I urged her to forget this unfortunate experience and emphasized that she would live to a ripe old age.

"But I would rather talk of the one serious problem that you do have," I stated with feigned seriousness.

"What is that?" she asked, her eyes widening with mounting concern.

"Your only real problem is sweaty palms."

She gave a loud sigh of relief and laughed nervously. She admitted that her hands were a constant source of embarrassment. As a teenager she had dreaded going to dances because she would leave a smudge on the boy's shoulder. She spent more time worrying about her sweaty palms as a youngster than about almost any other problem.

I told her that she accentuated the problem by the way she shook hands. "If you shake hands briskly and aim for a firm handshake, no one would detect anything. But as you have a limp hand and introduce it hesitantly, the other person's fingers slide slowly over your entire palm, promptly detecting that you have sweaty hands. In fact, you announce the problem and thereby aggravate it. But if you shook hands properly, palm touching palm, it would not be as readily obvious. Let's try shaking."

For the next several minutes we experimented in handshaking. After a while, beginning to relax, she was amused and clearly relieved. She was discharged that very day and had no further heart problems.

How could her internist have erred so egregiously? The presence of mitral valve prolapse (MVP), when accompanied by extra heartbeats originating in the ventricle, the so-called ventricular extrasystoles, is widely regarded by doctors as potentially life-threatening. This is a misconception. MVP is a completely benign and trivial condition. In the United States there are probably about 25 million individuals with MVP. Fewer than one in five thousand will encounter any problem as a result of it. In my mind it rates in importance with freckles. It is more prevalent among young women — as many as 15 percent exhibit this condition — but occurrence of sudden death among young healthy women is so rare as to be almost unheard of. Yet thousands, like the woman just described, are terrorized. Worse still, a number have died from medication with dangerous and unnecessary antiarrhythmic drugs.

How do such wrong views pervade the medical profession? The reason for the dire interpretation by a primary care doctor relates to the contemporary culture of medicine. Much of the understanding of disease, its diagnosis and management, is shaped by academic physicians who practice in tertiary-care hospitals. These doctors do not see ordinary, garden-variety medical problems; they see extraordinarily complex and complicated problems. A patient with MVP would not be referred to a teaching hospital except with significant arrhythmia, stroke, or bacterial endocarditis, extraordinarily rare complications of the condition. When academics publish articles about MVP, they may accurately indicate that 10 percent or more of the patients they studied had serious complications. In my own practice, I have seen more than twenty patients with MVP who have suffered a cardiac arrest. But I directed an arrhythmia clinic drawing patients from all over the United States and abroad. God only knows how many millions of people constituted the population base of referral. It is sheer fallacy to generalize the incidence of a condition to a population at large on the basis of attending to inmates of a nursing home or members of the military. In the former one deals with the sick and senile, in the latter with the young and healthy.

Whatever the condition, whether as trivial as MVP or as terminal as heart failure, the patient expects hope from the doctor, affirmation and help to lessen this problem and the problem of living in general. This is best accomplished when the doctor is optimistic in temperament and assuring in counsel. Certainty is conveyed not merely by words but by avoiding excessive modifications in lifestyle. Multiple prohibitions undermine certainty and rob life of its quality.

Physicians at times assume the role of religious zealots. Ecclesiastics of old frequently abjured all bodily pleasures and overwhelmed sinners with fear of hellfire and eternal damnation. The physician, in pursuit of the more temporal mission of delaying death, also commonly proscribes pleasurable activities. This may deny the elderly and sick their few remaining satisfactions.

I am reminded of a medical joke. A patient asks a doctor what he can do to live longer. The doctor intones a long list of don'ts, including nearly everything he enjoys. The dismayed patient asks, "If I deny myself all those things that make life worth living, will I live longer?" The quick response is "No, but it will seem that way."

I try never to impose categorical restrictions on a patient unless the facts are indubitable. Even when data are decisive about the harmful effects of a particular food or behavior, flexibility and moderation are preferable to rigid prohibition. The patient who proclaims that he hasn't eaten an egg in ten or more years generally does not do as well as the one who occasionally indulges. The reason is straightforward. Compulsive behavior is fear-driven. If one thinks of eggs as life-threatening, one must be constantly on the alert. Such vigilance, according to the distinguished American physiologist Walter B. Cannon, engages an ancient neurophysiologic system that prepares for fight-or-flight behavior. This system evolved over millions of years to permit an animal instant readiness for deadly struggle or fleeing. During such an activated behavioral state there is an increased circulation of adrenaline, entrainment of sympathetic reflexes, acceleration of heart rate, and elevation of blood pressure. A wealth of scientific evidence indicates that animals chronically on the alert are much more disposed to heart abnormalities.

Chance of survival is improved, whatever the illness, when the subject has cultivated a relaxed and philosophic attitude toward life, especially one accompanied by a sense of humor. Three hundred years ago, the great English physician Thomas Sydenham mused that "the arrival of a clown exercises more beneficial influence upon the health of a town than twenty asses laden with drugs."

A doctor must be an embodiment of optimism. It has been my conviction that a physician should always search out a ray of light even under the darkest circumstances. When the outlook is doubtful, an affirmative attitude promotes well-being if not always recovery. My motto has long been "Do not have the doctor limit the patient. Let the limits be set by the patient." I have avoided restricting and burdening patients with fears and don'ts. This approach has resulted in many astonishing surprises of survival against all medical odds, some that can be regarded as truly miraculous. The following illustrates the gratifying result when a physician, serving as a patient's advocate, is charged with buoyant optimism.

ONE LAST FLING

I always welcomed the professor's visits. He was a lanky man with a boyish mien, a shock of graying hair, large gray eyes illuminating an intelligent face; squinting slightly, tilting his head to one side, he never quite looked at me but through me. I deeply admired him, not so much because of his great accomplishments in jurisprudence but largely because of the dignity and equanimity he displayed as a patient.

Twelve years earlier he had suffered a massive myocardial infarction that left his heart looking like a punctured tire. I realized the magnitude of the injury when visualizing his heart and lungs with fluoroscopy in the dark. I could see nothing moving in the center of his chest, only a large immobile glob. Not even a tremor was detectable. Anxiously, I shouted, "Professor T.," wishing to assure myself that he was still alive.

"Yes, Doctor, do you wish me to take a deep breath?"

"Yes, of course," I responded, relieved as I followed his cue and inhaled deeply.

On being discharged from the Peter Bent Brigham Hospital after weathering many dangerous complications as a result of the heart attack, he insisted that he wished to go on with his life minimally encumbered by the heart condition. He asked how long he had to live. Prognosis, I told him, is in God's province. "The Greeks were even wiser than we are, but their gods could predict very little. They understood that prophecy required complete knowledge of everything in the universe. We can't even foretell the weather a week hence, and you want me to be a soothsayer about life," I said, equivocating.

He tolerated my circumspection, but insisted on a ballpark figure, saying I owed him this information so he could plan the few years remaining. Believing that I was overstating by at least 50 percent, I responded, "Certainly five years." He never again broached the subject and went on living a full life, teaching at the Harvard Law School, sailing in summer to the northern waters of Newfoundland and Labrador, traveling to Cairo and the Far East. After he exceeded that magic number, he never chided me for being a poor prognosticator.

Twelve years later, he was still active but increasingly afflicted with severe congestive heart failure, life-threatening irregularities of the heartbeat with showers of ventricular extrasystoles, atrial fibrillation, and recurrent paroxysms of pulmonary edema.

While participating in a symposium in Philadelphia, he was seen to doze off, and a friend of his who was sharing the dais later told me that he saw Professor T. suddenly drop his head to the table. After ten or more seconds, the professor shook his head as if far too long underwater, took deep stertorous breaths, his eyes glazed as though having lost consciousness. This was a keen observation. When we hospitalized Professor T., the grim reality was promptly apparent. He was having short bouts of ventricular tachycardia at rates of nearly 300 beats per minute. This dangerous arrhythmia is a prodrome of sudden cardiac death. At a rate of 250 beats per minute and higher, effective heart pumping is seriously compromised even in a normal heart. In a sick heart it ceases entirely. The professor's very impaired ventricle just collapsed into contractile quietude and stopped pumping blood to perfuse body and brain. These are mini-episodes of cardiac arrest, but they spontaneously revert. If one such episode persisted, it would end Professor T.'s life.

The professor was progressively more limited and had to be hospitalized frequently to be bailed out from pulmonary edema, from which he nearly suffocated several times. The arrhythmias grew ever more ominous and frequent. The manipulation of drugs that he required would have challenged Solomonic wisdom. I was therefore shocked one day, in early summer, when he asked whether I would permit him to go sailing to Iceland with a group of younger friends. At this point, though he was frail and his lips were blue, he was still very lucid and quite determined to undertake this grueling junket.

I was momentarily flustered. Instead of responding instantly with a big fat *no*, I tried some evasive verbal maneuvering, knowing how much the annual sailing venture meant to him. I inquired about the size of the sailboat, how cramped the quarters would be, whether it would be possible to adhere to a low-salt diet, who would accompany him, how much he would have to exert himself, and so forth. It was clear that he saw this trip as a final adventure capping the end of his full and productive life. I did not have the heart to tell him no.

Once I decided that the sailing trip must not be denied, I turned to the practical nitty-gritty. First I worked out a method for him to treat his pulmonary edema, urging him to carry a tank of oxygen on the sailboat, and giving him Syrettes of morphine and diuretics. I rehearsed with him what he needed to do once he detected a rattle and wheeze and breathing became hurried and difficult. These were signs, I explained, that his lungs were overloaded with fluid and the outlined steps had to be undertaken without delay. My great concern was the increased intake of salt from ocean spray. Finally, I insisted that he contract with a helicopter company to evacuate him in case the congestive heart failure grew intractable.

He went off in fine fettle psychologically but looking wretched physically. Thereafter I had many restless moments. My unease grew with the summer and I berated myself for irresponsibility. Why had I let a dying man with end-stage heart failure and oft-recurring ventricular tachycardia go sailing off across the Atlantic? I could rationalize it somewhat if the direction were south, but they were heading to the chilled north, to Iceland, of all places. I began to scan the obituary pages, which I had never perused before or since. The summer dragged.

Came autumn, my impatience grew. I lacked the courage to telephone his home, but one day I noted Professor T.'s name on my roster of scheduled patients. At least he was still alive. I hadn't done him in! When he finally arrived, he looked better than I had seen him in several years. His cachectic, wasted look had been replaced by a healthy tan and windblown glow, and his spirits were buoyant.

"Professor T., did you have to use the helicopter?" I asked.

"Yes, indeed" was his curt reply.

"Oh, my God! It was a mistake on my part to let you go." Before he could respond, I continued, "Was your pulmonary edema bad?"

He looked perplexed. "Yes, we used the helicopter, but it was not only for me," he explained.

"Were there other cardiac patients sailing with you or was there a serious accident?" I inquired incredulously.

"Neither. The boat got stuck in a huge ice floe. There was no way out. After being stranded for a week, the crew pleaded with me to call the helicopter to enable them to return to their jobs. They were grateful for my foresight."

This was to be his last visit. Professor T. died several months later, exactly twelve years after the heart attack. It was a chastening experience, showing the weakness of the doctor's prognostic ability when confronting human will.

My aim in relating these stories is not only to emphasize the value of optimism and of communicating certainty, but the fact that medicine still requires navigating through largely uncharted waters. Many think that since we are living in the age of science, much of the guesswork is taken out of the practice of medicine. We select the right tests and computer printouts flash the exact diagnosis for which there is an effective remedy. If it were only so! I am not persuaded that it will ever be that simple. So-called medical facts are biologic approximations; outcome data and prognosis are statistical, and their application to an individual patient invariably requires a choice among diverse management options. An experienced physician knows that far too frequently the domain of science does not extend to a majority of clinical problems.

Effective patient management requires appreciation of the art of healing, in which one is guided by experience, by the recall of a similar case, and by the exercise of common sense. A sense of humility, too, is an asset, for any prescription or advice has a substantial measure of conjecture. Much medical data is increasingly based on epidemiological studies of large populations. A doctor, however, confronts a single, singular individual. There is never any certainty as to where the individual fits on the normal statistical distribution curve. Statistics may present probabilistic truth, but they shroud souls and obscure individuality.

The doctor, loyal to his or her calling, craves certainty while immersed in doubt. Yet doubt cannot delay the urgency to treat and the necessity to heal. The essence of true professionalism is to act even when the state of knowledge is inadequate. The cure needs to be prescribed immediately. The ache will not wait for the definitive study that is years away, and many clinical problems are unique, exceptional, never before encountered by the practitioner and never to be overcome by statistical battering rams. The data will frequently be soft, the patient will need to serve as his or her own control, and the cure will have to be invented if no textbook addresses the patient's precise problem. One ends up searching for the soft intangibles to substitute for nonexistent hard data. When confronting uncertainty, the physician has to be an ombudsman for the patient. But advocacy requires caring. Only then can the physician somehow surmount the agony and absurdity of human decision.

9

Extraordinary
Healing Techniques

THERE IS another dimension to medicine beyond the uncertain, one that derives from its scientific infrastructure. I have lived through a revolutionary period in medicine, a revolution continuing at full gallop. Monumental scientific discoveries and extraordinary technologic innovations have drastically altered the face of medicine. When I entered medical school, pneumonia was still a fatal disease, polio was a dreaded scourge, and inflammation of the mastoid was a ubiquitous pediatric problem that drove young mothers to distraction.

There was no cure for bacterial endocarditis. Rheumatic and syphilitic heart disease victims filled the wards of the Johns Hopkins Hospital. Cardiac surgery had been only timidly initiated. There was no medical answer for a host of major ailments from dysfunctional and painful hips to detached retinas. Hemodialysis for kidney disease was still some years in the future. Caring for patients with renal failure was a nightmare — they would retch and itch without even momentary respite from total body discomfort. As with many other conditions, we doctors stood helpless and offered only empty words to assuage the colossal misery. I vividly recall, during my internship, one such patient with end-stage kidney disease. Not finding him in bed, I went searching and discovered him hanging in the men's room. When I pulled him down, I regarded his survival as a triumph — until he confronted me with unspeakable rage, sobbing convulsively. I still remember his words: "You are not a doctor! You are a Nazi storm trooper!"

The diseases that caused so much suffering, such as syphilitic heart disease, polio, and the common earache, have nearly disappeared. Some, like smallpox, have been totally eradicated. We live in a new and unprecedented era of medicine, with a new culture affecting both doctors and patients. The near miraculous therapeutic innovations are sharply targeted on precisely defined diagnoses. Subjectivity no longer has a role in defining where the pathology resides. Therapeutic success has little to do with the character, personality, or charisma of a physician. The key elements in a successful outcome relate to the doctor's professional competence and technical skill. Unlike the preceding age, it matters little whether the patient has faith in what the doctor prescribes. Lobar pneumonia, formerly a consistent killer, is cured by antibiotics irrespective of the patient's feeling about the physician who prescribes the drug or degree of confidence in the remedy.

In this modern epoch, the growing intimacy between medicine and science promotes an illusion that they are identical. It leads doctors to trivialize the importance of bedside manner, fosters neglect of comprehensive history-taking, and diminishes the investment of self in promoting humane interactions with patients. The focus shifts from healing to curing as though these were adversarial rather than complementary systems.

For patients, the scientific revolution enhances expectations of instant cure whatever the sickness. Health concerns grow. For many, these have become their paramount preoccupation and a major subject of conversation. The media are full of medical news and employ correspondents exclusively devoted to health matters. The health complex has become this nation's largest industry and the greatest single drain on social resources. While people are healthier and live much longer than in the past, their tolerance for discomfort has diminished as their fears of sickness have mounted. This relates in no small measure to Americans' exposure to around-the-clock medical hype. In the current cultural climate, trivial symptoms are often viewed as potential harbingers of a fatal disease. Norman Cousins captured the scene: "Most people think they are going to live forever until they develop a cold, when they think they are going to die within the hour."

Another aspect of the new cultural milieu is a widespread disenchantment with scientific medicine. In a survey conducted by the Harvard School of Public Health in 1994, only 18 percent of those questioned were satisfied with the American health care system. Alternative therapies are continually gaining in popularity. In a survey reported in the *New England Journal of Medicine*, researchers interviewed a selected sample of 1539 English-speaking adults demographically representative of the U.S. population. They found that 34 percent had used at least one unconventional therapy during the preceding year. These included relaxation, chiropractic, massage, megavitamin dosages, and lifestyle diets, for example, macrobiotics. The alternative medical therapies were sought mainly for chronic, non-life-threatening conditions such as backaches, headaches, allergies, and the like. Although these therapies were resorted to by all social groups, affluent, educated whites under the age of fifty used them most frequently. The authors of this report estimated that Americans make more than half of their annual 813 million health visits to providers of unconventional therapies.*

Why do people increasingly seek out alternative therapists in preference to primary care physicians? Probably because orthodox medicine does not provide relief for whatever ails or troubles them. At present, about 25 percent of patients who visit an American doctor are successfully treated. The other 75 percent have problems that scientific medicine finds difficult to resolve. After being shuffled among a bevy of specialists and subjected to costly and invasive technologies, many patients, frustrated, turn away from conventional medicine. The power of this disaffected lobby was demonstrated when Congress compelled the National Institutes of Health to establish a branch devoted to

---

* D. M. Eisenberg, "Unconventional Medicine in the United States: Prevalence, Costs, and Patterns of Use," *New England Journal of Medicine* 328 (January 28, 1993): 246–252.

research in alternative medicine. It was charged to investigate a roster of issues, from psychic healing to homeopathy, acupuncture, herbal medicine, and the like.

In my own practice as a highly specialized cardiologist, the problems of more than half my patients do not relate to their heart conditions but to the stresses of living. I have learned that few patients search for alternative therapies when physicians focus on healing as well as using the powerful scientific tools at their disposal. Healing and improving a patient's well-being frequently require imagination in devising approaches that assuage discomfort or relieve a complaint. Sometimes a doctor may have to resort to unconventional techniques in order to improve a patient's well-being. These are not taught in medical school but are discovered through clinical experience and sanctioned by common sense.

Early on, I saw that Dr. Samuel A. Levine was not loath to scare patients into changing an unhealthy lifestyle. He would get into an oxygen tent surrounding a patient's bed, which had been painstakingly made up by a nurse. For those having difficulty in breathing, the tent provided a cool, humidified, oxygen-enriched, comfortable mini-environment. Crawling into the narrow confines of the tent, Levine would position his face close to that of the sick patient. Touching the patient's nose with an index finger, enunciating each syllable with clipped speech, he intoned as though delivering a hex, "If you smoke again after this heart attack, you will die." He would extricate himself from the oxygen tent without another word. So powerful was the spell he wove that I never heard of any patient who had been exposed to it resuming smoking, many of them going so far as to avoid the company of anyone who smoked.

Again I take to heart the words of the Siberian doctor who told me, "Every time a doctor sees a patient, the patient should feel better as a result." Visiting a terminally ill patient in the hospital, when little I do can make a difference in the outcome, I recall the heavyset Siberian. I turn the pillow over so that the patient, whose head was resting on a wrinkled, wet surface, can lie on a smooth, cool covering. After I have left the room, the patient sometimes asks the nurse, "Who was that nice doctor?" How little it sometimes takes to make someone feel better. At times a trivial intervention may appear extraordinary to a patient and leads to a more satisfied life.

DREAMS OF AN OMELET

Mr. H. was a schoolteacher in his mid-fifties, gentle, thoughtful, and undemanding. He worried much about his health, which was quite understandable because he had seen doctors so often throughout his life. Childhood rheumatic fever left him with diseased heart valves, primarily the mitral valve, which became tightly stenosed. It opens into the left ventricle, the heart's major pumping chamber, and when the mitral valve is narrowed, blood backs up, congesting the lungs. At a relatively early age, Mr. H. had to undergo mitral valve surgery, but fortunately he'd had a good operative repair and could live an unencumbered life. This was interrupted by his contracting bacterial endocarditis. This life-threatening inflammation of the lining of the heart and its valves necessitated six weeks of intravenous antibiotics. The infection destroyed his valve and he had to have another operation. The course was difficult, but nonetheless he had fared well since.

Surprisingly, with many things to be concerned about, he was culturally in tune by worrying about his cholesterol. Although he was free of risk factors for coronary disease, and his arteries were normal, he was on a rigorous low-animal-fat diet. "My wife is very strict with me; she makes sure that not a crumb of cholesterol passes my lips."

When I saw him at Christmas, I asked what he would wish for most in the new year. Without hesitation, he responded, as though the thought had long been percolating, "I dream of an omelet." He continued, "I have not had an omelet for ten years. My wife tells me it is poison for me because of my heart condition."

I explained that his type of heart problem does not require rigorous avoidance of cholesterol. "As a matter of fact, I am now prescribing an omelet for you once a week, always on Sunday." To make sure that his wife would believe the incredible, a cardiologist prescribing an omelet, I wrote a letter accompanying the prescription of a two-egg omelet once weekly. When he next visited, he was beaming. "I look forward to Sunday as never before." His eyes lit up. "Doctor, it is the best gift I have had in a very long time."

COMPLEMENTARY MEDICINE AND ACUPUNCTURE

Acupuncture is one alternative medicine technique that is most commonly sought for a variety of difficult health problems. The word "acupuncture" conjures up magic from China and the hope of gaining instant relief for whatever hurts. The origins of acupuncture are lost in antiquity, but it is known to have been used during the time of the fabled Yellow Emperor, Huang Ti, who is presumed to have lived around 2650 B.C. and is discussed in the earliest known medical text, the *Nei Ching* or *Classic of Internal Medicine,* written by many scholars in the third or second century B.C. It was first introduced to the West in the seventeenth century by Jesuit missionaries sent to Peking, yet remained little known here until about fifty years ago, when the French sinologist and diplomat Soulié de Morant published an extensive treatise on the practice.

Acupuncture is based on a philosophical belief system deriving from ancient Taoist teachings. The essential principle envisions a struggle between opposites, the yin and the yang, which constitute the basis for the universe and everything else. (See David Eisenberg, *Encounters with Qi: Exploring Chinese Medicine* [New York: Norton Press, 1985].) Disease is represented as an imbalance of these opposing yet complementary and indissolubly linked forces. Within the unity of these opposites is the ubiquitous *ch'i* (qi) which gives life its vitality. The health of an individual depends on the proper balance of ch'i; disease is the consequence of either too much or too little ch'i. Acupuncture fundamentally aims to reestablish a balance and normal flow of this ethereal substance.

The body is a pincushion for about one thousand acupuncture points, which follow an invariable topographical pattern on the body surface. The lines that link a series of points associated with a particular organ, designated meridians, extend from head to toe and are pathways for the flow of the mythical ch'i.

While a mainstay of medical healing over five thousand years for a fifth of humankind, acupuncture was never once mentioned during my medical school days. However, during early doctoring, I encountered several patients who swore by it, and intrigued by the idea that sticking and twirling needles in some mysterious points in the skin could prove therapeutic, I read the meager literature then available in English. It did not win a convert. What turned me off were the pretentious claims ascribing efficacy for every imaginable ailment from acne to xanthomas, including bronchitis, diabetes, epilepsy, hypertension, impotence, infertility, migraine, and myopia, as well as nephritis, peptic ulcer, sciatica, and much else. Like the snake oil of yore, nothing was outside its all-powerful dominion.

I was also troubled by the absence of any anatomic or physiologic rationale. For example, the back of the neck joining the skull is a point for the gallbladder, while the wrists are points for the lungs. Depression is a disease of the liver, while fear is a disease of the kidney, and both will respond to acupuncture points along the respective meridians for these organs. I found it impossible to believe that sticking a needle in a foot could improve liver function, thereby alleviating a morbid mood of depression, and found it incredible that objective evidence supporting the efficacy of acupuncture was lacking after five millennia of use. Medicine has, with great difficulty, exited from the quagmire of subjectivism, and few are ready to replace the certain compass of science with the uncertain predictions to be garnered from tea leaves and folk tales.

My skepticism was sundered, however, by a personal encounter with acupuncture. While tobogganing as a youngster, I seriously injured my back, and years later, in the mid-1960s, I experienced episodic bouts of severe back pain and sciatica.

The conventional treatment included extended periods of strict bed rest, and several times I was kept immobilized in bed for up to six weeks. Unwilling to cope with the unpredictabilities of episodic invalidism and beginning to have neurologic deficits, I underwent disc surgery. The cure was good for about five years. Thereafter, back pain recurred but did not compel long periods of bed rest.

In 1973, I was a participant in the first delegation of American cardiologists to the People's Republic of China. The group, headed by Dr. E. Grey Dimond of Kansas City, Kansas, consisted of eight prominent specialists in the field. I flew from Boston directly to Canton with brief refueling stops in Seattle and Tokyo. Arriving in Canton at the end of the long grueling flight, I began to experience severe lower back pain, which soon completely disabled me. Even the soft mattress in the Chinese hotel felt like a medieval torture rack. The only relief came from lying on the floor as long as no one walked close by. My American colleagues, though outstanding medical authorities, hadn't the foggiest idea how to deal with an excruciating backache. The best they could offer was Tylenol and codeine, which someone had brought along in case of a toothache.

In desperation, I asked my Chinese hosts, who were eager to be helpful, whether they could arrange any traditional treatment for the back pain. They obliged and I was taken to an institute of traditional medicine. I undressed to my shorts, and after little if any history-taking, two massive men resembling Japanese sumo wrestlers appeared. Each grabbed a leg, seeming to pull at right angles to each other. The pain was the most severe that I had experienced, and I felt I was about to be bisected. When they let go for a moment, I jumped off the table, saying I was cured. Back at the hotel I was in more agony than before. Moaning with unremitting pain, for which narcotics provided by the Chinese afforded no relief, I relented and begged for acupuncture.

The acupuncturist who arrived was a small, frail, and unprepossessing man. He had me roll over on my stomach and inserted a long, thin acupuncture needle in my upper buttocks. I felt nothing as he twirled the needle. Disappointed that I had no sensation, he reinserted the needle, seemingly in the same spot. I complained of an uncomfortable heaviness and tingling, and my buttocks muscle seemed to resist rotation of the needle. The doctor was delighted with my discomfort and muttered something that sounded like "dechi." Later I learned that de ch'i meant "obtaining ch'i," getting the vital energy to flow. After several minutes, he suggested that I stand up and walk. I categorically refused. Astonishingly, the torments of just a few minutes earlier had begun to diminish, and I was not about to reactivate them by engaging in foolhardy experiments. Furthermore, I wished to bask in the marvelous sensation of being nearly pain free.

The acupuncturist continued to insist that I stand. I rose without assistance and walked some steps without severe pain. Where minutes before a hot poker seemed to be held tautly against my sciatic nerve, I now felt only a little stiffness and numbness. While physically I felt good, psychologically I was in a state of shock. He came back the next day and, in addition to needling, carried out moxibustion, in which the lighted end of a slow-burning stick of herbs, a Chinese mugwort that glowed like a hot charcoal, was brought close to my skin at the very spot he had previously acupunctured. This resulted in further improvement in my ability to walk without pain. In the past, given the severity of the pain, it would have taken a month or longer of absolute bed rest to gain some relief. Now, after three days, I could walk comfortably. A week later I climbed the Great Chinese Wall and had no difficult during the direct return flight from Hong Kong to Boston. I remained free of a significant backache for about a year.

Had such a miraculous cure been reported to me by someone else, I would have been skeptical, but there was no evading the reality of what had transpired in my own flesh. Either I was a suggestible psychoneurotic or there was some objective merit to acupuncture. As might have been expected, I chose the latter option. Recalling the words of Saint Augustine, "There are no miracles, only unknown laws," I no longer thought of it as "quackipuncture." I began to search for the science.

In China we had occasion to see much of what they called acupuncture anesthesia in both Western and traditional clinics. Chairman Mao had said, "Chinese medicine and pharmacology are a great treasure house, and efforts should be made to explore them and raise them to a higher level." In practice this meant acupuncture, herbal medicine, and massage. Our visit came in the midst of the "great cultural proletarian revolution." Mao's every utterance was an unbreachable commandment. Any failure to comply enthusiastically was sufficient reason for imprisonment or deportation to a life of drudgery in the countryside, or even worse. It was therefore a heyday for acupuncture, the merits constantly being embellished with extravagant claims of remarkable cures.

Even discounting the ideological hoopla, it was nonetheless impressive to observe its effectiveness in diverse surgical operations as a substitute for anesthesia. We saw thyroidectomies, brain tumor removals, and heart surgery performed in wideawake acupunctured patients. Witnessing the repair of a hole in the heart made the most enduring impression on me. The patient, a young man in his early twenties with a ventricular septal defect, walked into the operating room of a leading Shanghai hospital. After shaking hands with each of the eight visiting Americans, he lay down on the operating table and the surgery was performed. The room was bare except for an oxygen tank, a sphygmomanometer, and a primitive-looking pump oxygenator. He was draped for the operation, an intravenous was started, and a thin rubber tubing to provide oxygen was inserted in a nostril. Several acupuncture needles were then inserted in his ear and in his left wrist. After about fifteen minutes he appeared to be dozing. He was then connected to the ancient bypass machine to provide external pumping of his blood.

The surgeon was masterfully skilled and extraordinarily quick. In no time at all he had opened the chest and electrically fibrillated the heart to stop its contractions. Ventricular fibrillation is an ultrarapid chaotic rhythm in which heart pumping ceases, enabling the surgeon to have a quiet field for his work. In the absence of an external assist pumping device, the patient would die within a few minutes.

Standing at the head of the operating table, I could intimately observe the patient's face. The entire scene was eerie and totally unreal for those of us trained in Western medicine. Several times during the operation, the patient opened his eyes and talked, though he was without any cardiac contractions. A distinguished American surgeon standing close by kept nudging me in disbelief and repeating, "Are you seeing what I am seeing?" He whispered that we were being subjected to some Chinese trick of mass hypnosis.

The patient moaned only twice, each time when the surgeon encountered excessive bleeding, which he had difficulty in clamping rapidly. As the patient was surgically draped and could not see what was going on in his own chest cavity, and as the surgeon remained silent, I was mystified as to the cues the patient was picking up. When the surgeon had the situation under control, the patient relaxed as well.

As the operation was coming to an end and they were closing the chest, I began to worry about how they would revert the fibrillating heart, for no cardiac defibrillator was in sight in the technologically empty operating theater. When the thoracic cage was closed, they rolled in a vintage defibrillator, indistinguishable from the one I had introduced more than a decade earlier (see Chapter 13). They placed the electrode paddles against the chest wall and delivered an electrical discharge, which instantly restored a normal rhythm. The doctors and nurses then lined up in front of me, bowed, and said, "Thank you for serving the people." The patient sat up, once again shook hands with everyone, seated himself in a wheelchair, and was rolled to the recovery room.

In the years since, the Chinese have acknowledged that acupuncture is not an effective substitute for anesthesia in all cases. It is no longer used for abdominal or gynecologic operations, and many individuals are not suitable subjects for it. Nonetheless, it is a remarkable technique for diminishing pain perception. Still mystifying is the basis for its effectiveness. Puzzled by how it worked, I visited the Shanghai Institute of Traditional Chinese Medicine, a pioneering center for acupuncture research. There I found irrefutable confirmation of the potency of acupuncture as an analgesic agency. I witnessed an experiment that would shock the sensibilities of many people.

A rabbit was harnessed in a cradle, immobile except for its head. Fixed in front of the rabbit's nose was a heating coil. When the electric rheostat was turned, the coil glowed red hot. Within a few seconds the rabbit moved its head away from the hot probe. This was repeated several times with an identical response. Several acupuncture needles were then inserted in one of the rabbit's hind legs, which were then attached to an electric stimulator. This time when the coil in front of the rabbit's nose glowed red, the head did not move. I watched with disbelief and horror as the tip of the nose began to char and turn black with an acrid odor of burning flesh. This single, yet decisive experiment dissipated all my doubts that acupuncture can shut off pain sensation.

But how is the perception of pain blocked by acupuncture? Chinese scientists offered several explanations. One related to the gating mechanisms in the spinal cord which can close when powerful stimuli enter the nerve network. According to this theory, the acupuncture stimulus serves as a red traffic light stopping pain information that arises in the peripheral nerve endings and preventing these noxious messages from reaching the brain. Another explanation offered was that acupuncture releases neuropeptides in the blood, which dull perception of pain. Supporting this second theory is the finding that infusing blood from an acupunctured animal into a second animal lowered the pain threshold for the second even though it had not been needled.

Dr. David Eisenberg, a careful student of traditional Chinese medicine, concluded, "There is sufficient scientific evidence that acupuncture can predictably and reproducibly alter pain perception in animals and in humans." He suggested that the pain relief may be due to the release of opioid-like endorphins. Indeed, the Chinese have reported on cases of addiction to acupuncture needling.* Such addicted individuals experienced withdrawal-type symptoms, suffering from lassitude, nausea, abdominal pain, and headaches when acupuncture was stopped. The symptoms were promptly relieved when acupuncture was resumed, suggesting that acupuncture stimulated the brain to produce such potentially addicting neuromediators like endorphins or enkephalins.

My personal experience with acupuncture and the observations I made during several trips to China raise profound questions in the field of neurophysiology and psychobiology. If stimulation of the subcutaneous nerve network can block painful nerve traffic so completely that the skull and chest can be opened without anesthesia, powerful agencies must exist at the body surface that can alter brain perception or interpretation of physical sensations. Can these be affected by means other than penetrating the skin? The fact that massage and mere pressure are also effective would suggest that needles may not be necessary.

Does acupuncture share a common neurophysiology with the placebo? The action of placebos is an important issue in therapeutics. Why does a simple sugar-coated pill change the most intimate body functions? Indeed, one may never be certain whether an effect ascribed to a drug is not partly or wholly owing to a placebo effect. Like drugs, placebos can induce serious adverse reactions. According to Dr. Herbert Benson, promulgator of the relaxation response, the effectiveness of a placebo involves three major elements: the belief and expectation of the patient; the belief and expectation of the doctor; and the doctor-patient relationship. These same relations are essentially operative in much of alternative medicine.**

I frequently practice what is referred to as alternative medi-

---

* Eisenberg, "Unconventional Medicine," 118.
** Eisenberg, "Unconventional Medicine," 12.

cine in treating problems for which I can find no scientific answers or helpful guidelines in the medical literature. One cannot always go by the book. The unique qualities of each person mean that what works for one may not prove equally effective for another. At times, off-the-wall measures are successful. It is certainly unlikely that a physician nowadays would resort to using hypnosis; more likely, a patient would be referred to an experienced psychologist. The present litigious age can open a doctor to significant penalties should a seemingly innovative approach fail, and the consequences are likely to be far worse if the procedure is truly novel and untested. The fear of litigation makes physicians hesitant, circumspect, and as a result, frequently ineffective.

HICCUPS AND HYPNOSIS

In the late 1950s, I was called to see a West Virginia physician who was a patient on the thoracic service of the Peter Bent Brigham Hospital. It was a routine consultation for preoperative cardiac clearance. Dr. E.W. was a depressed Afro-American man, cachectic and wrinkled, who appeared much older than his fifty-three years. He was awaiting exploratory thoracotomy for a left lower lung lesion. Cancer was suspected because he had smoked three packs of cigarettes a day for thirty years. This was in the days before the elegant methodologies permitted definitive diagnosis of cancer without resort to surgery. The patient's most striking aspect, however, was the frequent, unremitting hiccuping that shook his long, wasted frame. The spasms, occurring only while he was awake, made him stutter and interfered with his eating.

For the past two years, Dr. W. had not had a momentary respite from hiccuping during waking hours. He had visited many medical centers in a futile search for a cure, but none of the prescribed remedies afforded any relief. He had even been subjected to a surgical severing of the left phrenic nerve, which partially paralyzed his diaphragm. Aside from making him somewhat breathless on exertion, this drastic procedure had not altered the continuing hiccups. A suicide attempt had brought him for psychiatric care to the Massachusetts Mental Health Hospital, where a routine admission X ray exposed a mass in his lung. Therefore he was transferred to our hospital, his condition deemed grave. The massive weight loss of more than sixty pounds, severe anorexia, and hiccuping were suspected to be the results of metastatic cancer.

I had never seen such a sad-looking human being. I was dismayed that in this day and age, modern medicine should stand defeated before a hiccup. In my medical note I expressed certainty that the condition could be effectively managed, speculating that the lung lesion was benign, the result of immobility of the left diaphragm.

When I returned from a trip some days later, my assistant, a postdoctoral clinical fellow, suggested that we see Dr. W., who had apparently become my responsibility. The fellow intimated that the patient was transferred to my service by the surgeons, who did not wish to be burdened with an intractable problem, especially since I was a self-proclaimed hiccup maven. My consternation grew as I reviewed Dr. W.'s voluminous chart. Any and every treatment for hiccups known to medicine had already been tried, from putting sugar on the back of the tongue, to inhaling whiffs of nitrous oxide, to sniffing garlic, to an array of exotic remedies, all without avail. Even the phrenic nerve crush, in a desperate attempt to alleviate his condition, had proved fruitless.

My discomfort mounted and turned into panic as I realized that I was no hiccup expert and had nothing significant or even trivial to suggest besides what had been tried many times. In fact, I had never dealt with a similar problem. What was I to do for this terribly depressed and disabled man? Dr. W. indicated, in fractured sentences, that if we could not clear up the hiccuping, he did not want to live, as it was sheer hell. It had disrupted his marriage, caused him to lose his medical practice, and made him a complete invalid and pauper.

For the next few days nothing occupied me except his damn hiccuping. Searching the literature was totally unrewarding.

One thought kept recurring, emitting the same cacophonous few bars, like a phonograph needle caught in the groove of a recording. If the hiccuping was due to a cancer irritating a nerve plexus, why did the hiccuping stop at night? If sleep shuts off the hiccuping, it probably results from a functional impairment rather than an organic lesion. This was a hopeful note. It might be impossible to determine the cause, but could we induce a state of relaxation that would effect relief similar to that obtained during sleep? Then out of the blue, eureka! Would posthypnotic suggestion be a useful approach? This was not an unexpected direction, considering that during the previous year I had worked with a group to study the cardiovascular consequences of chronic stress induced by means of posthypnotic suggestion.

Undeterred by the fact that hypnosis had not been previously employed for intractable hiccups, I turned for help to a brilliant psychologist, Dr. Martin Orne, at Massachusetts Mental Health. Though very young, he was already recognized as a leading authority on hypnosis, and since he had been a co-investigator in our earlier research, I knew him well. When I called to relate the clinical situation, Orne affirmed that hypnosis was a reasonable therapeutic approach.

"Can you see him this afternoon?" I inquired.

"Out of the question. You caught me as I am racing to the airport."

"That's okay. The man has been hiccuping for two years, a few days longer won't much matter. We'll expect you immediately when you return," I replied. My disappointment turned to dismay when he told me he'd be in California for six weeks.

"What am I to do then?" I implored despairingly.

Orne, in his imperious German accent, responded that I should proceed without him. "It is straightforward. You will hypnotize Dr. W. the way you watched me do for a year. You will encounter no problems." Then he gave me simple instructions on the art of hypnosis, admonished me never to mention hiccups while the patient was hypnotized, wished me good luck, and left me on my own.

The next day I hung a sign outside Dr. W.'s hospital room: DO NOT DISTURB. THERAPY IN SESSION. I had rarely been so anxious. Clearly I was deep in the soup. There seemed no reasonable way to retreat. Hypnotizing Dr. W. turned out to be easy. He was a ready, willing, and highly motivated subject. As I was not permitted to talk about hiccups by the ultimate hypno guru, I kept muttering, "You are now relaxed, very relaxed, you are very, very relaxed." This Buddhist mantra sort of muttering made me very sleepy but had absolutely no effect on the hiccuping. Nothing seemed to happen. The séance, which took place each morning, required about twenty minutes. Day after day as my measure of desperation increased, there was absolutely no change in the frequency of the hiccuping. Meanwhile, strange murmurings, sly looks, and unsuppressed giggles among the nursing staff greeted me whenever I arrived for a session. They were no doubt wondering what was really going on behind the closed doors.

One day, visiting Dr. W., I hit on the idea of asking him to keep a daily count of the exact number of hiccups. This chore sounds idiotic, but there was a plan to this seeming folly. I provided him with a notebook and suggested a method for record keeping. Just before hypnotizing him, I asked the number of hiccups for the day. The first day it was 43,657. While he was under hypnosis, it was possible to allude to the problem without saying the no-no word "hiccup." Before ending the session I simply suggested that the next day the number would be fewer than 40,000. The day dragged interminably until the next visit.

The following day, before I even sat down, the question was on my lips. "And what is the number today?" I solemnly asked, concealing my tremulous apprehension. Dr. W. responded, without emotion, that it was 38,632. I could hardly contain my excitement. Since the number of hiccups had dropped almost exactly 5,000, I decided to aim for such a reduction every day. I was not yet ready to declare victory, but for the first time there was a glimmer of light at the end of a long, dark tunnel. In the next hypnosis session I suggested, "Tomorrow it will be fewer than 34,500." The next day it was 34,289. Each day I reduced the number by 5,000, and each time the hiccups dropped by almost exactly that amount.

When we were down to about 15,000, the improvement was noticeable. Dr. W. grew less depressed. For the first time he was hopeful, even smiling now and then. We began to talk constructively about his returning home and picking up the pieces of his wrecked life.

When we reached 5,000, I slowed the tempo. He later commented that traveling in a car, in the past, had made the hiccups intolerable. By that time he was down to zero, and I suggested during a session that while he was driving, the number would remain zero. We took a spin in my automobile, and he did not emit a single hiccup. Dr. W. acknowledged that he was cured and that it was time to return home.

This entire enterprise had taken more than three weeks during which I had been in an unspeakable state of anxiety. I repeatedly asked myself, Why am I indulging in such idiocies, completely out of my depth, becoming the laughingstock of colleagues and undermining my medical career? Fear of malpractice was not yet on the horizon, but clearly I was malpracticing. It was the first and last time I dabbled in hypnosis, in large part because I never encountered a similar problem. Were I to do so, would I pursue a similar tack? Most probably.

A doctor partakes of two cultures, the dominant one that of science, the second that of the art of healing, which is indispensable for the full success of the science. In time the domain of science will no doubt extend to include within its province more of what ails human beings. However, it will never displace the art. There will always remain ample space for alternative therapies that find their roots in traditions other than science. The fundamental reality is that the soul is not encompassed by the brain. Medicine cannot abandon the healing of aching souls without diminishing its relevance for the human condition.

10

Malpractice
Corrupts Healing

PHYSICIANS, when asked what ails medicine, invariably put the medical litigation jungle at the top of the list. According to a view widely shared by doctors, hungry ambulance-chasing lawyers have corrupted the practice of medicine, conjuring up and exaggerating real or imaginary medical misdeeds. The malpractice craze is blamed for every health care ill, including the outrageous price of drugs, the upward spiraling hospital charges, the exorbitant fees of medical specialists, as well as the mechanistic character of modern medicine and the erosion of the doctor-patient relationship. Some medical leaders believe that genuine reform of the health care system requires rectification of the "malpractice mess."*

At any medical conclave, the audience warms to even a poor speaker if the discourse is spiced with anti-lawyer anecdotes, which are not hard to come by. Indeed, in a society such as ours, with more lawyers in Manhattan than in a country the size of Japan, a litigious culture rides the waves. Medicine is not exempt; on the contrary, the health profession is a significant target.

Medicine acquired its halo in small communities during the early decades of the twentieth century. Rigorously trained physicians knew enough to make a difference. Even when ignorant about the medical condition, which was often, a doctor was at

---

* J. S. Todd, "Reform of the Health Care System and Professional Liability," *New England Journal of Medicine* 329 (1993): 1733–1735.

the patient's home, keeping vigil at the bedside. Hospitalization was the exception. The doctor knew the patient as a person, was familiar with the family, and had a sound notion of the prevailing psychological and social stresses. In present-day America, this idyllic scene has vanished. In the large urban sprawl where most of the population resides, a doctor confronts a stranger. Worry about litigation contributes to an unease that may lurk before the first salutation. There is rarely time for civilities such as a handshake or small talk. The doctor, constrained by the clock, may have only twenty minutes for a visit. Questioning therefore focuses on the chief complaint, which commonly has little to do with the real reason for a patient's visit. Worse still, even the limited time available may be interrupted by telephone calls and other intrusions. The physical examination is as cursory as the history-taking and is concentrated on the area where the imagined primary complaint is lodged.

Such brief and often frustrating encounters cannot address a patient's deeply felt problems; at most, they may temporarily satisfy an immediate complaint. When history-taking is given short shrift, the doctor is likely to be lost in a sea of dire possibilities, warranting a diversity of technological interventions. In contrast, a careful history, a thorough physical examination, and a few simple routine tests provide about 85 percent of the basic information required for a correct diagnosis.* Costly technologies and invasive procedures are far less rewarding, accounting for about 10 percent of the significant data for securing a diagnosis.

The fear of litigation and the lack of thoroughness during the initial encounter encourage testing and invasive procedures. The logic is that if all diagnostic options are covered, accusations of negligence can easily be refuted in a court of law. This kind of defensive medicine is the basis for minor problems receiving comprehensive workups. I learned this fact from my postdoctoral fellows who, to supplement their meager income, often moonlight in emergency services or in the medical wards

---

* J. Hampton, *British Medical Journal* 2 (1975): 486–489.

of small community hospitals lacking house staff. In past years, such coverage meant being a physical presence and available for the rare problem and provided a golden opportunity for the fellow to catch up on medical reading or much needed sleep. This is no longer the case. After a weekend of moonlighting, postdoctoral fellows arrive for morning hospital rounds sleep-deprived and brimming with fatigue. Coverage now requires attending to numerous tests and responding to complications resulting from the many procedures. Formerly, when a youngster fell off a bicycle and scraped a shin, attention to the injured area was all that was required. Now, before he can be sent on his way, one needs to rule out a host of unlikely and hidden injuries. One fellow explained, "I do these stupid things just to cover my ass."

It is ironic that the quest for avoiding litigation sets the very stage for the legal entrapments it aims to avert. In the best of all possible worlds, any procedure used on a patient should carry a minimum unavoidable incidence of complications. No procedure is completely safe. Even an innocuous intravenous stick can become a source for infection or the nidus for a blood clot. The commonly practiced cardiac catheterization results in a life-threatening complication once in about every four hundred procedures. Also, a single test is rarely single, often leading to additional tests to confirm the original results, thereby multiplying the chances for adverse reactions.

Any routine, well-standardized medical test is wrong about 5 percent of the time, providing either false-positive or false-negative information. A false-negative result means that the test fails to detect a condition that is present. In my mind, the opposite error, a false-positive result, is far more serious, as it serves as an invitation for a host of other tests and procedures. For example, if an exercise stress test is positive, showing electrocardiographic changes compatible with coronary heart disease, a doctor often orders an invasive coronary angiogram, which is extraordinarily costly and fraught with additional complications. If the test is positive, it may be repeated; should the second test be negative, the result remains inconclusive. A third test is necessary, and only if it is normal may one entertain the possibility that the initial result was in error. It may be weeks or months before the situation is clarified, dispelling the cloud of heart disease, cancer, or another serious disease. The more tests, the more erroneous information is dredged up. In the case of a false-positive result, one is led on a wild-goose chase in attempting to discover a condition that does not exist. In the case of a false-negative finding, a condition is missed that needs to be addressed. In either case, there is a disconcerted and angry patient.

The penchant for procedures and tests is compelled by the very nature of medicine. Many problems a doctor encounters lack a ready explanation, but whether one is available or not, a bothersome complaint must be treated. It takes much experience for a physician to master the art of navigating the sea of uncertainty, particularly today when doctors crave certainty more than ever. Medical education inculcates the concept that medicine is a scientific discipline, an idea reinforced during house staff training within a hospital burgeoning with advanced technologies seemingly capable of providing insights into all problems.

Another element that drives testing is the fact that young physicians are filled with encyclopedic information of all the mayhem that can afflict a human being. The less experienced the physician, the less skilled he or she is in discriminating between what is likely and what is highly improbable. It takes much leavening experience to appreciate that oddities are rarely encountered and to know when it is appropriate to launch an intensive search operation.

These factors explain the reason house officers prescribe a long diagnostic rule-out list including much esoterica for nearly every new hospital admission. The stereotypic justification for all this investigative mayhem is offered as a question: What if the patient has this or that unusual disorder? Since the inexperienced house staff largely determine what studies are carried out, little wonder that technology is extensively engaged. It should be no surprise that many complications occur even in the best of hospitals. The dangers multiply not only because of the high concentration of young health professionals having modest experience and inadequate senior supervision but because all the technologic heavy artillery is at their beck and call. These factors make a hospital a hazardous place for sick people.

I still recall with pain the tragic sequence of events that befell one of my hospitalized patients. He was a distinguished professor, a scholar of international renown, and I had taken care of his coronary heart condition for slightly more than twenty years. Hospitalized on the surgical service for removal of a bladder tumor, he sustained a minor heart attack during the night of the second postoperative day. The surgical resident on duty, presuming the patient had mild congestive heart failure as well, decided without any consultation to insert a Swan-Ganz line to monitor heart pressures. In this procedure a catheter is introduced through a neck vein, slipped through the right ventricle, and wedged in a branch of the pulmonary artery. This permits measuring pressures in the critically important left ventricular chamber and helps monitor fluid balance of sick patients. In theory it provides valuable information, but in practice it is rarely if ever indicated. In the professor it was certainly unwarranted.

The next day, I learned from the nurses that my patient grew quite agitated about having a catheter inserted in his heart. As the catheter entered the right ventricle, it precipitated ventricular tachycardia which rapidly degenerated to ventricular fibrillation, resulting in a cardiac arrest. After a prolonged and trying resuscitation, he survived for only five days. When the resident was questioned on the rationale for the invasive procedure, he responded that it would have been malpractice to deny him hemodynamic monitoring. In an eighty-year-old man who had sustained a minor heart attack, the procedure was completely without justification.

Although such a tragic episode is exceptional, the media convey an image of a jungle of misdeeds and gross negligence, a raging epidemic of medical incompetence in this country. "The carnage from malpractice is astonishing. If you add up all the deaths each year from crime, from motor vehicle accidents, and from fires, they will not equal the estimated 80,000 people who die in hospitals annually from some form of medical practice."* The report continues that scores of thousands are left paralyzed, brain damaged, blind, or horribly disabled as a result of medical incompetence.

One can indeed cite individual cases of unimaginable incompetence causing untold tragedy. What rankles the public is the hesitancy of physicians to blow the whistle on a grossly incompetent colleague. A case that gained wide media coverage was that of a forty-four-year-old man who checked in for routine low-back surgery. Expecting to be discharged within several days, he spent six months in the hospital and was discharged with catastrophic brain damage requiring seventy pills daily merely to control seizures. The tragedy was the fault of an alcoholic anesthesiologist who gave the patient more than ten times the prescribed dose of a sedative, then did not monitor vital signs during the operation. There is no excuse for doctors to remain silent in the face of such egregious incompetence and gross malfeasance.

While infliction of hurt should never be justified, it nonetheless needs to be seen in perspective. Incompetence accounts for an infinitesimal percentage of the mistakes that lead to human suffering and loss of life. In my view, most mistakes are caused by well-trained physicians who bypass careful history-taking, indulge in rampant use of technology, and thereby injure far more patients than incompetent doctors do. Regrettably, the focus of criticism is on the outrageous case, not on the less newsworthy but more serious problem caused by the current culture of medicine.

Even more disability and death result from the excessive prescription of drugs, from polypharmacy, and from drug interactions than from the inappropriate use of technology. Nei-

* B. Herbert, *New York Times,* op-ed page, August 10, 1994.

ther surgery nor invasive procedures cause a fraction of the damage that is done with pharmaceuticals. Rarely a week passes without my encountering one or more patients suffering from adverse drug reactions.

Early in my career I learned that even the most meticulous physicians at times make costly errors in prescribing. While I was still in fellowship training, Dr. Samuel Levine asked me to see Mr. G., one of his out-of-town patients, who was staying in a hotel. It was way past midnight during a winter blizzard. Over many years Mr. G. had suffered from advanced coronary artery disease and congestive heart failure for which he had been treated with digitalis. I found him seriously ill with severe cardiac congestion, lungs filled with fluid, and his heart racing at 160 beats per minute with perfect clock regularity. The rhythm was readily identified as paroxysmal atrial tachycardia with block (see Chapter 11), a disordered heartbeat brought on by digitalis overdose. Because of the raging snowstorm it was difficult to obtain an ambulance. While waiting, I gave him potassium chloride, an antidote for this type of digitalis poisoning. Several hours later Mr. G. reverted to a normal heartbeat and his congestion improved.

But how had he become poisoned from digitalis? The next morning Levine did not believe that digitalis could have been the culprit, as the patient's drugs and dosage had not changed. He received only a weekly mercurial diuretic to leach out fluid and a daily dose of digitoxin. Levine showed me his office notes confirming that Mr. G.'s 0.1 mg daily dose of digitoxin had not been altered over several years.

But Mrs. G. recalled that when they visited Levine three months earlier, he had written a new prescription for digitoxin pills, which was filled in a local drugstore. Playing Sherlock Holmes, I went to the pharmacy, inspected the prescriptions on file, and was taken aback to find a prescription in Levine's fine distinctive handwriting made out for twice the dose the patient had been taking. Written clearly was 0.2 mg daily, not 0.1 mg. Levine was utterly mortified when I told him and could offer no explanation for this grievous error. He was fully aware that giving a sick cardiac patient twice the prescribed dose of a highly toxic drug could have proved lethal. It was a sobering lesson that even good doctors are not eternally vigilant.

One cannot outlaw human error, and even the best doctors make mistakes. The widely held medical point of view is that most malpractice suits are frivolous and lacking in merit. The intense emotion of doctors on this issue is understandable. Few events are more demoralizing to a physician than being confronted with a subpoena to hand over all records on a patient. The chill of guilt, the need to invest endless scarce time in meeting with lawyers, the disruption of tranquillity, the shame of being accused of a misdeed, coalesce into an unfathomable sense of misery. The offending physician feels wronged, and with time this feeling is transformed into seething anger. Unfortunately, I have seen it directed against other patients, which fosters the atmosphere for further malpractice suits.

The shock of a malpractice suit is worsened because doctors are so convinced that, as stated by organized medicine, "The quality of medical practice has never been higher; the standards have never been more strictly defined; the caliber of individual practitioners is historically unsurpassed; the volume and intensity of review activities are unprecedented."* Something is out of kilter.

Malpractice in American hospitals has been studied extensively. Only 1 percent of patients are injured through medical error while hospitalized, but with 30 million hospital admissions annually, even such a small rate of error amounts to 300,000 cases of negligent care, or approximately 800 daily. The public, however, is not as litigious as the media and the medical profession would lead one to believe. In fact, suits are far fewer than instances of negligence or malpractice. A Harvard study found that only 1.53 percent of patients who were harmed by medical treatment actually filed suit. In the United States there

---

* J. M. Vaccarino, "Malpractice: The Problem in Perspective," *Journal of the American Medical Association* 238 (1977): 861–863.

are eight times as many instances of negligence as claims for compensation and fourteen instances of negligence for every successful claim for compensation. The study concluded that "litigation infrequently compensates patients injured by medical negligence and rarely identifies and holds the provider accountable for substandard care."* Even in the litigious atmosphere of the United States, the chance of a doctor's being sued after a negligent event is only one in fifty.

Also unfounded is the widely held view of organized medicine and the insurance industry that malpractice lawsuits are a substantial factor in the surge in health care costs. Only 1 percent of health care expenditures are attributable to issues of professional liability.** On average, doctors spend 2.9 percent of their gross income on malpractice insurance, just a shade over the 2.3 percent they spend on their "professional car upkeep." It is the insurance companies more than the victims of malpractice who are collecting the loot; for example, in 1991 malpractice policies earned them $1.4 billion in profits.

So why all the hullabaloo? There is more than meets the eye. While doctors are genuinely terrified of being sued, the surge of defensive medicine has a subconscious motivation. The fear of malpractice has grown as a rationalization for lucrative procedures, especially invasive ones. The higher the litigation frenzy, the higher the incomes of doctors. The case of the Swan-Ganz line is an illustration. There was a time when nearly half the patients having an anterior transmural myocardial infarction

---

* H. H. Hiat et al., "A Study of Medical Injury and Medical Malpractice: An Overview," *New England Journal of Medicine* 321 (1989): 480; L. L. Leape et al., "The Nature of Advanced Events in Hospitalized Patients," *New England Journal of Medicine* 324 (1991): 377; A. R. Localio, A. G. Lawthers, T. A. Brennan, et al., "Relation between Malpractice Claims and Adverse Events Due to Negligence: Results of Harvard Medical Practice," *New England Journal of Medicine* 325 (1991): 245–251.
** "Medical and Hospital Professional Liability: A Report Prepared for the Texas Health Policy Task Force" (Austin: Tonn and Associates, 1992), and B. Beckman et al., "The Doctor-Patient Relationship and Malpractice," *Archives of Internal Medicine* 154 (1994): 1365.

had these lines inserted. The justification was that this was an effective way to monitor heart function in a sick cardiac patient. A doctor earned several hundred dollars for inserting such a line in addition to a fixed daily fee for keeping it in. The doctor had little to do while the patient was bearing the discomfort. In my view, the procedure offered little if any useful information that could not be obtained by a far simpler, less traumatic, and less costly approach, namely, examining the patient.

On the basis of my experience in directing an active coronary care unit for more than a decade, I estimate the complication rate of a Swan-Ganz line to have been about 10 percent, ranging from unsightly hematomas in the neck to serious infections and life-threatening arrhythmias. In fact, the fear of malpractice has become a rationalization for excessive indulgence in lucrative procedures. The popularity of a procedure is a function of its financial rewards. When reimbursement for the Swan-Ganz procedure was reduced, so was its use, even though the clinical rationale remained unaltered.

WHY DO PATIENTS SUE?

Patients who sue doctors or hospitals consistently say that the prime reason is a perceived lack of caring. Another reason is the impression that a doctor was unavailable when needed or abandoned them. Still another common answer is that a doctor ignored the patient's concerns and failed to consider his or her perspective. It appears that litigation resulted more from miscommunication than malpractice per se.

It requires intense determination, driven by a high concentration of anger, to take legal action. The long and frustrating process requires an enormous investment of time and emotional energies. Furthermore, in most instances the judgment is against the plaintiff. Although many physicians believe that the majority of litigations involve trivial or imagined wrong, they invariably involve major injuries. The incidents for which doctors and hospitals are sued are of a serious nature, frequently resulting in long-term disabilities affecting work, social life, and family relationships. In one study, anatomic deformities or death were involved in 52 percent of malpractice suits, while emotional impairment was the basis for an additional 20 percent. More than 70 percent of the suits are against surgeons, obstetricians, and emergency room physicians. Most malpractice suits were suggested by health care professionals who subsequently provided care.

A British report on malpractice indicates that an original injury is not enough to spur a malpractice suit; insensitive handling and poor communication after the original incident are also required. The claimants were disturbed by the absence of explanation, by what they interpreted to be a lack of honesty, a reluctance to apologize, or their complaints being dismissed as neurotic. More than a third would not have opted for litigation had they received an explanation or apology.*

In this British study, three reasons were generally advanced for initiating legal action: first was a sense of altruism, to prevent a similar injury being visited on friends or neighbors; second was a desire to expose the truth of what actually happened; and third and least important was to gain monetary restitution for suffering. Similar American studies also show that most patients sue merely to receive an explanation or in the hope that staff will be called to account, and learn a lesson from their trauma, rather than for financial reward. The lawsuit becomes a way of compelling a physician to assume responsibility for the outcome and share the anger and suffering the patient has endured. One patient sums up the sentiments of many: "If I were to use a couple of words, they would be 'accountability' and 'justice.' To be more explicit, there seems to be an all-pervasive attitude that doctors are somehow above and beyond the normal restraints the rest of humanity have to abide by."**

* C. Vincent, M. Young, and A. Phillips, "Why Do People Sue Doctors? A Study of Patients and Relatives Taking Legal Action," *Lancet* 243 (June 25, 1994): 1609–1617.
** A. Simanowitz, "Standards, Attitudes, and Accountability in the Medical Profession," *Lancet* 547 (1985): ii.

AVOIDING MALPRACTICE

The dictum often heard in medical circles is that every doctor is vulnerable to a malpractice suit, irrespective of competence and care. It's the luck of the draw. The implication is that "in terms of protection, the only available mechanism is the purchase of liability insurance."* I believe, however, that doctors who worry about being sued probably will be. Fear of litigation, when uppermost in a physician's mind, sets the stage for it. Defensive medicine has two consequences: it maximizes procedures fraught with potential complications and sets up every patient as a potential adversary. Defensive medicine distorts professionalism and dehumanizes medicine. The patient, instead of relating to a friendly and caring physician, encounters disinterest and hostility. This environment undermines communication, and when the patient grows more surly and visibly dissatisfied, the doctor increasingly suspects that his client is potentially litigious. When the relationship is poor, failure of a promised outcome, a seemingly exorbitant medical bill, or a complication from a drug or procedure set litigation wheels in motion. This mad dynamic has the inevitability of a self-fulfilling prophecy. The patient has little compunction about litigating against an indifferent stranger.

Contributing to frivolous litigation is the prevalent unrealistic expectation of what medicine can do. Patients with chronic disease arrive in hopes of magical cures but are rapidly disabused of the notion. The arthritic joint pain does not yield to any of the current wonder drugs. The impaired breathing of emphysema is likewise recalcitrant to a doctor's bag of tricks. Most chronic diseases, whatever the organ involved, have no sure cure, but these conditions are made more tolerable if the patient is treated with respect. Even small overtures of kindness by a doctor are long remembered. I have often marveled at the infrequency of litigation against alternative medicine practitio-

* Vaccarino, "Malpractice."

ners and chiropractors. Litigation against a compassionate physician who invests time with patients is equally rare. What these practitioners have in common is that they engage in sympathetic listening.

These observations, though self-evident to me, seem to have minimally affected some doctors. For instance, a patient inquiring about aspects of postoperative care is brushed off by his surgeon. "I did my job in the operating room. The nurse will answer your questions," he says as he stalks away. Another patient asks me to provide a photograph of the surgeon who a week earlier replaced his aortic valve. My initial thought, that the surgeon made a deep impression on this grateful patient, rapidly fades away with these plaintive words: "I have no idea what he looks like; the only time he was with me was in the operating room when I was unconscious. He never visited before or after the operation." These small embers can ignite a malpractice conflagration.

Preventing litigation begins with the recognition that medical mistakes are inevitable. In most domains of life, an error can be merely an inconvenience. The artist might need to erase a line or at worst discard a canvas, but in medicine, there is a traumatized human being at the receiving end of the mistake. As every patient is unique, medical work is essentially experimental, uncertain, and prone to error. It follows that a doctor can never be certain how a particular individual will respond to a treatment, but a sense of personal fallibility diminishes the occurrence of very big bloopers. Being constantly on guard against oneself is not an easy way to live, but it ensures that the fundamental Hippocratic principle, "First do no harm" (*Primum non nocere*), is rarely breached. To paraphrase Berthold Brecht, the objective of medical science is not to open a door to infinite wisdom, but to set a limit to infinite error. But ironically, the rigorous self-doubt of science is foreign to the medical tradition.

When serious injuries occur, it may be difficult to ascertain the cause or the responsible party, but I tend to fault the physician for not exercising a clinical imagination and anticipating what could go wrong. This was brought home to me by an incident with my mother. In her early nineties, she lived alone, was still vigorous intellectually, and insisted on her much vaunted independence. However, one day, late in the afternoon, I found her looking disheveled, still in her nightgown. Without our greeting each other, she announced that she was fed up with suffering and wished to die. Her appetite was gone, she did not have the energy to lift a spoon, but what was far more disconcerting was that she could not think straight. She insisted that she did not have a fever or any new pains and that her several drugs had not been changed. I inspected her medicine cabinet anyway and found a vial of 0.25 mg digoxin pills rather than the 0.125 mg she had been taking for the past ten years. It turned out that she had run out of the drug three weeks earlier, while her physician was away. She had reached someone covering for her medical group who called a local drugstore for a refill. Through some error in communication, 0.125 was doubled to 0.25. Since my mother had macular degeneration and was nearly blind, she could not read the label on the new bottle, and the pills were nearly alike in size and color. She was clearly poisoned by this vital medicine that had helped keep her from heart failure. She could have died from this simple error.

Once an error has been committed, how should a doctor explain it to a patient? Doctors receive no instruction in medical school or thereafter on how to cope with error. The reflex tendency is to fudge, to cover one's tracks, to shift responsibility, to obfuscate, or to withdraw rather than come forward to admit the mistake. During hospital training, my seniors admonished me never to write in a patient's chart anything that would suggest an act of negligence or acknowledge a misdeed. I have encountered doctors who were even loath to express regret when someone died for fear that it would be interpreted as an admission of guilt, leading to liability.

Keeping quiet and hoping the error passes unnoticed is the worst policy. Adverse outcomes must be anticipated, addressed, and apologized for. Physician withdrawal behind a professional mien is interpreted as a lack of caring and fosters a patient's sense of abandonment. Acknowledging error is powerful and humbling stuff.

I recall the dread I experienced after nearly doing away with a patient. Mr. K. was in atrial fibrillation, but instead of the racing pulse which is the rule, his heartbeat rate was consistently forty per minute. I interpreted this as owing to a block in the conduction system from atrium to ventricle, which filtered out the flurry of fast impulses. This led me to conclude erroneously that Mr. K. did not need digitalis, the standard medicine to slow the heart rate in the presence of atrial fibrillation.

About a month after discontinuing digitalis, he arrived at the Peter Bent Brigham Hospital semistuporous with fulminating pulmonary edema, the rhythm still that of atrial fibrillation but racing inordinately. Mr. K. appeared in extremis and required a ventilator and tracheal intubation for several trying days during which it was uncertain whether he would recover. The reason for this near-death complication was evident. Apparently his conduction system was not impaired as I had suspected. In fact, it was completely normal and accounted for the runaway rate during atrial fibrillation, discharging at 190 beats per minute. In someone with severe cardiac muscle disease, the ultrarapid beating precipitated galloping heart failure.

On his recovery, Mr. K. promptly surmised what had transpired and I was not surprised that he brimmed with hostility toward me. I promptly acknowledged my serious misjudgment, and out of guilt and contrition counseled him to sue me for malpractice. He assured me that this option was uppermost in his mind. About three months later he showed up for an office visit. When I asked why he was a glutton for punishment by returning to the doctor who had nearly killed him, he replied, "You are quite right. You nearly killed me. From now on you will therefore be especially careful how you treat me. If I go to another joker he may not be as attentive and do me in for good." As an afterthought, he added that what had made him return was that I did not try to justify but was "ready to face the music."

"Be plainer with me — let me know thy trespass by its true visage," pleads a character in Shakespeare's *Winter's Tale*. An injured patient expects the same. Admitting error and offering a deeply felt apology clears the air. I am not aware of a case where apology led to litigation, and I have often known such forthrightness to bond doctor and patient in a closer relationship of trust and friendship.

In my view, malpractice is largely the consequence of depersonalized medical practice. The experience of my medical group, the Lown Cardiovascular Center in Brookline, Massachusetts, provides evidence that when practice is time-intensive rather than technology-intensive and focused on the primacy of caring, there need be little worry about litigation. This small group of five doctors has practiced together for about twenty years without a single malpractice suit. I am familiar with other such groups' similar results.

An instructive example of the value of this approach was my experience with Mrs. B., whom I saw annually for several decades. She had several serious cardiac problems, including coronary artery disease, hypertension, cardiac arrhythmia, and disabling peripheral vascular disease. When she developed a large abdominal aortic aneurysm, an outpouching of this large artery that could have ruptured, she insisted on having the surgery in Boston under my care rather than in Miami, her home, even though she had limited economic resources. The operation went well, the recovery uneventful. On the seventh hospital day, being readied for discharge, she began to experience abdominal pain. The hospital, adhering to regulations for Diagnosis Related Groups,* insisted on her leaving, but I persuaded the surgeons that she needed to stay until the nature of her complaint was clarified. Since it was already Friday and there

---

* Diagnosis Related Groups (DRG) creates diagnostic categories and assigns for each a specified duration of hospitalization derived from a large database of hospitalized patients. Individual exceptions are allowed, but only after a bureaucratic hassle.

were no family members in Boston to take care of her, hospital authorities agreed to keep her until Monday.

Arriving at the hospital late Monday morning, I found that Mrs. B. had already been discharged. The surgical house officer assured me that her condition had improved and she had flown back to Florida. Six weeks later, Mrs. B. called from a Miami hospital with a tale of woe. When I had seen her over the weekend, the pain in her belly had grown progressively worse. With little relief from analgesic drugs, she spent a few sleepless nights. Early Monday morning, the surgical resident insisted that since nothing had been found to account for her discomfort, she was experiencing "healing pain," which would resolve with time. She protested that she was terribly sick, but the resident humored her and was certain that everything would turn out well. In any case, the hospital would not permit a further extension, as she had already stayed far longer than her condition warranted. During the flight to Florida, the pain grew unbearable and she was horrified to find herself sitting in a pool of blood. Unbuttoning her skirt, she saw her intestine spilling out from a disrupted abdominal incision. An ambulance was waiting for her on the tarmac at the Miami airport, and she arrived at the hospital in septic shock and remained critically ill for many weeks.

I was mortified at what had transpired. The DRG rule enforcement leads to management of patients according to an arbitrary numerology rather than a patient's condition. It compels doctors to practice a brutal, Procrustean brand of medicine. I was certain that Mrs. B. would sue the hospital, the vascular surgeon, and me, but no suit was brought.

During her annual visit about a year later, I inquired why Mrs. B. had not sued us for malpractice. She said that her family and her Florida physicians urged her to do so and she had engaged a lawyer who felt that it was an "open-and-shut case." However, she refused to proceed, because, she said, "I was told by the lawyers that I couldn't sue the hospital without suing you. I would rather die than do that."

Many errors that lead to malpractice litigation could be mitigated just by listening to the patient. No example is more telling and tragic than that of Betsy Lehman, a *Boston Globe* health columnist. She died suddenly at age thirty-nine at Boston's Dana-Farber Cancer Institute near the end of a grueling three-month treatment for breast cancer. She did not succumb to her disease, but to a massive overdose of an experimental anti-cancer drug that destroyed her heart as she was readying to go home. The autopsy report found no visible evidence of breast cancer in her body. The egregious error was not the fault of a single inexperienced and overworked intern; it was a horrendous mistake overlooked by at least a dozen physicians, nurses, and pharmacists, including some of the senior staff. For four consecutive days she was given four times more than the highest permissible dose, yet no one took note. It was compounded over several days while the patient was complaining bitterly about her severe reaction to the medication, but no one was listening! Lehman alerted her doctors repeatedly that something was dreadfully remiss. Yet despite the fact that she was a well-known personality in the health field, her complaints were ignored.*

Even more incomprehensible is that shortly before the Lehman tragedy, another woman was similarly poisoned and left with severe permanent heart damage. The hospital ascribed it merely to "human error." These incidents occurred at one of the world's most prestigious cancer hospitals, a flagship institution for oncologic research in this country. If it can happen at Dana Farber, it can happen anywhere. No system is fail-safe unless the patient is central in the minds of those who administer drugs or procedures.

I return to my central thesis. Our health care system is breaking down because the medical profession has been shifting its focus away from healing, which begins with listening to the patient. The reasons for this shift include a romance with

---

* Richard Knox, "Doctor's Orders Killed Cancer Patient," *Boston Globe*, March 23, 1995.

mindless technology, which is embraced in large measure as a means for maximizing income. Since it is uneconomic to spend much time with patients, diagnosis is performed by exclusion, which opens floodgates for endless tests and procedures. Malpractice suits should be viewed as mere pustules on the physiognomy of a sick health care system. They are not what ails medicine in the United States, they are the consequence. The medical care system will not be cured until the patient once again becomes central to the doctor's agenda.

III

Healing the Patient:
Science

❦

11

Digitalis:
The Price of Invention

FOR MORE THAN forty years, I have engaged in cardiovascular research in addition to my clinical practice. Research enriched my knowledge of medicine and honed my scientific perspective; despite a high dosage of drudgery, experimental work has been a heady adventure. The triumphs of discovery made me feel the way I imagine a mountaineer must feel on reaching the top of a hitherto unscaled peak.

My earliest investigations focused on the then most popular heart medicine, digitalis, a drug whose introduction in 1775, by the British physician and botanist William Withering, marked the beginning of the modern era of cardiac therapy. Dr. Withering noted that an old woman herbalist in Shropshire, England, had been successful in curing dropsy, that is, edema, "after the more regular practitioners had failed." She employed twenty or more herbs, but Dr. Withering, an astute botanist, rapidly determined that the active ingredient was digitalis, found in the leaves of the purplish foxglove plant. As he ran a large clinic for poor people, he experimented freely and promptly defined the remarkable therapeutic effect of digitalis. Believing he had discovered a new diuretic, he described it in the minutest detail in his classic book, published a decade later.*

One might imagine that a drug in continuous use for more than 150 years would hold few surprises for doctors, but as a

---

* William Withering, *An Account of the Foxglove and Some of Its Medical Uses* (London: M. Swiney, 1985).

young researcher in 1950, I soon realized that even experienced medical practitioners were not too clear about when and how to use this medicine. Erroneous ideas were passed, like religious writ, from generation to generation, from one medical textbook to another.

Digitalis had become the cardiologist's mainstay for good reason. First and foremost it strengthens the force of cardiac muscle contraction, thereby addressing the central problem of the failing heart, impaired pumping. Excessive fluid, sequestered in body cavities and manifest in swollen ankles, is excreted. Unhealthy weight is shed rapidly and in large amounts. Breathing is improved. The racing pulse is reined in. The patient can walk without puffing. Stretching out in bed is no longer accompanied by choking cough. For the first time in weeks the patient gets a night's sleep. The draining fatigue, which makes the smallest effort an insuperable chore, dissipates.

Not surprisingly, digitalis has been referred to as the wonder drug. The wonders, however, do not come without a price. At full therapeutic action, the patient receives a near toxic dose. Side effects, frequently insidious, are marked by a loss of appetite, dizziness, vertigo, and a discomforting fullness in the head. But the appearance of cardiac arrhythmias, some auguring death, is far more dangerous.

A distressing yet empowering experience relating to the use of digitalis occurred at the beginning of my medical career in 1950. The senior resident on the female ward at the Peter Bent Brigham Hospital asked me to see one of Dr. Samuel Levine's newly admitted elderly patients. Mrs. M. was in heart failure with congested lungs and massively edematous swollen legs. Breathing oxygen did not improve her rapid and labored respirations. One factor for the congestion was her extraordinarily rapid heart rate, a staccato 190 beats per minute. Even a healthy heart decompensates when driven three times its normal rate, but Mrs. M.'s heart had been seriously impaired by childhood rheumatic fever.

When I met Levine that morning, I urged him to see Mrs. M.

promptly, as she was by far the sickest patient on his service. While admiring the thoroughness of Levine's history-taking and the meticulous craftsmanship of his physical examination, I was dismayed to hear him prescribe a large dose of digitoxin (one of the family of digitalis drugs) and a mercurial diuretic. Without thinking, I burst out, saying, "This combination will kill her. She will surely die within the day." Levine's eyes narrowed with ill-concealed anger. Lips barely moving, he said, "Record your opinion in Mrs. M.'s chart, exactly as you just stated." He quickly stalked away.

On finishing the brief note, I sat, my energy drained as though I had just climbed the Bunker Hill Monument. The day that had just begun dragged as if the clock had been inadequately wound while I was hoping against hope that my foolish prognostication would prove wrong. A visit to the ward late that afternoon, however, dissipated any prospect that Levine's prescription would ameliorate Mrs. M.'s perilous condition. The extra dose of digitalis had not slowed her heartbeat; on the contrary, her heart was racing even faster. Because of delays on the busy ward, she had not yet received the diuretic that I was certain would deliver the coup de grace. Panic prevented me from thinking through the options. Forty-five years ago it was unthinkable for a mere pup of a trainee to question, let alone countermand, medical orders of a senior attending physician, especially one as distinguished as Dr. Levine.

The next morning I raced to see Mrs. M., but her bed was empty. She had died during the night. The resident told me that the diuretic finished her off. As she began to pass large quantities of urine, her situation worsened by the moment. Her heart rate reached 220 beats per minute, she turned blue, gasped, and died. Resuscitation was not attempted, as the technique was not to be discovered until a decade later.

While horrified at the outcome, I confess with shame that I was more troubled about the possibility of losing my fellowship than at the tragic fate that had befallen Mrs. M. My career as Levine's fair-haired boy, so promising the day before, was seemingly at an end.

I waited with a heavy heart for Levine's arrival, for I dreaded telling him about Mrs. M. As soon as we met, Levine asked about her. With bowed head, I whispered that she had died during the night. Levine walked briskly away, barking out, "Follow me!" I followed, feet dragging, feeling like a man about to be sentenced for an unspeakable crime. When we came to his small office, he locked the door. Looking ashen, he startled me with the words "What did I do wrong?"

Recalling the moment nearly a half century later, I am still shaken by the sizzle of intense emotions and the unexpected reversal of roles. The convict was expected to pass sentence on the revered judge. An inexperienced medical upstart was being asked to render an opinion about the improper use of digitalis by one of the great cardiologists, whose forte was clinical pharmacology. For me, this was Levine's supreme moment as a human being. Never had I encountered someone with the moral rectitude to confess such a grievous misdeed, in the process abasing himself before a young student.

I explained to Levine that Mrs. M.'s heart rhythm disorder at the time of admission was a hitherto undescribed cardiac mechanism that I had recently discovered and designated as paroxysmal atrial tachycardia with block (PAT with block). Usually, it was an expression of digitalis poisoning. In the presence of PAT with block, administering more digitalis was like attempting to extinguish a blaze by pouring gasoline on it. With each increment of drug, the heart rate accelerated, and when it reached more than 200 beats per minute, the heart abruptly catapulted into ventricular fibrillation, the mechanism of cardiac death. Having seen the arrhythmia emerge under similar circumstances and hearing Dr. Levine prescribe more digitalis, I could not contain my dread at the tragic outcome, which was made inevitable by the addition of a diuretic drug. PAT with block most commonly developed in patients who had received excessive digitalis and were then leached of body water and salts, or electrolytes, with a diuretic.

Levine listened attentively without a single interruption. When I finished, he asked a few questions and then commented, "Bernie, I appreciate your teaching me. I should have been less proud and paid attention to what you said." He never again referred to this event, but thereafter he turned to me for advice on the use of digitalis drugs in particular patients.

What Levine did not know was that I had experienced a similar tragedy as a result of my own ignorance. Sadly, my new-found expertise on the use of digitalis had also come at high price. The year was 1948, when I was a junior assistant resident (JAR) at the Montefiore Hospital in the Bronx, dedicated to chronic care. Many terminally ill patients or those with intractable chronic problems were transferred to Montefiore for long-term care from all over New York City. As a JAR, I had enjoyed almost complete autonomy. The responsibilities were enormous, and at times awesomely misplaced. Supervision was largely by senior residents, doctors in training, who had only one more year of clinical experience than I. The attending physicians, who were officially in charge, limited their oversight to the brief morning rounds. The training of doctors was accomplished at a cost to life and limb of the economically disadvantaged, for the house staff was in complete command in the wards where these patients were admitted.

There is a tendency to gild memories of the past, "the good old days." Yet reflecting on hospital care fifty years ago, I can plainly see that enormously positive changes have been wrought since. Hospitals now are far safer, patients are better informed, drugs are far more carefully dispensed, operating rooms are vastly improved. The most important development is that the patient has much more of a say in what is being done. In retrospect, the mayhem committed within hospitals five decades ago staggers the mind.

It was past midnight when a thirty-year-old woman was rolled onto my medical ward at Montefiore. Ms. W. weighed only eighty-nine pounds. She was feverish, pathetically pale, and her muscles were wasted. Her eyeballs dangled like dried prunes in largely empty sockets, her skin hung in loose dehydrated folds. Her problems, though numerous, were largely the result of the odd combination of anorexia nervosa and ulcerative colitis. Intractable diarrhea was draining her vital body fluids while her anorexia precluded oral replacement.

Being inexperienced, I fixated on her rapid heart rate, 170 beats per minute. Digitalis was the premier drug to contain the speeding heart. Because of the state of her gastrointestinal tract, the drug had to be given intravenously and that very week I had read about an old but extremely effective French digitalis agent, ouabain. It could be administered only by vein and was ultra-rapid acting, seemingly ideal for Ms. W. Because it was past midnight, no one was around to offer me guidance.

Judging her situation critical, I hooked up an electrocardio-gram and injected in her one remaining vein a bolus of what I thought was a small dose of ouabain, one-fifth the usual dose. Nothing happened for five minutes. Then abruptly Ms. W. began to flail her arms and thrash around like a fish out of water. Her mouth grimaced monstrously, repeatedly opening in a wide yawn as though she was hungering for air. Instead of slowing, the heart kept speeding. Within several minutes she turned a ghastly shade of purplish blue. As I looked down on the strips of electrocardiographic paper, the rhythm turned chaotic, proclaiming the death knell pattern of ventricular fib-rillation. Small bundles of wasted muscle twitched agonally, grasping for the last molecule of oxygen from the no longer circulating bloodstream. Transfixed into helplessness, I stood quavering as though watching a murder committed on a 3-D movie screen. Ms. W. was dead within eight minutes of receiv-ing the injection.

The next morning at medical report, guilt, coupled with a lack of sleep, enhanced my throbbing sense of foreboding. Without omitting any details, I bluntly told the medical staff what had happened and showed them the remarkable electro-cardiographic strips. I craved punishment, yet no one faulted my judgment or behavior. On the contrary, I was treated with the respect accorded a heroic soldier in the trenches. The only comments were: "Don't take it so hard," "Win some, lose some," "This is the price you have to pay to become a doctor,"

"To gain experience you have to take a few hard knocks," and other such meaningless platitudes meant to show solidarity.

The most galling comment was "You took a calculated risk." Yes, I did the calculating, but the patient took the risk without having been given a chance or choice. The chief of medicine, a kindly fatherly figure, consoled me with the words that good judgments come from experience, "but experience is the name we give to bad judgments."

It was unreal! A summary execution had taken place but no moral tremor was felt. Granted, the action was not premeditated and it arose out of ignorance, but when is ignorance a mitigating justification for such a transgression? Within five minutes after I had related the tragic event, everyone turned to the next case without the slightest trickle of indignation. A patient had been prematurely dispatched to the hereafter, and these very well-trained doctors, who were good human beings, had commiserated with the physically scratched culprit, apparently indifferent to his dead victim.

A week later, when the patient's blood chemistries returned, I was startled at the profound derangement in electrolytes, including potassium, sodium, and chloride. I did not immediately connect the extremely low potassium, only 1.6 milliequivalents, about one third of the normal concentration, with her extreme sensitivity to the digitalis drug ouabain. The relation between potassium and digitalis had not yet been discovered.

Later that year, when I knew more, I reexamined the patient's electrocardiogram. It was clear that on admission her heart rhythm had been sinus tachycardia, a fast heartbeat, the normal physiologic response to stress either physical or psychological. In such a clinical situation, digitalis is ineffective in slowing the tachycardia. This still did not account for her striking sensitivity to digitalis. The patient had not received any digitalis before the fatal small dose and the postmortem examination was unrevealing, showing a perfectly normal heart muscle, intact heart valves, and widely patent coronary vessels. In the absence of heart disease, even a massive overdose of digitalis, while it can poison, does not kill. According to the knowledgeable chief cardiologist at the Montefiore Hospital at the time, young people with normal hearts could consume buckets of the stuff. In searching the published literature, I came across someone who, in a suicide attempt, took 200 times the dose I had administered and survived. Why then this marked sensitivity?

I had little time to sleuth for an answer. House staff training was arduous, with duty on alternate nights and alternate weekends. The patient load was high, with many of them on the verge of death. Arriving home weary, I would find that my two young children were hungering for fatherly attention, and my wife, cooped up in a small apartment, away from friends and family, was starved for companionship. I had little chance to brood or obsess about my fatal error, and the unsettling experience sank to the depths of my consciousness but continued to exert a magnetic subliminal force.

The following year, as senior resident, I had more time to reflect, and the sad Ms. W. began to reappear in my thoughts when I was trying to relax or before I fell asleep. Like a toothache constantly tongued into consciousness, the woman's death haunted my mind, the memory of her stirred up by the numerous patients I saw with digitalis intoxication. Many of them were receiving a fixed dose of digitalis, and a toxic state was provoked by the administration of a mercurial diuretic. No sooner had the copious flow of urine stopped than the patient began to feel wretched with nausea, vomiting, dizziness, and weakness. The heartbeat grew irregular from salvos of ventricular extrasystoles. In sick elderly patients, digitalis toxicity was a particularly ominous condition, commonly auguring death.

In the mid-1930s, Levine had provided the most widely accepted explanation for diuretic-induced digitalis intoxication. He reasoned that when a diuretic acts on the kidney to rid the body of excess salt and water, the fluid cannot reach the kidney without traversing the heart. Levine surmised that since digitalis was distributed throughout the body, fluid mobilized by the diuretic contained substantial quantities of the drug. Diuresis was therefore equivalent to administering more digitalis by redistribution from body stores. Levine was convinced that he had proved his hypothesis when he demonstrated that edema fluid leached from patients taking digitalis contained enough of the drug to stop a beating frog heart. In short, the cause of the digitalis poisoning induced by administering a diuretic was due to heart muscle being exposed to more digitalis, which Levine designated as diuretic redigitalization.

This theory had little relevance to Ms. W.'s case. She had never been given diuretics, and before receiving ouabain had not been exposed to digitalis drugs. Some other mechanism must be found to account for her supersensitivity to digitalis. This conclusion stimulated me to examine Levine's hypothesis more critically. According to his theory, digitalis poisoning should occur only in patients with sizable diuresis, while those with meager urinary outputs would not experience this redigitalization phenomenon. The ugly fact was that I could detect no such clear-cut relationship. At times patients who barely voided in response to the diuretic appeared massively poisoned; others who lost gallons of fluid, weight loss of ten or more pounds, showed not a scintilla of digitalis overdose.

To test Levine's theory, I administered extra doses of digitalis to patients who had experienced digitalis poisoning after a diuretic. The dose I prescribed far exceeded the amount that Levine suggested could be present in the fluid secreted after the diuretic. Nonetheless, not a single patient developed digitalis poisoning from that single additional dose. They did not experience any of the typical symptoms nor did they develop the telltale arrhythmias of overdigitalization. For me, Levine's hypothesis was demolished. But I had not identified the X factor that was being washed out of the body, which accounted for the increased sensitivity to digitalis.

If the diuretic was washing something out of the body, what could it be? Ms. W.'s case, like Banquo's ghost in *Macbeth*, hinted at the answer. The haunting refrain to her abrupt death crystallized into a question: Does low body potassium affect cardiac sensitivity to digitalis? Searching the medical literature,

I found that a San Francisco cardiologist, John Sampson, discovered in the early 1930s that potassium could abolish ventricular extrasystoles, or extra heartbeats, a frequent expression of digitalis overdosage. But this left unanswered the essential question about the potential adverse relationship between low potassium and digitalis drugs.

If potassium was the X factor, then a reduced concentration of blood potassium should be found only in those who had symptoms of digitalis poisoning after receiving a diuretic and not in those without such symptoms. To my delight this proved to be the case. But my concept had not yet been proved with the rigor demanded by science. To do so it was necessary to replicate experimentally what happened to Ms. W., specifically demonstrating that a diuretic drug sensitized the heart to digitalis only when it leached out substantial amounts of body potassium, thereby resulting in an abnormal blood concentration of potassium, a condition designated as hypokalemia. If my hypothesis was correct, sensitivity to digitalis after a diuretic should be a function of the extent to which the blood potassium was lowered by the diuretic.

The experiment was easier to describe than carry out. How could I show that a patient who had not been receiving digitalis became more sensitive to the poisonous action of digitalis by virtue of a diuretic-induced loss of body potassium? This seemed like an insoluble conundrum. Then, as frequently transpires, the insoluble became straightforward. Again the memory of Ms. W. suggested an answer. Why not use a short-acting digitalis drug like the one I gave her to titrate the dose required for provoking mild toxicity? If my view was correct, patients who had lost potassium after a diuretic would require substantially less digitalis to reach a toxic endpoint. The experimental design was now apparent: administer a short-acting digitalis drug to patients before and after a diuretic. For this I needed a safer drug than ouabain, more rapid in onset of action and more prompt in total dissipation of cardiac action.

I searched all the different forms of rapid-acting digitalis drugs available, but none fit the bill. Then I learned that Dr.

Charles Enselberg, a cardiologist at the Montefiore, was experimenting with a newly synthesized digitalis agent, acetyl strophanthidin. This drug, a first cousin to ouabain, could be given to a full digitalizing dose within a couple of minutes and was totally eliminated from the body within less than two hours. Overdosing could not lead to serious toxicity, since the drug was rapidly dissipated. It was ideal for the study I had in mind. At the time there were no human-use committees to rule on what was permissible to do to patients. No informed consent was required. All that was necessary was to ask permission from the chief of service. The answer was invariably in the affirmative. In fact, one gained brownie points by showing a penchant for research.

My enthusiasm waxed day by day, my emotions churning at high speed. I rapidly recruited ten patients with heart failure who had not yet been given digitalis and gave them by vein the amount of acetyl strophanthidin they would tolerate. Two hours later, when the titration was completed and all the drug was eliminated from the body, they received a mercurial diuretic. Over the next twenty-four hours, every drop of their urine was collected to measure their excretion of potassium. The following day I again titrated their tolerance for acetyl strophanthidin. Some patients took much less drug to reach toxicity the second time, while others tolerated exactly the same dose. In order not to bias results, I asked Dr. Ray Weston, a research cardiologist, to analyze the data. When he showed me the final outcome, I could not contain my elation. The patients who showed no change had lost no potassium and their blood potassium remained unaltered. On the other hand, those who during the second administration of acetyl strophanthidin were more sensitive and could tolerate far less drug had lost large amounts of potassium in the urine. This was corroborated by a marked decrease in the blood potassium concentration.

Without any fiscal support or technical assistance, I was forced to do all the scut work. The investigation did not free me from the heavy clinical load as resident. It meant that my fourteen-hour working day was extended by several hours, but the excitement of the work, the important clinical implications, revved up extraordinary energies. The drudgery and sleepless nights were well worth it. The research resulted in my first medical publication. Meager as the article was, a mere four pages, it was widely noted and cited. The work was editorialized in the *Journal of the American Medical Association* as well as in the leading British medical journal, *Lancet*. Both deemed it a milestone study.

Digitalis poisoning was a leading cause of fatality among patients with heart failure, and my discovery that diuretic-induced loss of potassium sensitized the heart to the toxic action of the digitalis drugs raised numerous questions that urgently needed to be answered. To continue the investigations it was important to obtain a cardiovascular fellowship in a leading research hospital. The Peter Bent Brigham Hospital (PBBH), now the Brigham and Women's Hospital, was the ideal institution in which to investigate the full ramifications of the digitalis-potassium relationship.

At the time, Dr. John Merrill was carrying out pioneering studies at the PBBH with the recently introduced artificial kidney, and hundreds of patients were being dialyzed annually. Many were in heart failure and receiving digitalis. Dialysis, in addition to removing metabolic waste products, was washing out potassium from the body. This offered a unique opportunity to determine expeditiously how removing body potassium affected patients receiving digitalis drugs.

A more profound attraction was the opportunity to work with Dr. Levine, though there was little if any chance of my gaining a fellowship with him. He took only one person for a single year and favored Harvard graduates, especially those who had matriculated through the PBBH house staff. Nothing was to be lost by applying, however, and to my surprise I was granted an interview.

I devised a bizarre strategy. From the medical grapevine I learned that Levine was impeccably honest and exceedingly proud and that he did not take kindly to being contradicted. I therefore decided to challenge his work. When I presented my unimpressive credentials, he asked, as anticipated, why I wished a fellowship with him. I answered that my aim was to prove him wrong on an important concept he had been promulgating. Momentarily startled, he inquired what that might be. I explained that his widely accepted theory about diuretic redigitalization was erroneous. He was barely able to restrain himself. "You obviously have not read our paper on this subject, because we proved with certainty in a frog heart preparation that edema fluid has large quantities of digitalis."*

I replied with a carefully prepared argument about the critical role that I had discovered for potassium, adding that the PBBH was the ideal place for me to continue my research. Then came my well-rehearsed punch line, namely, that every good scientist, like Levine, believes that next to the promulgation of truth, the public recantation of error was the greatest virtue. Levine's hostile demeanor when we parted indicated that there was not the remotest chance of my procuring the appointment. But Levine proved himself to be a man of principled integrity. Although his ego was bruised, he nonetheless offered me a job, though he duly punished me for my chutzpah by not permitting me to work on digitalis for more than a year.

But in my second year, Levine freed me to work on the drug. Within short order, we decisively proved the digitalis-potassium relationship. It alerted doctors to the importance of potassium loss in the genesis of digitalis intoxication and heart arrhythmias. It led them to prescribe supplementary potassium when administering diuretics and stimulated introduction of a new class of potassium-sparing diuretics. Our findings were summarized in a number of publications and in a book that became a medical best seller. Barely thirty years old, I was catapulted into a world authority on the most important heart drug at the time. During the 1950s, the subject of my extensive lecturing was exclusively "The Use and Abuse of Digitalis." Once, while introducing me as the guest speaker at a medical

* M. A. Schnitker and S. A. Levine, "Presence of Digitalis in Body Fluids of Digitalized Patients," *Archives of Internal Medicine* 60 (August 1937): 240–250.

meeting in a small city in Michigan, the chairman became flustered and spoke approximately as follows: "It is a great privilege for our hospital to be addressed by Dr. Lown, the world's leading digitalis poisoner." Suddenly, Ms. W. in her terminal agony appeared before my eyes. Guilt gnawed like an ulcer.

The work on digitalis and potassium led to my lifelong appreciation of every drug as a potential poison in disguise, which was hardly a novel observation. Paracelsus, the medieval alchemist and physician, wrote, "All substances [drugs] are poisonous; there is none that is not a poison. The right dose distinguishes a poison and a remedy."

As he usually did, Shakespeare stated it more poetically. In *Romeo and Juliet*, Friar Lawrence searches for a potion to put Juliet in a sleep simulating death. On encountering a flower with medical powers, he reflects:

> Virtue itself turns vice, being misapplied;
> And vice sometime's by action dignified.
> Within the infant rind of this small flower
> Poison hath residence, and medicine power.

My research work on digitalis led to a number of further significant advances. It aroused interest in cardiac arrhythmias, since digitalis drugs can provoke every conceivable heartbeat derangement. For the first time, doctors learned that atrial rhythm disorders could follow excess digitalis. The research also led to the abandonment of long-acting digitalis drugs like digitalis leaf, digitoxin, Gitaligin, and other such preparations. My agitation for the use of digoxin led to its universal acceptance, and legions of lives have been saved through the safer use of the digitalis drugs.

Although in death Ms. W. left a legacy of life, I remain convinced that good ends rarely justify bad means. The tragedy I inflicted on Ms. W. occurred early in my life and honed my moral sensibilities in confronting the myriad of problems a doctor faces. I became sensitized to the fact that far too often in medicine, as in the world at large, reasonable goals propel evil deeds. Foul means often pollute good ends. Few would contest that prolonging life is an unquestioned good. Yet in aiming to prolong life, health professionals frequently inflict indescribable misery. Worse still is the rationalization that good intentions provide sufficient sanction for questionable acts. I am persuaded that the moral fiber frays when means and end are sundered.

12

A New Medical Tradition

DR. SAMUEL LEVINE was the first to emphasize the harm of bed rest for cardiac patients. He became deeply convinced of this as a result of his extensive clinical experience in treating patients with heart failure and especially by one particular patient who started him thinking about the potential adverse effects of bed rest.

In the late 1930s Levine was called to see a very sick man with far advanced congestive heart failure. As a consultant, Levine was expected to pull a therapeutic rabbit out of his clinical top hat. However, physicians had tried every known measure in this case. Levine noted that the patient was restless and his lungs were heavily laden with fluid. He reasoned that if the patient were to sit upright in a comfortable chair, gravity would shift the fluid from his lungs, where it choked off the exchange of oxygen, to less harmful depots in dependent limbs. As Levine prescribed, around-the-clock care of the patient seated in a chair led to his unexpected recovery.

Many such observations persuaded Dr. Levine of the negative consequences of bed rest, especially for patients with heart failure. Among a long list of complications he included atelectasis, or collapse of lung lobes predisposing to pneumonia; pulmonary embolism; lung congestion; prostatism; urinary retention; thinning of bones; and constipation. Bed rest, he reasoned, was most harmful for those who had suffered an acute heart attack, the very people for whom prolonged periods of absolute bed rest were prescribed.

In the early 1950s, patients with a diagnosis variously described as acute coronary thrombosis, acute myocardial infarction, or merely a heart attack were confined to strict bed rest for four to six weeks. Sitting in a chair was prohibited. They were not even allowed to turn from side to side without assistance. During the first week, patients were fed by a nurse. Moving the bowels and urination required a bedpan. For the constipated, which included every patient, precarious balancing on a bedpan was embarrassing as well as agonizing.

Medical insistence on rigorous bed rest was based on a sacrosanct therapeutic principle, the need to rest a diseased body part, be it a fractured limb or a tuberculous lung. Unlike a broken bone, which could be immobilized in a cast, or a lung lobe, which could be collapsed by inflating a chest cavity with air, the heart could not so readily be rested. The only approximation to the principle of rest for the diseased heart was to diminish its workload. The lesser burdening of the heart during recumbency was manifested by a slower heart rate and lower blood pressure, both indices of reduced oxygen usage and therefore of lessened cardiac work. Thus, bed rest was traditionally equated with heart rest.

But was that the case? Surprisingly, no one had studied the issue, though every other aspect of care for those with heart attacks had been extensively investigated. This was yet another of the numerous examples of medical tradition derailing healthy skepticism and impeding commonsense approaches.

At the time, hospitals lacked coronary care units. Patients with heart attacks were admitted to any medical ward where beds were available. There were no monitors for heart rhythm surveillance. The importance of arrhythmias as a cause of death was unrecognized. The Peter Bent Brigham Hospital had only two electrocardiographic machines, one of which, on a large mobile cart, served all the inpatients who could not be wheeled to the heart station. Cardiac drugs for heart attack victims were limited to digitalis glycosides, antiarrhythmics such as quinidine and procainamide, anticoagulants such as heparin and warfarin, morphine, and various sedatives. Since patients were restive and anxious, they were kept heavily sedated, which undoubtedly contributed to the high complication rate and the inordinate mortality. The dreaded complications of a heart attack were shock, lung edema, and the common and life-threatening pulmonary embolism.

Heart attack patients presented a major challenge to the nursing staff, including their having to feed the victims three meals a day, help maneuver dead weights precariously onto a bedpan, and maintain morale under conditions fostering hopelessness and depression. Nursing was further complicated by the fact that many who required oxygen had to be placed in special tents surrounding their upper bodies. To obtain adequate oxygen concentration, bed sheets had to be tucked snugly to prevent air leaks. Patients resembled immobile, swaddled infants. In this solitary confinement, they could not be heard over the racket of the pumping of oxygen and were barely visible through the fogged plastic tent. At the time, 35 percent of heart attack patients admitted to the Brigham died.

On morning rounds, Levine frequently commented that the outcome would be much better if the patient were treated while sitting in a comfortable chair. When I asked whether he had studied this issue, he responded that he was too busy and too old for such an undertaking. Foolishly, I volunteered to pursue it, and Levine readily accepted my offer. Although I knew that the project would be a chore, I didn't expect it to be an act of martyrdom. It didn't enter my mind that a tradition was about to be breached — the type of trespass that invariably stirs dust storms of opposition. For a brief period I had alienated Levine himself, for he was writing an opinion piece on the hazards of bed rest for the sick cardiac patient and invited me to be a coauthor. Instead of expressing gratitude, I declined to lend my name. Not yet having done any of the work, I didn't think it was ethical for me to pretend I had made a contribution. Levine was deeply offended, however, and in the ensuing fifteen years of our association he never again asked me to join him in authorship. We were off to a rocky start.

To carry out this study, I had to meet patients diagnosed

with heart attack immediately on their arrival and persuade the house staff to prescribe the large, comfortable lounge chair we had had built especially for the purpose. We aimed to get patients out of bed on the first day of admission. My pleading and arguments generally were to no avail. Asked to cite the supporting literature, I could not comply, since none existed. Most doctors viewed it as an unethical misadventure. When I insisted, some called my attention to the Nuremberg trials and the immorality of unjustified medical experimentation. On entering a medical ward, I was occasionally greeted by a Nazi salute, a clicking of heels, and a "*Sieg heil!*"

My tactic for circumventing house staff opposition was to bring Levine to the bedside. He acted as a sheriff, determined to maintain law and order, arriving at a scene of civil disobedience. Teaching hospitals were then organized as a series of feudal fiefdoms. Each senior physician, usually a private practitioner, was the lord of his own manor and could practice largely as he wished without interference from the chief of the medical service. House staff were as obedient as if they were serving in the military. The disciplining hand was invisible, but it was clearly perceived by highly ambitious young professionals impatient to advance. Levine's instruction to get a heart attack victim out of bed therefore was not bucked, but this did not prevent several interns and residents from venting their anger at me.

The idea of moving a critically ill patient into a chair was regarded as off-the-wall in spite of its emanation from a great authority. Several times, behind Levine's back, an angry intern would shake his fist at me, muttering, "We'll get you later, Lown." But even with Levine's sponsorship, patient recruitment was initially slow and halting. While the Brigham admitted, on average, one heart attack patient daily, we were lucky to recruit a single patient a week for chair treatment.

Witnessing even one patient in a chair rapidly won converts, however, and the study gained momentum. In short order I was deluged at all hours with calls to put patients in a chair. Levine's ukase was no longer necessary, and during five months eighty-one patients were so treated. At the beginning they were placed in a chair for half an hour; by the end of the first week of hospitalization, they remained seated throughout most of the day.

Compared with patients managed by other physicians with strict bed rest, ours did remarkably well. Levine eschewed psychiatric explanations, ascribing the benefits to mechanical factors. He resorted to the same line of reasoning that rationalized bed rest, but reversed the argument. In essence, he said, an upright posture reduced the heart's workload. In the prone position, gravity pooled blood into dependent parts of the body; with a decreased blood volume to pump, the heart worked less. The explanation made no sense. How could a patient's sitting up for thirty to sixty minutes out of twenty-four hours have such an extraordinary, long-lasting beneficial effect, especially as the heart rate and blood pressure were raised by sitting up?

My observation of many patients with myocardial infarction treated both with strict bed rest and the more liberal chair regimen suggested a different explanation, one that had more to do with psychological than physical factors. To be well one minute and seriously ill the next is a major psychological shock. To be told that the discomfort came from a heart attack carried the dire connotation of disability and death. The ominous implication was reinforced by the physician's insistence on complete bed rest, proscribing all activity, even to prohibiting movement in bed. The patient was left to the mercy of forces over which he or she had no control. Adding to the anxiety was the absence of a way to assess the extent or speed of recovery. A patient's inevitable restlessness and agitation were combatted with large amounts of bromides and later barbiturates. Pain invariably was severe and long-lasting, requiring large doses of narcotics. The combination of these factors led to a multitude of complications, many life-threatening.

Lying in bed for twenty-four hours, in addition to being uncomfortable and unnatural, sapped physical strength and undermined the psychological resolve to recover. By the third week in bed, depression was the rule, and many patients lost interest in surviving. By contrast, patients managed in a chair did not consider themselves hopelessly ill. After all, in our culture the act of dying takes place in bed, so there was some sense of safety in being out of it. The progressive increase in time allowed out of bed provided a gauge for judging progress. The patient was made an informed and active participant in the healing process. This empowerment, I came to believe, was the critical factor, far more potent in allaying fear and dissipating anxiety than any reassuring words from the medical staff.

In following these patients, I noticed many other salutary changes. Within a day after admission, they no longer looked sick or wan. Their pain readily responded to small doses of morphine. Though their condition remained serious, their outlook was upbeat, and they were impatient to resume normal living. Patients in chairs promptly began to harangue the staff to let them walk and to press for an early discharge.

Other outcomes were also striking. In nearly 30 percent of bed-treated patients who died, pulmonary embolism was the cause of fatality. This dreaded complication, resulting from thrombophlebitis in leg veins, was not observed in any of the eighty-one patients who were treated in a chair. In retrospect, I believe the result was hardly surprising. Anxiety increases coagulability of blood, and total immobilization contributes to sluggishness of blood flow. The recumbent posture also impairs lung ventilation, which serves as a bellows sucking blood into the chest, facilitating venous return of blood to the heart from the periphery. Calves compressed by lying in bed additionally impede venous flow. All these factors act in concert to cause phlebitis in the legs, with clots that tended to propagate to the lungs, resulting in the dreaded pulmonary embolism.

In the chair-treated patient, these factors were diminished, if not totally absent. Another complication also vanished, the hand-shoulder syndrome, a painful and disabling arthritic condition involving a frozen left shoulder accompanied by a swollen, red left hand. Various theories were in vogue for the striking changes in the hand. The one that held sway at the time ascribed the condition to a reflex from the injured heart muscle that traversed the autonomic nervous system and constricted small vessels, diminishing blood flow to the hand, designated a sympathetic neural dystrophy. Immobility was a critical factor in its development. While I encountered at least fifty patients with the hand-shoulder syndrome in the days of strict bed treatment, I do not recall ever having seen the condition again after the chair became standard treatment.

Despite dire predictions, getting very sick patients out of bed during the early throes of a heart attack did not result in any complications. As our published report stated, "The most encouraging aspect of this type of care for patients with acute coronary attack was the continued sense of well-being and high morale. This was especially apparent in those experiencing their second or third occlusion. Their invariable comment indicated that the current episode was easier to bear."*

In January 1951, Levine had suggested that I write a first draft of our experience, to be presented at the meeting of the prestigious Association of American Physicians. The group met annually in May in Atlantic City. When I asked how much time I had, Levine said that since it was already a Thursday, he expected a completed draft the following Monday. Anticipating that he would give me at least four or more weeks for this chore, I was speechless. At that time my only writing experience was my two-month struggle to complete the four-page report on digitalis and potassium.

I worked around the clock without sleep. Not having mastered typing, I wrote and rewrote numerous drafts of the fifteen-page article by hand. As requested, I handed in the manuscript on Monday, anticipating sharp criticism and extensive editing. Over the ensuing few days, as Levine offered no comments, my unease mounted. I assumed that he found the manuscript pitiable and didn't want to hurt my feelings by saying so. Finally, no longer able to contain myself, I asked what he thought of the chair manuscript. Levine matter-of-factly

---

* S. A. Levine and B. Lown, "'Armchair' Treatment of Acute Coronary Thrombosis," *Journal of the American Medical Association* 148 (April 1952): 1365.

indicated that he liked the draft and had sent it off unaltered. I was particularly surprised that he had changed little of the discussion section, since he was convinced that circulatory factors were primarily responsible for the salutary effect of chair treatment, while the discussion section of our report emphasized the role of psychological factors. In any case, the paper was promptly accepted for presentation.

As soon as we arrived in Atlantic City, Levine gathered his colleagues, some of America's leading physicians, and prepared a claque to comment following the usual ten-minute presentation. Indeed, no sooner had he finished his talk than they leaped forward with effusive statements praising the innovative quality and historic significance of Levine's report, which would revolutionize the care of heart attack patients. No one rose to contradict the pretentious remarks. A person sitting beside me, unaware of my association with the manuscript, confided, "This new method will some day be referred to as the electric chair, not the armchair treatment."

I later realized that our study had been poorly carried out, since it was uncontrolled, anecdotal, and the sample was too small to permit any certain conclusions. Nonetheless, it exerted a profound effect on the care of patients with heart attack. Until our work, patients were kept in the hospital for a month or longer. Within a few years after its publication, the period of hospitalization was reduced by half. The range of activities permitted to patients was enlarged, and self-care became the norm. The hateful and dangerous bedpan was abandoned; walking was allowed earlier; hospital mortality was reduced by about a third. Considering the fact that in the United States about one million people suffer heart attacks annually, perhaps as many as one hundred thousand lives were salvaged each year by this simple strategy. Rehabilitation was hastened and return to work was accelerated. The time required for full recovery was reduced from three months to one month.

I continue to be troubled by the ways in which doctors rationalize treatments that are not only without merit but draconian punishments to boot. Why subject heart attack victims to rigid bed rest that could only increase misery and lead to major complications in patients who already had a life-threatening condition? This was not just a small error, it was a colossal misjudgment. Why were the deleterious consequences of strict bed rest not detected sooner? Why had this aspect of patient management never been investigated, either for its clinical justification or the duration of treatment? Until our publication, no systematic studies of bed rest had been reported in the medical literature. Generally, quietude in the face of a misguided approach relates either to matters of ideology or to an economic advantage.

Medical dogmatism, in the past as well as today, is sustained by a multiplicity of factors, foremost of which is the uncertain terrain doctors constantly traverse. Every patient is an act of discovery. Faced with myriad variables, a doctor can never be categorical about an outcome. What works for one patient is not only ineffective for another but may be injurious and even lethal. In fact, an experienced physician appreciates that individual outcomes are never predictable except statistically in a large universe of individuals to which a particular patient may not even belong. Yet when confronting pain, infection, hemorrhage, life-threatening arrhythmia, and so forth, doctors cannot delay action until knowledge is certain. One could be waiting for Godot. Paradoxically, human beings, when compelled to act, learn to justify a chosen course with an assurance unwarranted by the depth of their understanding. This was clearly the case with enforced bed rest for heart attack victims.

Another factor relates to the need to persuade a patient of a therapeutic option. To remain in control, a doctor often resorts to a simple stratagem of painting a grim scenario (see Chapter 5). A dire prognostic outcome, as well as a severe therapeutic regimen, communicates that the physician clearly understands the condition and is tutored in the latest science, and it conveys a sense of authority. The gravity of the diagnosis stuns both patient and family into quiet acquiescence. By contrast, if the situation is presented as less threatening, the doctor is deluged with questions. Because many of these are unanswerable, they expose the doctor's scientific pretensions. The current tendency to involve patients in decision making has not dissipated medical dogmatism. Therapeutic dogma, however, is no longer a secure citadel for the opinionated.

In reflecting on some of the other reasons for the practice of strict bed rest, I believe they related to the sad truth that doctors had little to offer in treating heart attack victims. When good answers are unavailable, bad answers emerge frequently. Therapeutic measures were palliative and merely reactive, from morphine for pain, diuretics and digitalis for heart failure, and the few antiarrhythmic drugs when the heart's rhythm went out of kilter. The ability to reduce the damage of a thrombosed coronary artery was totally lacking. The revolutionary thought of dissolving the obstructing clot did not burst on the scene until the introduction of thrombolytic therapy in the early 1990s.

The original theory of lessening the heart's work was not without merit. The general idea, that if the heart expends less contractile energy, muscle damage is reduced, was conceptually sound, and there was a perverse logic for presuming that the bed is the most suitable place in which to achieve heart rest. Don't we go to bed when we are tired? Doesn't sleep rejuvenate? Don't doctors plaster-cast a broken limb to protect it from stress? Such simplistic reasoning had been responsible for bloodletting, stomach freezing, using X ray for peptic ulcers, and it accounted for a host of other reasonable but unproved procedures.

Another reason that detrimental effects of prolonged bed rest were not discovered earlier has to do with the antimentalist tradition within scientific medicine. By that I mean physicians' utter insouciance to psychological and behavioral factors. Doctors had and still have little appreciation that churning emotions derange the functioning of every organ in the body, be it heart or intestine. While anatomy, physiology, and biochemistry were revered, psychiatry had been peripheralized and was merely tolerated. The adverse consequences of enforced bed rest, predominantly emotional, were misperceived and largely ignored.

One final factor related to medical economics: the longer a patient remained hospitalized, the higher the physician's income — an effortless gain at that. Following the first few critical days, the patient's condition stabilized, with little going on, as the infarcted heart muscle healed and formed a scar. There was not much for the physician to do except make a daily brief hospital visit that required but a few minutes to earn a substantial fee.

The patient, having been consigned to total inactivity, was in a state of unquestioning hibernation. The only event to be anticipated, with impatience and unease, was the doctor's daily visit. Moses descending from Mount Sinai could not have been greeted with more reverence. Every syllable was regarded as divine revelation. Bed rest was therefore accepted as the panacea. A patient who was treated in a chair and was soon feeling well was not a candidate for prolonged hospitalization. The hospital, of course, had a vested interest in keeping beds fully occupied.

Curiously, I have received invitations to lecture on every subject I have researched except chair treatment for acute heart attacks. While the impact of our work was substantial and profoundly changed the treatment of coronary thrombosis, the study has rarely if ever been cited in the medical literature. Yet in the number of lives saved, it was a significant medical breakthrough.

One might argue that doctors are not interested in loss of control or reduction in income. Yet the economic motive was not the decisive one, as I learned during many visits to the former Soviet Union. Soviet physicians and hospitals had absolutely no economic incentive to prolong hospitalization of patients with acute heart attacks because the socialized health care system provided a fixed salary for doctors. I was therefore astonished to find that twenty or more years after our study was reported, patients in the USSR were still confined to bed for a month or longer after a heart attack. When I questioned this, I was given an ideological rather than scientific answer, namely, that in a capitalist society, based on exploitation of the working class, it was necessary to get patients rapidly back to their jobs whatever the health consequences. On the other hand, in a socialist society, human welfare being paramount, patients were kept at rest until the infarct totally healed. Little did I realize that chair treatment was a nefarious device to promote capitalism!

Perhaps the most important lesson I derived from this experience is that many medical practices are not soundly based. They are sustained, as is true of other human pursuits, by an inertia supported by fashion, custom, and the word of authority. The security provided by a long-held belief system, even when poorly founded, is a strong impediment to progress. General acceptance of a practice becomes the proof of its validity, though it lacks all other merit. In the words of the great nineteenth-century French physiologist Claude Bernard, the innovator's talent is in "seeing what everybody has seen, and thinking what nobody has thought." Once a new paradigm takes hold, its acceptance is extraordinarily rapid and one finds few who claim to have adhered to a discarded method. This was succinctly captured by Schopenhauer, who maintained that all truth passes through three stages: first, it is ridiculed; second, it is violently opposed; and finally, it is accepted as being self-evident.

13

The Shock That Cures:
DC and Cardioversion

IN THE LATE 1950s, doctors were largely helpless in treating tachycardias, the sustained, rapid beating of the heart. Tachycardias, which can originate either in ventricles or atria, arise when an abnormal electric source usurps the heart's physiologic pacemaker. The normal pacemaker, the sinus node, is a small comma-shaped structure, no longer than a pencil eraser, located in the right atrium. It emits more than 2.5 billion pulses during a lifetime with a remarkably clocklike regularity of approximately 70 beats per minute. Furthermore, it knows when more or less blood has to be pumped and adjusts the heart rate accordingly. With strenuous exercise the sinus node speeds up to a rate of 160 beats per minute or faster, and when sleep puts the body in a state of hibernating quietude, it may slow down to 30 beats per minute or less. To allow this fine-tuning, the sinus node is richly innervated, serving as a downlink station in the flow of information from brain to heart.

With a tachycardia, the heart rate is no longer physiologically attuned to bodily needs for blood flow. The heart races like an automobile with its accelerator stuck on the floor, and the abnormal source for electrical activity makes the heart impervious to all nervous regulatory influences. The rate can exceed that seen during strenuous exertion and remain there with rigid constancy. When the abnormal pacemaker is located in the ventricle, the ensuing ventricular tachycardia threatens survival. The danger stems partly from the rapid heart rate, ranging from 150 to 280 beats per minute, far higher than a normal heart can sustain for any duration. It is also due to the fact that when the heartbeat is initiated outside the sinus node, the electrical activity does not flow along the heart's normal conduction system; instead, it is transmitted haphazardly, and the heart muscle is therefore activated in a helter-skelter fashion. The result is a disorganized heart muscle contraction largely ineffectual in propelling blood. To make matters worse, ventricular tachycardia emerges in patients already suffering from serious cardiac ailments, usually far advanced coronary artery disease. These patients tolerate a disorganized heartbeat poorly; formerly, few survived long enough to be hospitalized. In fact, ventricular tachycardia commonly constituted the brief prodrome for sudden cardiac death.

Tachycardias originating in the heart's upper chambers, the atria, are far better tolerated. The most common of all the tachycardias, atrial fibrillation, probably afflicts as many as one million Americans. In this arrhythmia, the atrium discharges at fiendishly rapid rates, exceeding 350 beats per minute or faster. These high rates are not sustainable by the pumping chambers, the ventricles, but fortunately the rapid bombardment of impulses cannot reach the ventricles without traversing a narrow bridge of conducting tissue, the atrioventricular bundle. This narrow inlet reduces the impulses reaching the ventricles by about two thirds. While the resulting rate is rapid and irregular, it is tolerated for months, even years. Once the heart rate is slowed with drugs like digitalis, one can live, without impaired cardiac function or symptoms, a long, largely unencumbered, life.

This is not the case with another form of atrial arrhythmia, designated as atrial flutter. In my early days in medicine there was no ready way to terminate this disordered rhythm, as it proved intractable to the few cardiac drugs then available. Not immediately life-threatening, with heart rates ranging from 120 to 160 per minute and the atrium discharging twice as fast, atrial flutter could be well tolerated for brief durations. However, when the arrhythmia persisted for several weeks or longer, the heart began to fail. Once congestion of the lungs set in, the course was unalterably downhill.

These various rhythm derangements were a challenge to cardiologists, and therapeutic failures were common. In the late 1950s, three drugs were used to restore a normal rhythm: quinidine, procainamide (Pronestyl), and the anticonvulsant diphenylhydantoin (Dilantin). Quinidine, the premier agent, was especially effective, taken orally, for combatting atrial fibrillation but was ineffectual by the oral route for ventricular tachycardia and could not be given intravenously or intramuscularly. In addition, many patients did not tolerate quinidine because of severe diarrhea, high fevers, or dangerous suppression of blood platelets. For ventricular tachycardia, Pronestyl was the standard-bearer, since it was the most effective of the three. When it was administered by vein, the speed of injection was limited by a drop in blood pressure. This was a hazardous complication, for the heart was already severely strained by the arrhythmia. The third drug, Dilantin, was rarely effective when the tachycardia came from coronary disease, the most common background for this disordered rhythm.

The hazard of these antiarrhythmic drugs was rapidly brought home to me early in my career. I was impressed that before drug treatment many patients were tolerating the ventricular tachycardia, experiencing only minor symptoms, some remaining unaware that their heart rhythm was out of kilter. Blood pressure was well maintained, even though the heart was pulsing away close to 200 beats per minute. However, soon after receiving an antiarrhythmic drug, the patients began to deteriorate, to feel sick and look as though the props were knocked out from under them. From that moment onward, the trajectory was unrelentingly and rapidly downward: blood pressure became imperceptible, a state of circulatory collapse developed, and recovery was unusual. However, if the drug was effective in restoring a normal heart rhythm, effective pumping action was rapidly restored.

* * *

This was the state of antiarrhythmic therapeutics when I first encountered Mr. C. A slightly built Scotsman with lively, sky blue eyes and thinning sandy blond hair, he was always cheerful, although at age fifty-four he had already suffered two crippling heart attacks. About once a week he developed ventricular tachycardia — at the onset of which he looked remarkably well. Though breathing rapidly, he would deny breathlessness or other symptoms. The sole complaint was palpitation, what he called a racing heart. The tachycardia always occurred at night, rousing him from deep sleep. He could not recall dreaming. My sleep was likewise disrupted, and many were the nights I raced to the hospital to meet an apologetic Mr. C.

We learned that administering Pronestyl in a formidably large intravenous dose consistently restored a normal heartbeat, but there were tense moments before this occurred. No sooner did the injection begin than his blood pressure began to plummet. Thereafter a seeming race ensued between the drug's adverse and salutary actions. The former impaired the heart's pumping function as Mr. C.'s lungs brimmed with congestion. Mr. C. turned blue from inadequate oxygenation, and his breathing grew increasingly rapid and uncomfortable. Anxiety among medical staff mounted as we waited with apprehension. Which would give way first, the arrhythmia or the heart? After a stressful hour Mr. C. would revert to a normal heartbeat, vital signs would rapidly be restored, and he was once again his chipper self. As we shook hands, he would vow never again to disturb my sleep.

Handshakes accompanied by earnest pledges were unavailing, as recurrences continued approximately once weekly. He could not identify any triggers, emotional or physical. Invariably the onset occurred past midnight. I began to consider a sleepless night a week as penance for some unconfessed medical sin. After the tenth such session, nervous fatigue was setting in. But little did I anticipate what was yet in store.

At 2:30 A.M. on Tuesday, November 3, 1959, I was wakened by a phone call from a nurse at the Peter Bent Brigham Hospital emergency ward. She announced matter-of-factly, "Your friend

Mr. C. is here to see you." When I arrived in the EW, he looked quite comfortable. His heart was beating at a rate of 170 per minute, which he could tolerate without evident compromise for many hours. With optimism based on numerous similar encounters, I assured Mr. C. that we would soon have him back to normal. This time, however, the usually effective dose of Pronestyl did not reverse the tachycardia but made him deathly ill. The heart rate, instead of slowing, accelerated to 212 beats per minute, while blood pressure receded to around 80 systolic and was difficult to measure. At this level of blood pressure only the brain and heart are being sustained, with circulation to other organs largely shut off. Signs of heart failure with lung congestion were in evidence. The next day we tried Dilantin without effect. By Thursday he looked more dead than alive, yet his eyes communicated trust because I had never failed him. I kept muttering inane platitudes about how we would soon restore a normal heart rhythm, not having the remotest idea how to achieve this. I began to feel the sizzle of panic.

As Thursday wore on, my staff and I were zombified from little sleep and our morale was frayed, the last scintilla of hope vanishing. But Mr. C. retained a flicker of optimism and tried to cheer us. "I'm sure, Dr. Lown, you will pull me through, as you did all the other times." Such comments made the situation more insufferable. A Bertolt Brecht aphorism kept spinning in my tired brain: "I admit it — I have no hope. The blind speak of a way out. I see."

By Friday morning Mr. C.'s breathing was labored, skin ashen and covered with a thin film of sickly cold moisture, lips a deep blue; Mr. C. was tossing restlessly as his brain agitated for more oxygen. His lungs were now totally flooded with congestion that was unresponsive to diuretics. We discontinued monitoring his blood pressure and he stopped cheering us on. With every word he spoke he fell into a prolonged period of coughing and gasping for breath. For the first time, his widely staring eyes articulated despair. The message was "You have failed me," or so I imagined.

Wracking my brain and reviewing for the umpteenth time

what could be done, I consistently came up with a zero. Then I recalled that only a few years earlier, Dr. Paul Zoll, an innovative physician-inventor from the adjoining Beth Israel Hospital, had wrought a medical revolution by introducing alternating current (AC) shock across the intact chest to treat ventricular fibrillation, the arrhythmia of sudden death. The device essentially tapped current emerging from an electric outlet and shocked the heart into a normal rhythm. It was a phenomenal breakthrough for those who had experienced cardiac arrest. They were in fact dead, and while AC failed to resuscitate a substantial number, at least the procedure was free of complication. No further injury could be inflicted on a dead person, but my patient was still very much alive and fully conscious.

Never having seen an AC defibrillator, I hadn't the remotest idea how to use one. A host of questions needed prompt answers: Was the shock painful? Was anesthesia required? Was there an appropriate voltage setting to reverse ventricular tachycardia? If the first shock failed, how many additional ones could be delivered? Did the electric discharge traumatize the heart or injure the nervous system? Could it burn the skin? Were there any hazards for bystanders? Was it explosive for the patient receiving oxygen? My head was migrainous from the avalanche of questions. There was no one I could turn to at the PBBH, for few had significant experience with a Zoll defibrillator.

I tried to call Zoll himself but, as luck would have it, he was out of town and could not be located. I talked with one of his knowledgeable coworkers who indicated that they had never used the AC defibrillator on someone with ventricular tachycardia. Hitherto everyone subjected to the Zoll treatment had experienced a cardiac arrest and was unconscious. The associate could not provide any helpful advice, and my resolve weakened. But on returning to the vigil at Mr. C.'s bedside, I threw caution to the wind. First I turned to Mrs. C., explaining that we might kill her husband by this untried procedure. Having suffered silently by his side throughout the long ordeal, she was well aware that we had reached the end of the road and that her husband could die at any moment. A woman of great resolve, she urged us to move ahead.

The next obstacle to overcome was recruiting someone willing to anesthetize a nearly dead patient. Afraid of losing precious time by appealing to men low on the totem pole, I turned to Dr. Roy Vandam, chairman of the PBBH Department of Anesthesia. It seemed unlikely that he would agree to become an accessory to what might prove to be a tragic misadventure. After explaining the therapeutic dilemma, despair in my voice, I asked if he could send one of his junior associates. He refused, indicating that this was not a job he could delegate to an assistant, and he would be there instantly. Indeed, he came running, carrying a small canister of nitrous oxide as the anesthetic, thereby ascending to a permanent niche in my private hall of fame.

As Mr. C. was about to be anesthetized, the director of the medical service barged in and stopped the procedure. Mr. C. was now stuporous and every minute's delay jeopardized his survival. The director bombarded me with questions: Was I experienced with AC defibrillators? Had I ever used the device on a patient with ventricular tachycardia? Had anyone performed such a procedure at the PBBH, or in Boston, or anywhere in the world? To each question my answer was negative. Finally he asked whether I understood that if the patient died the hospital would be legally liable and might confront a large malpractice suit. When I remained nonplussed, he insisted that I obtain clearance from the hospital's attorney. I refused, but as a compromise noted in the patient's chart my sole and exclusive responsibility and acknowledged the hospital's opposition to my proceeding.

This bureaucratic hassle cleared, Mr. C. was anesthetized. We then applied large plate electrodes on the right and left side of his chest, and as soon as Dr. Vandam gave the signal, everyone jumped away from the bedside as I delivered an electric jolt. For the next minute the electrocardiographic stylus went haywire and we could not tell whether the tachycardia had been abolished. However, listening to Mr. C.'s heart with a stethoscope,

I heard the happy tidings of a slow, strong, regular lub-dub. These heart sounds gave me a goose-pimply thrill, recalling my first hearing, as a youngster, the opening bars of Beethoven's Fifth Symphony.

Mr. C. woke up almost immediately, as though from a restful siesta, an angelic smile on his red lips. He soon didn't need the oxygen or the pressor drugs to support the circulation. A miracle had been wrought. Mr. C. recovered rapidly, becoming fully ambulatory within a day. I approved his and Mrs. C.'s going to Florida for a deserved holiday, little anticipating that this fine man was soon to confront the most grueling chapter of a long saga.

Exactly three weeks later, on a Friday morning, Mrs. C. telephoned that her husband was back in ventricular tachycardia and hospitalized in Miami. I reassured her that the large university hospital undoubtedly possessed an AC defibrillator and all I would have to do was speak to his doctor. Referred to the director of the cardiology service, I painstakingly detailed the patient's recent history and explained that he would die if not shocked out of the rhythm disorder. None of my arguments and entreaties made the slightest impact, and a friendly discussion rapidly turned angry as he categorically refused. The purported reason was that the use of an AC defibrillator for ventricular tachycardia had not been reported in the medical literature. He was unswayed by the fact that our experience was too recent to have been published and added that no one could assure him that he would not face a malpractice suit were something to go wrong.

I asked incredulously, "You will let this man die without trying a method that has worked on him?"

"I am afraid, Doctor, I cannot carry out a newfangled procedure that is not documented even by an abstract in the literature."

Foolishly, I urged Mrs. C. to fly her husband to Boston. About two hours later she called from Miami International Airport in a state of agitation. No air carrier would board a critically ill patient. It was 2:00 P.M. and the weekend was rapidly approaching. My behavior was unconscionable. At my suggestion, a dying patient had signed himself out from a hospital against advice and was lying unattended on a gurney at a busy international airport. I was despairing about what to do. He had to get on a plane to Boston immediately. By four in the afternoon, not knowing where else to turn, I decided to visit the professor of aviation medicine at the Harvard School of Public Health, Dr. Ross McFarlane. Instead of calling, I felt it would be more effective to barge in without stopping at the secretary's desk. I found him in the midst of a meeting with two men. Paying no attention to the visitors, I recounted my tale of woe and the dire medical emergency. Professor McFarlane was completely unperturbed by the intrusion. "You couldn't have chosen a better moment," he said, laughing. His visitors, who had come from Washington, D.C., were key officials in the Federal Aviation Authority. They immediately got on the phone and began to call the chief executives of various airlines on the Boston-Miami route. They finally reached the chairman of the board of Eastern Airlines, who approved Mr. C.'s boarding the Boston-bound flight, departing Miami at about 7:00 P.M. and arriving at Logan International Airport about 10:30 P.M.

I was elated, but at about 10:00 P.M. the telephone rang and I picked it up to hear what sounded like an overseas call. At first I could not make out what was being said, but finally realized that the captain of the Eastern Airlines plane was calling to report that Logan Airport was fogged in and the flight was being diverted to New York's Idlewild. He wondered what should be done about the very sick passenger. I urged him to contact an ambulance service to transport Mr. C. to Boston. About 1:00 A.M., Mrs. C. was back on the line, hysterical. Apparently the ambulance took them into Manhattan before realizing that the Brigham was not in New York but in Boston. As a local ambulance, it was not permitted to go outside the precincts of the city. It took another hour to get Mr. C. into a private ambulance, and with the dense fog that night the drive to Boston was slow. They arrived at the hospital at eight o'clock Saturday morning.

We were ready, but Mr. C. was in extremis, semistuporous, more dead than alive. When the electrical shock was discharged across the chest, instead of resuming a normal rhythm, the heart was catapulted into dreaded ventricular fibrillation. Repeated shocks were to no avail. We opened up his chest without sterile technique. It was awful, messy and bloody. I shocked the heart directly, thereby delivering a higher electrical charge and restored a normal mechanism. But this time there was no quick recovery. He remained critically ill from both heart failure and raging infection, and when he was finally discharged after more than six weeks, he was an old and ailing man. Mr. C. did not survive long thereafter. My victory had turned into a calamity.

But why had the discharge precipitated intractable ventricular fibrillation, a much more malignant arrhythmia than the disorder being combatted? A search of the literature proved unrewarding. Not a single report addressed the possible adverse effects of AC on the heart. Zoll's method was sweeping the world, yet no one had documented the possibly dangerous consequences resulting from its use.

Aware of the potentially malign effects of AC, I began to visit operating rooms where heart surgery was performed. In these operations the heart frequently fibrillated and AC was applied directly to the heart to reverse the arrhythmia. Sometimes, when repeated shocks were required, the operating room smelled like a hamburger joint from the seared heart muscle. Needless to say, there was an inordinate amount of mortality associated with heart surgery when electrical resuscitation was required to restore an arrested heart.

No one focused on the adverse effects of the AC defibrillator because the cardiac arrest being treated was equated with death. If the patient did not recover, there was an abundance of other reasons for the fatality without implicating the defibrillator. The surgeons, rather cavalier, told me that if an AC defibrillator caused heart damage, it was a small price to pay for a patient's survival. But if I was going to treat arrhythmias in living patients, the procedure had to be nearly totally complication-free.

I outlined a series of straightforward experiments to test the safety of delivering AC across the closed chest, as was done in cardiac arrest. I had no funds and my grant applications were rejected, largely because of my lack of engineering credentials, but also because the use of electricity to treat ordinary arrhythmias struck many as outlandish. The project was rescued by Dr. Fredrick Stare, my chief and the remarkably visionary chairman of the Department of Nutrition at the Harvard School of Public Health, where I had a small animal laboratory. He urged me on, and for the next few years underwrote all the research costs without once worrying me about the large sums being expended.

In a number of animal experiments, I rapidly demonstrated that alternating current was injurious to the heart. It provoked every rhythm abnormality in the books, traumatized heart muscle, caused a leaching out of muscle potassium, and induced electrical burns. If enough shocks were given, the heart became permanently dysfunctional.

For a number of theoretical physiological reasons, I decided to test direct current (DC), but needed someone with expertise in electrical engineering. Fortunately, and quite accidentally, I met a brilliant young electrical engineer, Baruch Berkowitz, who rapidly comprehended the problem and proved decisively innovative. In a year of intense animal experiments, we showed that one of the numerous DC waveforms we had studied was consistently effective in reversing the most intractable ventricular fibrillation, which could not be budged by AC. To test the limits of the system, we cooled the heart, acidified the blood, and reduced the oxygen tension to a fraction of normal, circumstances that made reversion nearly impossible. Even under these difficult conditions, DC consistently restored a normal rhythm. Furthermore, it did not injure the heart the way AC did. In the closed chest animal, even after 200 successive high electrical energy shocks, there was no detectable heart damage. In effect, we had developed a nearly foolproof defibrillator. I had been searching for a method of dealing with cardiac tachyarrhythmias and ended up with a new and improved defibrillator.

For the first time, ventricular fibrillation did not exact an inordinate mortality. Not only did the DC defibrillator provide a new approach for resuscitating patients who died suddenly, it also widened the horizon for cardiac surgeons. During a coronary bypass operation the surgeon requires a nonbeating heart to enable the placement of a small vein or arterial grafts to bypass obstructed coronary vessels. The heart is arrested by inducing ventricular fibrillation, during which circulation to vital organs is maintained by an external pump oxygenator device. DC defibrillation provided, for the first time, a safe way to restore a normal heart rhythm. The great progress in heart surgery over the past three decades would not have been possible without a DC defibrillator.

The first surgeon to comprehend the importance of this breakthrough was Dr. Don Effler, director of cardiac surgery at the Cleveland Clinic. In 1962, shortly after developing the DC defibrillator, I met Effler at a meeting of the Sun Coast Heart Association in Tampa, Florida, where we were both guest lecturers. At the end of the day, while sitting by the swimming pool, I explained my work on the defibrillator. He evinced only slight interest and I forgot about this conversation until many months later, when Effler showed up at my modest laboratory in a Harvard School of Public Health subbasement. He had flown in for the sole purpose of learning about the new device, and his group became the first to employ the DC defibrillator. It is perhaps no accident that the Argentinean surgeon Dr. René Favoloro, working under Effler at the Cleveland Clinic, performed the first coronary bypass surgery a few years thereafter.

More than twenty years later, Effler wrote me a long letter reminiscing about the DC defibrillator and concluded:

> This letter was prompted by a question from my secretary, who asked me to define serendipity. I gave her the classical dictionary definition but then told her of my trip to Tampa, my par-

ticipation in a medical panel, my leisurely walk to the poolside bar seeking a cool drink and relaxation in the sun — and how I ended up with DC defibrillation, which made a profound difference in my morbidity and mortality rates then and now. The legendary Prince of Serendip always found a treasure when he was looking for something else — It's a beautiful story.

The DC device swept away the AC defibrillator despite substantial rearguard resistance from the latter's manufacturer, and within several years the DC defibrillator was the only instrument in use. A nagging question remained, however: Why not use the defibrillator for arrhythmias other than ventricular fibrillation? To do so we would have to be absolutely certain that direct current with the particular waveform employed was not injurious to the heart. With extensive experiments on animals, I became aware of a fly in this ointment. The so-called safe DC waveform could in fact provoke ventricular fibrillation. This happened infrequently, perhaps once in a hundred trials, and seemed completely haphazard in its occurrence. While this was of no consequence in a heart already afflicted with ventricular fibrillation, as in the case of cardiac arrest, it was absolutely unacceptable for treating less malignant arrhythmias.

We soon discovered why this happened. Each time the heart beats there is a brief interval in the cardiac cycle that is susceptible to ventricular fibrillation. This is true in a normal as well as a diseased heart. The interval is referred to as the ventricular vulnerable period and occurs early in the heart cycle, during inscription of the T-wave of the electrocardiogram. This is a brief interval during which the heart recovers from having been stimulated to contract and returns to a resting phase ready for the next electrical discharge. The vulnerable period is extremely short, lasting anywhere from 0.02 to 0.04 seconds, but when an electrical impulse occurs during the vulnerable period, it triggers the potentially fatal arrhythmia. We learned this through extensive experimentation, unaware that physiologists had known it for fifty years.

Once we realized the cause for the ventricular fibrillation, we could use the direct current defibrillator with much greater safety. Using a simple electronic timer, we triggered the electric discharge to fall outside the vulnerable period of the cardiac cycle. I designated this method of timed DC discharge cardioversion, the introduction of which wrought a veritable revolution in cardiology. For the first time, all rapid heart action episodes could be readily terminated. This was true of atrial fibrillation, atrial flutter, ventricular tachycardia, and a host of other disorders. Cardioversion gave a significant impetus to the creation of coronary care units, centers to care for patients suffering from heart attacks who are highly susceptible to diverse cardiac arrhythmias. Even more gratifying than improving cardiac care generally, however, was simply restoring that miraculous lub-dubbing for patients who were disabled with intolerable flip-floppings in their chest. Within hours they would forget how the heart can nag and gnaw.

In human affairs, resolution of a problem invariably brings new challenges in its wake. While a cardiologist used to see a patient with ventricular tachycardia once in a great while, it is now a common occurrence. Whereas in the past it was unusual for someone to have survived two or three bouts of ventricular tachycardia, we now see patients who have experienced several hundred attacks of this disorder. A new field of arrhythmology was spawned, resulting in innovative technologies for diagnosis and management of these patients. Countless lives were saved. What amazed me is how rapidly, seemingly overnight, this was adopted worldwide and became standard treatment everywhere.

14

The Coronary Care Unit

DIRECT CURRENT (DC) defibrillation provided ample proof that sudden cardiac death was reversible and survivable. It had the potential of saving many lives, but by the time emergency medical technicians reached a victim of cardiac arrest, efforts at resuscitation often proved futile. Following a cardiac collapse, the victim's door of life remained ajar for a short interval, then was shut forever. After five minutes, irreversible brain damage set in and the heart grew less willing to resume a normal mechanism.

To avoid a terminological Tower of Babel, it should be made clear that doctors use many terms interchangeably, albeit without scientific rigor. For example, cardiac collapse may denote a fainting spell, a loss of blood pressure, or a stoppage of the heartbeat. Cardiac arrest results from cessation of the heartbeat which, if not promptly reversed, leads to sudden death. Heart attack, synonymous with myocardial infarction and coronary thrombosis, is also used to designate sudden death.

Three decades ago it was generally accepted that sudden cardiac death was caused by a massive heart attack. The belief was that the attack was initiated when a thrombus or clot abruptly blocked a large coronary artery, that is, by an acute coronary thrombosis. Since the thrombus-obstructed vessel could no longer carry blood to the heart, the heart muscle segment that was deprived of the blood carrying oxygen and vital nutrients soon died and eventually became a scar. The remaining heart muscle, with patent coronary arteries, was unaffected except by the increased workload and had to strain to circulate a normal volume of blood to the body but with less pumping muscle.

The blocked coronary vessel also injured the electrical conduction system. This jeopardized survival even more than the damage to heart muscle. In bypassing the dead tissue, the flow of electric current became dispersed into eddies, which at times grew chaotic. In some patients these progressed into veritable electrical storms engulfing the entire heart. The disorganized heart rhythm — ventricular fibrillation (VF) — was the prodrome to cardiac arrest (see Chapter 13). To diminish the toll of ventricular fibrillation, I then reasoned that if patients in the earliest throes of a heart attack could be expeditiously hospitalized in a special monitoring unit with a DC defibrillator at the ready, their chances for survival would be vastly improved, for they could be resuscitated in the event of ventricular fibrillation.

During the early 1960s, I urged the establishment of what I thought would be a first such special coronary care unit at the Peter Brent Brigham Hospital (PBBH), but I was disabused of the notion that this was an original idea when Dr. Grey Dimond, then professor and chairman of the Department of Medicine at the University of Kansas, came to visit. He told me of a lifesaving miracle wrought by Dr. Hughes Day, a general practitioner in Bethany, Kansas, who had already organized the first coronary care unit in the United States. This breakthrough spurred me on to greater enthusiasm in trying to develop a coronary care unit at my hospital.

Central to my thinking was deciding how to protect cardiac patients against ventricular fibrillation. During VF, the heart was dying not because activity had stopped but, on the contrary, from a surfeit of tumultuous electrical activity. Closer observation of the fibrillating heart showed it to be a veritable quivering can of worms, caused by electric currents scurrying hither and thither, colliding with or canceling out one another, only to reemerge from nowhere in mad disorder. If this chaos was not stopped within several minutes it put an end to the heart's organized contraction and the heart was said to be fibrillating. Once this happened the patient would die within minutes unless revived by an electrical shock.

As I noted earlier, the electric spark responsible for setting off the heart's contraction normally originates in the physiological pacemaker of the heart, the sinus node (see Chapter 13). From there the stimulus traverses along preexisting conduits wired into the heart, which permit a sequential activation so that pumping proceeds from the apex toward the base where the valves are located. The consistent pattern of this steady electrical rhythm generates effective pressure, propelling blood forward through heart valves into the great vessels, thereby distributing the flow throughout the body. Ventricular fibrillation, by disorganizing electrical activity, disorganizes the heart's mechanical activity as well and stops its pumping action.

Once ventricular fibrillation emerges, as I have already emphasized, time is of the essence, seconds are precious. If this lethal rhythm disorder is to be instantly corrected, the patient cannot be far from a DC defibrillator. The coronary care unit (CCU) was equipped not only with the defibrillator itself but also with the electronic technology for identifying the exact moment when the potentially lethal arrhythmia emerged.

Even though the revolutionary innovations of DC defibrillation and cardioversion were first employed at the PBBH, I could not interest the administration in building a coronary care unit. I tried to persuade the distinguished chief of medicine, Dr. George Thorn, but while he endorsed the idea, he thought it unlikely that the board of trustees would approve, as the Brigham was planning to build a whole new hospital in the next few years and had no money for this project in any case. I was growing impatient because three more units had already opened in Miami, Philadelphia, and New York.

The year was 1963. I discussed the need for a CCU with my mentor, Dr. Samuel A. Levine, who did not require much persuading and promptly became a powerful ally, turning over his entire research fund for this project. The American Optical Company, which had been the first to manufacture DC defibrillators and cardioverters, donated all the necessary electronic equipment. The hospital could not resist such an attractive offer and finally allocated space for a four-bed CCU, the first in New England and the fifth in the world.

These early CCUs, before the opening of the PBBH unit, were essentially focused on cardiopulmonary resuscitation. The aim of monitoring was to intercept the earliest onset of ventricular fibrillation, the lethal arrhythmia of sudden death. A major instrument was the bedside monitor attached to the coronary attack victim, which kept the heart rhythm under continuous surveillance and set off an alarm if there was any change. A properly trained group of nurses was constantly on the alert and ready to intervene skillfully with a rehearsed and well-disciplined repertoire of activities in the event of a cardiac arrest. The prevailing atmosphere was that of a fire station, one surrounded by a large wooded area during a long dry spell with an incendiary on the prowl.

The moment an alarm went off, however, the less well-trained house staff took command. A headlong rush ensued, even though the majority were false alarms owing to electrocardiographic artifacts. When a bona fide cardiac arrest did occur, the space around the dying patient was packed with nurses, interns, residents, fellows, medical students, technicians, and orderlies. Voices were strident, high-pitched with excitement. The doctors, unlike the nurses, had no plan of action, but they exercised their authority. Since the ignorant are the most certain of what is right, the least experienced called the shots. More bicarbonate; The venous line is clogged; He needs to be zapped again; Can you feel a pulse?; Everybody step aside; The leads aren't on; Damn it, why isn't the defibrillator plugged in?

The following anecdote was then circulating. A patient arrives at a CCU with a minor heart attack. He is frightened, anxious, eager to know what is going on. Everyone is too busy saving lives to bother. Surrounded by awe-inspiring technology, the only sound he can hear is the amplified staccato beating of his heart. All he can see is the luminescent oscilloscopic screen with oft-repeated identical squiggles, which he rightly interprets as his heartbeat. Come evening, he despairs of ever hearing the verdict, whether it will be life, invalidism, or worse. A janitor comes to mop the floor. The patient turns to this man for information. "Tell me, buddy, what's going on?" "I dunno, but I can tell you one thing. You hear that beep, beep, beep? You better not let it stop. If you do, prepare for misery. Ten people in white will rush in and beat the crap out of you."

When the coronary care unit in the PBBH was opened in January 1965, I put an end to the circus atmosphere that prevailed in other CCUs when a cardiac arrest occurred. The essential aim, however, was the same: to resuscitate patients with acute myocardial infarction who had experienced cardiac arrest. Displaying the ubiquitous ventricular arrhythmias, the new oscilloscope monitors, strategically located around the unit, gave me an inkling of the future. The patient was being displaced in the roster of priorities. The nurses, rather than hovering at the bedside, fearing to miss a dangerous extrasystole, harbinger of possible malignant arrhythmia, were riveted by the electrocardiographic displays on the large TV screens at their stations.

The PBBH unit was revolutionary in several respects. It was built with an eye to diminishing psychological stress factors; the lights, for example, were on a rheostat so patients would not be aroused by a burst of bright lights when staff entered. Quiet was emphasized. Patients who wished to listen to a radio had to use earphones. As surgeons are invariably loud, boisterous, and threatening, a sign was posted at the CCU door: SURGEONS, DO NOT ENTER UNLESS CONSULTED. The unit was designed to maximize privacy while permitting direct visual contact with the nursing station, that is, patients could see the nurses, and vice versa. In endless exhortations to staff, I emphasized that a tranquil, low-key environment was essential if they were to sense a patient's mood and state of anxiety. Only when quiet reigns can one detect a low moan and the submerged turmoil of despair.

Nurses were upgraded from medical underlings, their historical role until then, to the level of fellow professionals. The nurses, like the doctors, carried a stethoscope. They participated in morning rounds and commented about patients, providing invaluable insights on what was troubling them — information the house staff rarely picked up themselves. An overburdened intern or medical resident on a fleeting visit to deal with some urgent clinical problem rarely took time to listen to the patient. We had teaching conferences for nurses, and I gave a weekly one-hour session exclusively for them. It was a new type of participatory nursing. Excitement was palpable and morale high.

With a cardiac arrest, nurses were instructed not to wait for doctors but to initiate immediate defibrillation. Exquisitely trained in cardiopulmonary resuscitation (CPR), they were more skilled than the medical house staff. While the latter received training in CPR, they had no time to practice. It was an aesthetic experience to watch a specialist nurse respond to a cardiac arrest. I am still in awe when I recall the time a slight nurse asked me to see a newly arrived patient. Since the unit was full, he was temporarily on a gurney in the treatment room. She told me very matter-of-factly that he was a forty-eight-year-old fire department inspector who had experienced a cardiac arrest a few minutes earlier. But as I walked into the room, the patient was free of apprehension or awareness of this near-catastrophic event. He commented, "I must have passed out for a moment."

From her story I gathered that while she was recording an electrocardiogram, he had developed VF. She had done the following: first, make sure that the chaotic pattern was not an artifact due to a disconnected lead, feel for a pulse, switch on the defibrillator, wait ten seconds until it stored sufficient energy, fix the proper discharge setting, apply conductive paste to the electrode paddles, position them on the chest, then deliver the jolt. She had accomplished all this within twenty-seven seconds! I knew the precise time because she had left the electrocardiogram running, which enabled me to ascertain the data. When the patient woke up a minute later, she had reassured him that he had a minor arrhythmia which would not recur. Both were unflustered, behaving as though what had just transpired was a routine event not worth many words. What extraordinary medical professionalism!

Nonetheless, I was dissatisfied with the focus on resuscitating patients. It would make more sense to prevent ventricular fibrillation in the first place rather than engage in heroics after the fact. The old adage of an ounce of prevention being worth a pound of cure was especially pertinent. Since VF was consistently reversible and patients did not seem the worse for it, the medical staff regarded the arrhythmia as innocuous. But was it? I began to observe rare patients with VF who could not be resuscitated. Even if a normal rhythm was promptly restored, during VF the heart was working away full blast, as though running a continuous hundred-yard dash, without a supply of oxygen and nutrients, since the circulation of blood had ceased. It stood to reason that even the briefest bout of VF worsened the damage already exacted by the blocked artery. We had to shift our emphasis from treating cardiac arrest to avoiding it. Easier said than done! One could not treat every victim of a heart attack to protect the one in seventy-five patients who might experience VF. How were we to predict who would experience VF? No information existed suggesting that VF had any recognizable prodromes. Merely identifying the patient to be protected was insufficient in the absence of a prompt-acting, safe, and effective antiarrhythmic drug. Those which were then available acted slowly, compromised the heart's pumping action, and unleashed a veritable swarm of adverse reactions. The task was daunting.

Even if we had a seemingly miraculous drug, how could we be certain it would protect everyone threatened with VF? For an infrequently encountered event, how does one select a therapeutic end point indicating that an effective antiarrhythmic drug dose has been prescribed? For me the problem was simplified by the fact that in the early spasms of a heart attack, patients had a profusion of skipped beats, ventricular extrasystoles. It was my view that these heartthrobs, by their frequency and type, identified the electrically unstable heart and therefore were indicators of susceptibility to VF. Diminishing, or better still, abolishing frequently occurring extrasystoles would prevent emergence of life-threatening ventricular fibrillation. These minor irregularities of rhythm would constitute a therapeutic target for defining the appropriate drug dose. In fact, we would administer the drug to abolish the extrasystoles and having done so presume it would ensure against the occurrence of VF.

With a suitable therapeutic target, such as the ventricular extrasystole, we could spell out the attributes of an ideal drug. A paramount requirement was that the antiarrhythmic medication would not further compromise the already injured heart. The drug had to be given by vein, thereby assuring immediate effectiveness. While exerting rapid antiarrhythmic action, it should not impair the heart's pumping action or compromise blood pressure. Moreover, it should be eliminated promptly by the liver or kidneys so that any adverse reaction would rapidly dissipate. No such drug was on the horizon, and in the unlikely circumstance that drug companies launched a type of Manhattan Project for discovering the ideal drug, it would take a decade or more to became available at the bedside. What we had to do was try to find a drug in the current pharmacopoeia that had unsuspected antiarrhythmic efficacy as well as all the other properties we were seeking.

I wrestled with this problem for many months. Suddenly there floated into my mind a strange yet appropriate image. I was in a 1950s operating room where a thoracic surgeon, Dr. Harrison Black, was performing a pneumonectomy. He did something unusual, dousing the heart with a clear liquid.

"What is it that you are spraying on the pericardium?"

"Oh, that's Xylocaine" — the trademark name for the local anesthetic lidocaine.

"Why?"

"It prevents irregularities of heart rhythm when I'm working on the lung," he explained.

My only familiarity with Xylocaine was having a dentist infiltrate my gum with this local anesthetic. I had never come across anyone besides Dr. Black who suggested that Xylocaine had antiarrhythmic properties. A review of the medical literature drew a blank, but I knew that surgeons were notorious for home remedies. Now that I was grasping at straws in my search for a new antiarrhythmic, I decided to give Xylocaine a closer look.

This was one of the many occasions when it was extremely useful to have a working animal laboratory in close concert with my clinical unit. Problems that could not be solved in the clinic were modeled in animal studies, and answers derived from those studies could be applied promptly at the bedside. The question posed this time was straightforward. Would lidocaine given intravenously during a heart attack abolish the prevalent ventricular extrasystoles?

We went to work with determination. After a dog's left anterior descending coronary artery was occluded, a multiplicity of ventricular arrhythmias developed within the ensuing twenty-four to thirty-six hours, which were refractory to the available drugs. Lo and behold, no sooner had we injected the lidocaine than all the ventricular extrasystoles were suppressed. It was as though a spigot had been turned, shutting off the flow of arrhythmia. It happened so abruptly, quickly, and totally that it left me perplexed. It was too good to be true. Sheer coincidence, I could hear myself muttering without conviction. But the results were confirmed by the fact that within fifteen to twenty minutes after lidocaine had been discontinued, the arrhythmia returned. Lidocaine caused no drop in blood pressure nor did it compromise ventricular pumping activity. We repeated the experiment dozens of times with identical results. My excitement knew no bounds.

At times impetuosity is rewarded. Within a week I brought lidocaine to the bedside without turning for permission to the Food and Drug Administration, which would have delayed its clinical use for years. I sent a memorandum to the staff instructing that all patients were to be given lidocaine if on arrival at the CCU they exhibited extrasystoles. From the dog experiments I extrapolated the human dose on a weight basis. Now this seems foolhardy, since there was no reason to surmise that dogs metabolized or excreted lidocaine identically to humans. Fortunately, what we had seen in dogs was replicated in patients. To this day the guideline for using lidocaine clinically remains essentially the same.

The ensuing weeks were extraordinary. We could shut off irregularities in heart rhythm at will merely by infusing lidocaine, and we could bring back these extrasystoles by slowing the intravenous drip. We established that lidocaine was safe even in the sickest patients and in those with severe heart failure. If complications resulted from lidocaine overdosing, they were eliminated in minutes by discontinuing the drug.

With the advent of lidocaine, the aim of coronary care changed dramatically from resuscitating patients with cardiac arrest to preventing its occurrence. During the unit's first year, using lidocaine on everyone admitted to the CCU with extrasystoles, we did not record a single episode of VF in 130 consecutive patients with a heart attack. This experience should have raised doubts about the need for such expensive units, which were then mushrooming all over the country and consuming billions of dollars. But I was too overwhelmed with the excitement to worry about economics or involve myself in long-range cost-benefit analyses.

Lidocaine swept into all coronary care units, intensive care units, and operating rooms. Sales of lidocaine skyrocketed. From a local anesthetic for dentistry it became a major lifesaving drug. An unfortunate consequence of its introduction was that we lost our entire team of great nurses. They were masters of cardiopulmonary resuscitation, but with lidocaine dripping into numerous veins, their skills were never challenged. With little of the old drama, the coronary care unit grew quiet, at least on the surface.

The nurses became demoralized, but my view was that the drama and excitement resided in the very fact that nothing was happening. People were recovering without hoopla, without residual scars in their hearts or souls. How fantastic! I could no longer ignite a spark in these nurses. My arguments were not rebutted. While listening with respect, they remained demoralized and shifted to other jobs. The extrasystole on the monitoring scope was riveting, the new technology was mesmerizing, and managing the machinery enhanced status. The human dimension was lost in the shuffle.

In retrospect it is evident, although I failed to appreciate it at the time, that we were on the threshold of a new age in medicine, where the excitement resided in the application of novel technologies more than in caring for individual patients. For some victims of a heart attack this was an entirely new ball game, as one patient brought home to me when he asked rhetorically, "What's the big deal about having a heart attack? It provided me a healthy rest for about a week. I wouldn't mind having another in five years."

Development of the CCU had many salutary consequences. It stimulated specialized intensive care units for other medical subdisciplines. It promoted nurses to a central role in intensive care units. The continuous monitoring of various cardiovascular functions improved care of the critically ill, and the mortality for patients with acute myocardial infarction was reduced by 50 percent. It stimulated research on every facet of a heart attack, confirming that the culprit event was a clot abruptly closing off a coronary artery. This knowledge facilitated the most significant breakthrough, introduction of thrombolytic therapy to dissolve the obstructing blood clot. The many advances would not have occurred without the research made possible in this type of a unit. Dissolving the clot in a coronary vessel has further reduced mortality from a heart attack to around 6 percent, a far cry from the one in three who succumbed a mere thirty years earlier. I am convinced that this remarkable lowering in mortality could not have happened without the advent of the CCU.

Of course, every silver lining has its cloud. Every advance exacts a cost. Medicine grew even more depersonalized. Technology took precedence and patients became secondary. A paradox of my life and its ultimate irony is that my research work facilitated that which I utterly deplore.

15

The Ventricular Extrasystole: Heartthrob or Harbinger?

EVERY NINETY SECONDS, around the clock, someone dies suddenly and unexpectedly from heart disease. In the United States the toll exceeds 400,000 victims annually, equaling that of cancer. Sudden death — the most catastrophic of all manifestations of heart disease — intrudes unannounced like a thief in the night. In approximately 25 percent of victims, death is the first and last indication that the patient suffered from a heart condition. It claims nearly 60 percent of all those afflicted with coronary heart disease.

It is incomprehensible that the leading cause of fatality in the industrialized world was largely ignored by the medical profession until the early 1970s. Death is the most concrete and most visible end point in medicine. How then is it possible that the mammoth problem of sudden cardiac death (SCD) had not been addressed when much lesser entities were recognized and amply researched? I believe that this paradox relates to how medical concerns and ideas are generated, promoted, and popularized.

A practicing doctor's interests are focused by the voice of the academician, and the academician's interests are in turn shaped by observations on his or her home turf, the tertiary-care hospital linked to a medical school. If patients with particular illnesses are not admitted to the hospital, their problems remain unnoticed. SCD victims did not make it alive to a hospital. They reached the hospital's outer perimeter, the emergency ward. This was a bypass rather than an admission, a brief way station where they were pronounced dead on arrival before being taken to the morgue. The rapid transit did not register on the academic mind, did not generate studies, resulted in no manuscripts, lectures, colloquia, symposia, and the like; it therefore made no impact. Likewise, deaths that occurred outside the hospital remained beyond the academic's visual field. Academicians' disregard of SCD led medical practitioners to suppose that the catastrophic sudden event was the result of a massive, irreversible heart attack. Unpredictable as well as unfathomable, it was an act of God before which health professionals stood largely helpless.

A paradigm shift to which several factors contributed began in the early 1960s. Among them was the introduction of the direct current defibrillator, which could shock patients out of ventricular fibrillation, allowing them to resume normal living. Many who survived had neither electrocardiographic nor blood enzyme changes indicating a myocardial infarction, or heart attack. These refuted the prevailing belief that sudden death was the consequence of a massive heart attack and showed instead that it was caused by a reversible electrical accident that led to ventricular fibrillation (VF).

Another factor in the shift originated at the Johns Hopkins Medical School in Baltimore. William Kouwenhoven, a retired engineering professor who was doing volunteer work in the surgical department, made the seemingly eccentric suggestion that rhythmic manual compression of the breastbone could substitute for the heart's pumping action. He demonstrated that this simple maneuver maintained adequate blood flow to such vital organs as the brain and heart for prolonged intervals after a cardiac arrest. It constituted a truly revolutionary discovery.

After a heart stops, it takes less than ten minutes for the brain to be irreversibly damaged, and even patients rushed directly to a hospital were invariably brain dead on arrival. Kouwenhoven's innovation lessened the tyranny of time, providing an interlude of tenuous survival frequently sufficient to transport a patient still clinging to life to the closest hospital for defibrillation.

A unique community project in Seattle, Washington, organized by Dr. Leonard Cobb and his coworkers, demonstrated that external chest massage initiated by bystanders was effective in resuscitating victims of cardiac arrest. With chest massage and mouth-to-mouth ventilation, they helped maintain blood flow to vital organs until the arrival of paramedics, who rushed the victim to the closest hospital for definitive defibrillation. Results were spectacular: nearly 30 percent of those felled by a potentially fatal heart stoppage recovered and were discharged alive from the hospital. However, other cities were unable to replicate the experience of Seattle, where nearly the entire community had been indoctrinated, trained, and committed. Furthermore, even with immediate resuscitation, 70 percent did not survive a cardiac arrest. It was evident that reducing the awesome toll of sudden cardiac death required identification of patients at risk and development of practical measures for preventing a cardiac arrest. Lidocaine was not the answer, because it was effective only when given by vein.

Extensive studies failed to uncover distinctive prodromes of sudden death. Since the majority of those experiencing a cardiac arrest had coronary artery disease, the usual coronary risk factors were not additionally informative. Electrocardiographic patterns were not distinctive. Even when a patient visited a doctor shortly before the fatal event, there was no complaint that could have alerted the physician of the impending catastrophe. It was of course possible that sudden death was happenstance, the expression of a chaotic process defying prediction, but I refused to accept that. My optimism was nurtured not by ideological preconceptions but by clinical observations during the early days of the coronary care unit (CCU). Among patients hospitalized with a heart attack, the greater the frequency of ventricular extrasystoles, the more predisposed the heart to life-threatening arrhythmias. The occurrence of VF was often announced by an abundance of ventricular extrasystoles. Was this also true of victims of sudden death? A significant difference existed between the two conditions. Cardiac arrest, unlike a heart attack, was not caused by the abrupt closure of a coronary artery. The experience with heart attack victims in the CCU therefore may have had little relevance.

Since sudden death came from VF, an arrhythmic event, the logical question was whether patients who died suddenly had demonstrated ventricular arrhythmias before the fatal event. If such arrhythmias were to prove helpful in identifying the threatened patient, they should manifest a distinctive pattern, occur frequently enough to be readily recognizable, and long antedate the cardiac arrest.

Might not ventricular extrasystoles, the seemingly trivial heartthrobs, be the indicators of risk for sudden death? The mere occurrence of extrasystoles, which may be felt by individuals as skipped beats or heart palpitations, is far too common to be meaningful. Since the days of the Roman physician Galen, extrasystoles have been recognized as innocuous. They are often bemoaned by the lovelorn, invoked by poets to depict a heart loaded with passion, and described by hypochondriacs as intolerable palpitations. The frequency of extrasystoles increases with age. By seventy, nearly everyone has skips in the pulse, most frequently causing no symptom at all. Many individuals have frequent extrasystoles over a lifetime without suffering ill effects. These observations were at odds with my hypothesis, reminding me of a remark by Thomas Henry Huxley: "The tragedy of scientific inquiry is that a beautiful hypothesis may be slain by an ugly fact."* Was my theory relating extrasystoles to sudden death merely an insupportable fancy?

Since the electrocardiograph was introduced at the turn of the century by the Dutch physiologist Willem Einthoven, physicians have been aware that extrasystoles differ from one an-

---

* Thomas Henry Huxley, "Biogenesis and Abiogenesis," in *Discourses Biological and Geological: Essays by Thomas Henry Huxley* (New York: D. Appleton, 1896).

other in many respects. For example, they may originate in the right or in the left ventricle, differ in morphology, appear early or late in the cardiac cycle, occur individually, in pairs, or in flurries, and discharge episodically or punctuate the heart's rhythm after each normal cycle without surcease.

Working with the defibrillator and cardioverter, I was impressed with the difficulty of causing fibrillation with electrical discharges even in animal hearts with obstructed coronary arteries. The electrical stimulus required was many times more powerful than the heart can generate — 50,000 times as strong as the jolt needed to induce a single extrasystole. Also, this stimulus had to be triggered in an ultra-brief interval located at the apex of the electrocardiographic T-wave. This interval, lasting only twenty thousandths of a second, was the vulnerable period of the cardiac cycle described earlier. Indeed, with every heartbeat, during a momentary speck of time, every heart is susceptible to ventricular fibrillation, a veritable hairsbreadth constantly separating life from death.

We concluded that a critical factor in inducing fibrillation was the relation between the vulnerable period and a strong electrical current. Only extrasystoles discharged early in the cardiac cycle, during the vulnerable period, are dangerous. While such early extrasystoles are common and readily recognizable, how they generated the current strength required to provoke the chaotic electrical activity observed in VF was unknown.

As frequently happened in my life, long-forgotten clinical observations unexpectedly ignited my memory. On a number of occasions in the CCU, where heart rhythm was uninterruptedly monitored around the clock, a patient, before experiencing a cardiac arrest from ventricular fibrillation, developed runs of two or three sequential extrasystoles or longer trains of successive beats. This led to questions that proved decisive. Do salvos of extrasystoles lower the vulnerable period threshold for VF? Does each sequential extrasystole incrementally increase the susceptibility of the vulnerable period until a beat is just sufficient to activate the vulnerable period? And how many such sequential early extrasystoles are needed to reach the critical juncture, when physiologic electrical energies suffice to trigger VF?

Once again, animal experiments provided a solution to the energy riddle. When we applied electric stimuli to the hearts of dogs to generate two successive extrasystoles in the vulnerable period, strikingly less energy was required to provoke VF during the second than for the first. If three sequential extrasystoles were discharged in the same manner in the vulnerable period, the threshold for VF was further reduced. When four extrasystoles were delivered, VF was provoked by the low energy electrical pulse. It was a breakthrough in our understanding of the genesis of VF, explaining how an innocent heartbeat could be the basis for a lethal arrhythmia that instantaneously extinguished life. The secret resided in the repetition of extrasystoles, each making only a small change in threshold, but cumulatively sufficient to trigger a lethal arrhythmia. It explained why such a multiplicity of ventricular extrasystoles, coming individually and in showers, often preceded sudden death.

These observations encouraged me to develop a way to classify extrasystoles in terms of their likelihood of provoking VF. Dr. Marshall Wolf, a postdoctoral fellow in my late 1960s training program, and I evolved a schematic classification of ventricular extrasystoles, also referred to as ventricular premature beats (VPBs). To confirm that our categories were clinically meaningful, we had to determine whether patients exhibiting repetitive extrasystoles — complex VPBs — were more predisposed to sudden death. However, we lacked a sizable population of coronary patients and the substantial resources to carry out a large clinical research project. Opportunity knocked, however, when I mentioned the idea to a close friend, Dr. William Ruberman, who was working at the Health Insurance Plan of New York. He had available, for unlimited follow-up, nearly two thousand men who had experienced a recent heart attack.

In a series of definitive experiments, Ruberman and his coworkers confirmed the risk potential inherent in complex VPBs. Patients with sequential and early extrasystoles interrupting the vulnerable period were five times more likely to die suddenly than coronary patients without VPBs. Despite these findings, no large investigative programs were instituted at the time to identify more precisely the patient at risk for sudden death. American cardiologists were ignoring this momentous challenge in large measure because it was completely outside the province of their experience. Also, if they could identify such patients, there was nothing they could do for them.

My mounting frustration led to a bizarre idea inspired by the pianist Van Cliburn. He had been unknown until winning the Tchaikovsky piano competition in Moscow, then overnight became an American cult figure. My craving was not for personal celebrity but rather to use the Soviets as a means of focusing on the neglected issue of sudden death. Suppose the Soviets were persuaded that this problem deserved national priority, would it not stir American interest? In the intense cold war competition then raging on all fronts, would it not grate on American national honor to permit the Soviets another first so soon after Sputnik? In 1966 I inveigled an invitation from Dr. Eugene Chazov, a leading young Soviet cardiologist, to address physicians in Moscow on sudden death. The lecture, to about eight hundred doctors, was a complete fiasco. No one seemed interested. I was told unequivocally that "sudden cardiac death is an American problem, a disease of capitalism due to stress in a dog-eat-dog society." This was absurd because coronary artery disease, the major predisposing condition for sudden death, was widely prevalent in the USSR, exacting a higher toll there than in the United States. The reasons were not difficult to find: widespread hypertension, obesity, smoking, crowded living quarters, a diet surfeited with animal fats, and above all, inordinate, unrelenting social stress from which many sought relief in the national pastime of alcoholism. Moscow left me disconsolate.

Four years later I was invited to deliver, before twelve thousand cardiologists, the Connor lecture, a keynote address at the annual meeting of the American Heart Association. The subject of sudden death thereafter took off in a multiplicity of directions, including epidemiological investigations, innovative research on drugs and antifibrillatory devices, as well as advances in the field of electrophysiology. In 1972 the Soviets, who had come to realize that sudden death was the leading cause of fatality in the USSR, invited me to help them deal with the problem.

In the ensuing years, extensive epidemiological studies, both here and abroad, have confirmed the VPB hypothesis. As clinical investigators, however, we could not remain satisfied with merely knowing who was prone to die suddenly. The aim of identification was to protect people against this tragedy. While there were a number of antiarrhythmic drugs, it was not clear in this case how to use them. Dr. Vladimir Velebit, a postdoctoral fellow in my group, made the disquieting finding that every antiarrhythmic drug then in use was proarrhythmic in some patients. That is, the very drug that one might employ to prevent sudden death could provoke malignant arrhythmias leading to sudden death. We failed to discover any distinctive cardiac factors that would identify a patient who might experience an adverse reaction to a particular drug. Each patient's response to a specific drug was unpredictable. Our extensive research led to a new approach designated acute drug testing in which brief electrocardiographic monitoring and exhaustive exercise on a motorized treadmill before and after a large oral dose of a specific antiarrhythmic drug screened for both an adverse and a favorable antiarrhythmic drug response.

An important finding was reported in 1982 by my colleague Dr. Thomas Graboys. Patients with severe coronary artery disease who had experienced a malignant arrhythmia were at inordinate risk for recurrence. In such patients, Graboys noted, the abolition of repetitive VPBs and those occurring early in the cardiac cycle strikingly reduced these patients' likelihood of dying suddenly. To abolish these VPBs required a highly individualized approach to drug selection as well as the use of drug combinations. We were aware that unless therapy was highly customized to the particularities of the individual patient, these antiarrhythmic drugs were likely to do more harm than good. Among effectively treated patients, the annual sudden fatality rate was only 2.3 percent as contrasted with a prodigious incidence of 43.6 percent among patients who continued to have threatening VPBs.

It was of course remotely possible that these patients would have survived without any antiarrhythmic drug, that their underlying predisposition to arrhythmia had spontaneously remitted. To address this question, Graboys and his coworkers postulated that if a drug was indeed protecting against the life-threatening arrhythmia, discontinuing it should cause prompt recurrence of the condition. For this study, he selected a group of patients who were experiencing adverse drug reactions and wished to get off the antiarrhythmic agent if this did not endanger their survival. Twenty-four patients who had been successfully treated for an average of thirty-one months comprised the study group. When the medication was stopped, only one patient remained free of dangerous arrhythmias. This finding lent support to the two concepts we had promulgated: first, that patients with malignant ventricular arrhythmias could be protected by individualized antiarrhythmic therapy, and second, that suppressing repetitive grades of VPBs by antiarrhythmic medication was an indication of long-term protection.

Yet I hasten to acknowledge that despite substantial progress, the toll of sudden death continues largely undiminished. In a significant measure this is due to a scarcity of social resources for solving the sudden death problem. When our national security appeared in jeopardy, we mobilized unprecedented intellectual talent and allocated unlimited fiscal resources for a Manhattan Project. In the past decade as many as four million Americans have died from a preventable electrical accident in the heart, but no such undertaking is in sight. While AIDS research garners a deserved $200,000 per victim annually, during the last decade the U.S. government has allocated approximately $25 dollars per victim for SCD research. The reason for this disparate investment is that sudden death has no constituency with political clout, except perhaps in the hereafter.

I find it painful to think of lives lost prematurely to a soluble problem. In spite of the numerous drugs available, none works definitively and safely. Further research is needed in the delivery of microamounts of antiarrhythmic agents, not only to the target organ but to the locus responsible for the arrhythmia. The implantable cardioverter/defibrillator is a significant advance. This electronic device serves as a constant sentinel of the heart's rhythm, and when an arrhythmia emerges it fires a preset electrical discharge directly to the heart. I do not believe that this costly instrument is the optimal approach to a problem of the formidable magnitude of sudden death. Far preferable would be preventing the emergence of VF, rather than episodically jolting a patient out of the arrhythmia, with all the ensuing psychological trauma of having experienced a near-death event. Other treatments are being introduced, for example, burning out the electrical focus or the tracts conducting the abnormal rhythms with radio frequency and other forms of energy. The goal of preventing sudden death is within reach, but every minute is costly; we are losing the most irreplaceable of all social assets — human beings in the prime of life.

In the mid-1970s, when I gained confidence about this subject, I was able to talk openly to my patients about sudden death, a subject I had dreaded until then. I would tell a patient with few risk factors, "You will not die suddenly," and explain why. As mentioned in Chapter 6, allaying the fearful anxiety of sudden death, which no doubt haunts many patients with coronary disease, instills the sense of ease and elation that caused my secretary to suspect me of giving them marijuana. They not only felt better but they *were* better, for the heart emptied of dread works under less stress, as a wealth of clinical and experimental data have shown.

Perhaps my most important achievement in nearly five decades of clinical research has been to help put sudden death on the medical research agenda as a legitimate scientific problem. The sense of futility has been dissipated. Sudden death is no longer a subject to be avoided in discourse between doctor and patient with heart disease. The predisposing factors are better understood and enough information has been amassed to define more precisely who is at high risk. The fear of sudden death need no longer instill morbid anxiety in patients with coronary artery disease.

In talking about my half century of research, I want to make crystal clear my unalterable commitment to and deep roots in the scientific medical community. I am convinced of the indispensability of scientific medicine and advanced technology to effective doctoring. From the vantage point of a clinical researcher, I have come to realize that caring without science is well-intentioned kindness, but not medicine. On the other hand, science without caring empties medicine of healing and negates the great potential of an ancient profession. The two complement and are essential to the art of doctoring.

In connection with my trying to interest Soviet cardiologists in the issue of sudden cardiac death, one anecdote remains to be told. Life's paradoxical unpredictabilities worked themselves out far differently than I had imagined. The Soviet connection, rather than galvanizing interest in sudden death in the United States, resulted in my lasting friendship with Dr. Evgeni Chazov. This in turn led to our cooperation in organizing the International Physicians for the Prevention of Nuclear War. In 1985, Chazov and I were honored to be the recipients of the Nobel Peace Prize on behalf of the organization we had founded to mobilize world opinion against the nuclear threat.

IV

Incurable

Problems

16

Caring for the Elderly: Problems and Challenges

"LIFE PROTRACTED IS protracted woe," bemoaned Samuel Johnson. Indeed, aging is frequently a story of mounting disrepair, with occasional galloping breakdowns in physical well-being and mental function. In Johnson's time the medical profession could do little to assuage the discomfort of aging or to enhance the quality of life, and today, despite the many scientific advances, the elixir of youth remains an unrealizable dream. Many regard old age as an affliction. In the words of Winston Churchill, it is "a foolish substitution for life." As a doctor, I take a more kindly view of growing old.

My earliest medical experiences taught me that the elderly cling desperately to their identities rather than merely holding on to survival. In so many words, they echo Shylock's plea in *The Merchant of Venice*. With a few minor changes, the appeal is contemporary: "I am [old]. Hath not a[n old person] eyes? hath not a[n old person] hands, organs, dimensions, senses, affections, passions? fed with the same food, hurt with the same weapons, subject to the same diseases, healed by the same means, warmed and cooled by the same winter and summer, as a [young person] is? If you prick us, do we not bleed? if you tickle us, do we not laugh? if you poison us, do we not die?"

While still in medical training I saw an old man who had been to every outpatient clinic in Boston without gaining satisfaction. At ninety-five, traipsing all over the city was no small ordeal. Why was he shopping around? Though he looked very old, he communicated a rugged determination to have his problem addressed. The man who accompanied him appeared like a somewhat younger brother; in reality, he was a seventy-year-old son.

Anguish was writ large on the old man's wrinkled face. Everything he ate provoked severe stomach cramps. The immediate penalty for swallowing a morsel of food was long-lasting and excruciating pains that caused him to moan and double over. Starvation had taken its toll. He had been reduced to a bag of wrinkled skin loosely robing a brittle skeleton. Abdominal angina had been diagnosed, a condition caused by narrowing of the arteries that supply blood to the intestines. The act of digestion called for more blood flow than his arteries could carry. The intestines, deprived of blood, went into spasms that provoked agonizing discomfort. He had been told that there was neither cure nor relief for the condition.

As he related his woes, the son, no doubt having heard this sad saga many times, appeared bored. He interrupted his father's plaintive recounting, muttering, "Dad, what do you expect at your age? After all, you *are* ninety-five."

Irritated by his son's uncaring comment, I blurted out angrily, "What has age to do with suffering? Of course I'll help you." My mouth dried in reaction to the hot air of my irresponsible words, which were mere bluff. I hadn't the vaguest notion how to help him.

A wide smile of relief wreathed the old man's face. "At last I have found my doctor. We don't have to look any further."

He showed up consistently at my medical clinic. Small frequent feedings, a few swallows at any one time, brought him modest relief, resting for an hour after eating lessened the pain, but more comforting to him was finding someone willing to listen. So little had been done to alter his chronic condition, yet he walked more erectly and no longer appeared depressed.

Several decades later I encountered another man of the same age. A New Hampshire farmer, he looked every bit of his ninety-five years. Curled up in a fetal position, Mr. J. slept through most of the day. His heart rate was fixed at 30 beats per minute from a blockage in the heart's conduction system, but I decided not to proceed with a pacemaker implantation. He did not complain of anything being wrong and did not need a more rapid heart rate to sleep his way to eternity. Long ago I had taken seriously the sensible adage "If it ain't broke, don't fix it." Occasionally a young woman I assumed to be his granddaughter sat by the bed. She looked about thirty-five and acted quite solicitous. At times she brought along her little boy, who may have been eight years old, a subdued, mirthless youngster. I tried to keep Mr. J. awake long enough to explain why it was senseless at his age to implant a pacemaker. At that very moment the granddaughter walked in, but he was once again snoring. I nudged him. "Wake up, your granddaughter is here with your great-grandson."

He roused with a start and looked more alive than I had seen him. "He ain't my great-grandson, he is my son, Billy." Then, with a good deal of civility, "Doctor, meet my wife, Mary."

I performed an instant intellectual somersault befitting the entirely new reality. "Mr. J., we have decided to give you a new pacemaker. The operation, which is a minor one, will be done later this afternoon."

After receiving the pacemaker, Mr. J.'s heart rate accelerated and more than doubled the number of beats per minute. Mr. J.'s torpor dissipated. He became quite an alert old man.

Between these two men flowed a wide river of experience in my dealing with the elderly. For most, death does not come in one swoop; instead, it involves a slow separation from one's self and the diminishing ability of the five senses to reach out and connect with the outside world. Hearing loss, in particular, is almost the invariable accompaniment of aging in the urban environment. The loud decibel assault on our ears takes its toll. A doctor may not realize that a patient is ashamed or unwilling to admit this impairment. I remember my painstaking explanation to an elderly woman of how to take her medications. After about ten minutes, watching her nod her head in seeming agreement, I asked her to repeat what I had told her. She responded, "What you said sounds interesting, I had better put my hearing aid in and have you repeat what you said. I couldn't hear a word of it."

I constantly encounter what Ronald Blyth Harcout called "the stunning contradiction between the lively mind and the senescent body in which it is entrapped." We grow unrecognizable to ourselves and embarrassed by our appearance. Our very presence seems to demand an apology.

The bulk of my patients are in the geriatric age range, with more than 60 percent past retirement. People are living longer and remaining healthy longer. Hippocrates chose fifty-six as the age of demarcation for senility. Today even the seventh decade of life is for many a period of robust living and fulfillment.

For many people, growing old is a passage to be dreaded, one marked by abandonment and loneliness. But for those adequately prepared, it can be embraced with the ardor of youth and an insight that young people rarely possess. I see quite a few elderly, who in their tenth decade are still creative and dreaming. As one ninety-year-old woman, long retired as a professor of art, told me, "Dreams are far more robust than memories."

Caring for the aged demands a readiness to imagine and a willingness to invent. Above all, it requires less reliance on drugs and more of a focus on rearranging the furniture of life. It demands being alert to the suggestions of depression. Expressing interest is no antidote against loneliness, yet it lessens the ache. Holding out the hope that life will continue encourages a patient to persevere. Setting objectives, searching for anniversaries, graduations of great-grandchildren, weddings, bar mitzvahs, christenings, all help the patient maintain a hold on life. A doctor probes for such events even as a coral diver plummets to great depths searching for a pearl.

The doctor develops strategies for keeping up the spirits of aged patients, such as setting the next appointment not so far in the future as to be hopelessly unreachable nor too near, suggesting a poor prognosis. I also encourage patients to bring me a good joke. One should not be ashamed to light a candle of cheer when all seems bleak, nor feel guilt when telling a fib that conveys a deeper truth. One should not hesitate to assure a patient that his or her life matters nor be embarrassed to show affection. Resisting the platitudes of formulaic medicine, the wise physician is not afraid to doctor.

Dr. D. was a long-retired physician with high blood pressure. His primary reason for living was to care for his Alzheimer-afflicted wife, who was eighty-eight and with whom he'd had a lasting sixty-five-year romance. She no longer recognized her children, and he was both her nurse and her housekeeper. A reedlike, gentle, and kindly human being, he walked unsteadily with a cane, and how he was able to do the shopping, house-cleaning, and laundry eluded me. Yet he was so full of cheer, so quick with gratitude, that everyone in our medical group looked forward to his semiannual visits.

He would come for encouragement and assurance, which we provided in abundance. He had been losing weight, and as a doctor, what was uppermost in his mind was whether this was due to some malignancy. During the physical examination he seemed to tense up when being weighed.

"Have I lost any weight?" he would ask with concern.

"Your weight is 134 pounds, unchanged since last visit," I fibbed. Actually it was 132. His face lit up. "That's good news indeed. I'm immensely cheered."

Now he had a brighter glint in his blue eyes and a readier smile. At his next visit his weight remained unaltered. By not telling the truth, I spared him six months of torment. Truth or lie can become a meaningless abstraction. The doctor, when motivated by goodness and love for patients, cannot lie but does not always have to tell the whole truth.

My elderly patients teach me the locution of circumspection and concern. They do not like to be reminded of advancing age, bombarded as they are with endless evidence of their physical dissolution. One patient, shortly before reaching her ninetieth birthday, visited an ophthalmologist because of blurred vision. While looking in her eyes with an ophthalmoscope, the doctor commented, "Your retina looks terrible!" He asked her age, and when she told him he said, "In that case it's normal." She related how miserable that made her feel.

ON LONELINESS

Many of my older patients are overwhelmed with loneliness. By the time they reach the mid-eighties, most of their contemporaries are gone. As they advance further into old age, their younger relatives begin to ail and die. There are ever fewer people to look in on them, and going out is often difficult because of rheumatism or incontinence or fear of embarrassment at forgetting the name of a close friend. Some patients imprison themselves in their own homes, but being alone speeds aging and further enfeebles. Absence of socialization dulls faculties, impairs speech, and shrouds waking hours with morbid apprehensions. The elderly do not fear death as much as the long act of dying, the bumpy road to final dissolution.

A stroke, a heart attack, a hemorrhage, a fall, or a fracture are distressing at any age, especially if one is alone. Tales and fears of such events are part of everyday conversation among the elderly. How often have I heard the story of an old woman found lying on the floor days after having sustained an immobilizing fracture. It is almost always a woman, because older women are more likely than men to fall and seven times more likely to sustain a hip fracture. Indeed, this is the most commonly diagnosed injury that leads to hospitalization for elderly women. The catastrophe is magnified because an independent and self-sufficient life is so often brought to an end by such a fracture. Ten to 20 percent of women with hip fractures die because of complications resulting from the injury, and 25 percent are institutionalized in a nursing home.

One elderly woman patient brought home to me the meaning of loneliness and the dread of living alone. Blessed with the genetic anomaly of rose-colored eye lenses, Mrs. S. was always fun to be with. Even at eighty-nine, life was an ongoing adventure for her. I was therefore taken aback when, during one visit, she appeared frightened, full of complaints, and depressed. This could not be the woman who only three months earlier had been so perennially optimistic, finding something positive to say even when the day was dull and cheerless. I asked if one of her few remaining friends had died or whether she was feeling ignored by her children. She denied that anyone close to her had passed away or that her family was less attentive.

Every bodily system had an ache or malfunction. Previously she was dismissive about constipation, incontinence, and rheumatism, but now these ailments had grown unbearable. Something was seriously wrong. But even after detailed probing, I could not locate the nidus of her discontent. There must have been a change in her life, but what was it? To my question about her children, she replied that they were fine. She would not let on that anything had changed, but perhaps my questions were too clumsily probing. When the examination was over, in the lingering final words before she was to depart, that meandering and unhurried leave-taking of the elderly, Mrs. S. brought forth a non sequitur. She casually mentioned how lucky her friend Mrs. O. was to be able to go off for a holiday with her family to Michigan.

My ears perked up. Why should I be informed about Mrs. O.?

"Where does your friend live?" I asked innocently.

"Oh, she lives in my building, in a room exactly below mine."

"What do you mean?"

"She has a room exactly below my room. We share a common pipe that carries hot water." Then she said, with a laugh, "It's our telegraphic system."

"What do you telegraph to one another?" I asked.

Every morning, she said, whoever awakened first banged the pipe to indicate she was still alive and well. Then she waited for the return signal from the other. But with her friend away, how was anybody to know whether Mrs. S. had died or, worse still, had a stroke or had fallen and broken her hip and was unable to reach a phone? As she shared her anxieties, she was forlorn and nearly tearful. "I can't wait until my friend returns. Life is so uncertain."

Then the old Mrs. S. asserted herself. "Doctor, I'm making too much of this. After all, she'll only be gone for two weeks." I reassured her that nothing would happen and promised to telephone her daily. Her old optimism was back as she walked out of the office a good deal steadier than when she'd come in.

ON HYPOCHONDRIASIS

I am persuaded that loneliness incubates hypochondriasis. Furthermore, our culture medicalizes age, as though growing old were a disease. No group is as preoccupied with illness and as surfeited with aches and disabilities. Is the dull ache behind the right ear a sign of a brain tumor? Are irregular bowels cause for an immediate revisit to a gastroenterologist? It is difficult for anyone, but particularly the elderly, not to be frightened and caught up by the endless alarms spewed out by the media. If you eat this or that, it predisposes you either to colon cancer or a heart attack. The conversation among the elderly is consistently focused on disease and spiced with anecdotes of the woe befallen those who have ignored early signs or trivial symptoms.

Solicitous family members add to the medicalization of life for the elderly. The guilt felt for neglecting a parent is translated into dread of a parent's dying. This is often expressed by urging medical attention for elderly parents, fueling their anxiety and resulting in numerous unnecessary visits to medical clinics.

Many elderly people are willingly entrapped in the burgeoning medical-industrial complex. Visits to doctors, like shopping, combat loneliness. For people who have nowhere else to go and are tired of looking at the same four walls, connecting with the health industry is a way of socializing. Shuttling from specialist to specialist fills up time in addition to providing the gratification of having someone listen attentively to one's problems.

It is disconcerting to me how people of all ages, but particularly the elderly, although proud of their common sense, can forgo reason when it comes to their own health. Some of the most intelligent patients I have encountered are among the most gullible and susceptible to deception, taken in by the latest nostrums as though these were communicated from Mount Sinai by a latter-day Moses.

Nowadays, nearly everyone is obsessed with cholesterol. One patient urgently telephoned me because his cholesterol level was found to be 220 mg, when a month earlier it had been 210 mg, an insignificant variation.

"But why repeat the test monthly?" I inquired.

"There is no harm, and I can afford it."

Another patient was more belligerent about a meaningless fluctuation in his cholesterol level. "Don't you think I should pay attention to a leading risk factor, considering that my dad died suddenly of a heart attack at age seventy-four?"

Preoccupation with cholesterol is a widespread affliction, but it is especially counterproductive for the elderly. Their diets are already impaired by dentures, constipation, lack of appetite, and intolerance for many nutritious foods. Mrs. T., in her late eighties when I first met her, was wasted and frail. I inquired why she had lost fifteen pounds over the past six months, a loss she could ill afford. She responded that there was nothing left for her to eat. "My cardiologist urges me to cut out animal fat to lower my cholesterol, my diabetic specialist advises me to reduce sugar, and my internist cautions that salt will cause me to drown in my own fluids." I counseled her to disregard the medical advice and eat whatever she liked. Within six months she regained weight as well as her feisty, upbeat spirit.

Another elderly patient complained to me: "Doctor, you haven't told me my cholesterol level."

"You have survived to ninety," I told him. "What difference will it make? You're on a healthy diet."

He asked, with mock seriousness, "What will I say at the dinner table? I feel embarrassed. Cholesterol is the major subject of conversation and I have nothing to say. It's worse than not knowing the president's name."

With cholesterol levels varying widely between different laboratories or even in the same laboratory at different times, the more the test is repeated, the greater the confusion and concern about the unaccounted variability. It is not unusual for the doctor to put a guilt trip on patients if their cholesterol is elevated. As many doctors determine the cholesterol level in their private laboratories, such anxiety is good for business. People, however, are unsuspecting and charitable to their doctors. As one intelligent retired scientist put it, "My doctor is very concerned about me. He takes my cholesterol once a month."

If education does not preclude gullibility about one's own health, lack of schooling is not an indication of lack of common sense. One of my elderly patients, self-educated and with biting insight, expressed utter disgust with the cholesterol craze. "There is little left to enjoy. Food is no longer a celebration. Every morsel, if it is tasteful, is sinful." She drove in to a gasoline station and the attendant asked, "Lady, what type gas do you want?" Her unthinking reply was "Fill her up with low cholesterol."

Overindulgence in testing is not limited to cholesterol. The elderly, more disquieted about disease lurking in any new symptom, are far more susceptible to technological assault than younger patients. Costly tests are ordered with unimaginable frivolity. Mrs. V. was elderly but in good health for her age and had no heart disease. I inquired what type of studies had been carried out at a local Boston hospital.

She tried hard to remember, a strained look on her pretty face. Then, with triumph, she said, "My annual whisper test."

"A whisper test; what is that?"

"Yes, a whisper test."

"You mean a breathing test, a vital capacity, where you blow all your breath into a tube?"

"No, no, it's nothing like that."

"Is it for the heart?"

"Yes, it looks inside the heart."

"You mean an echocardiogram?" I asked with uncertainty.

"Yes, yes an echo, a whisper test!"

The echocardiogram is invaluable for diagnosing valvular disease and myocardial abnormalities. Why was it performed in a completely healthy person? Why repeat it annually? Perhaps the charge of about $800 per test, of which $500 is clear profit, accounts for its popularity.

Even the very smart businessman is not above the tomfoolery of technologic assault. Mr. N. had been "Mr. Wall Street." In his prime he was a no-nonsense person, and when I saw him in consultation at his elegant estate on Long Island, he proudly spoke of the devotion and meticulous care afforded him by his physician. Weekly and sometimes daily, his doctor personally recorded an electrocardiogram. "My doctor is really watching over me." He led me into a library exclusively dedicated to housing his electrocardiographic records, where many thousands of them were stacked from floor to ceiling. Fortunately, he did not insist that I examine them. One or two electrocardiograms annually for Mr. N. would have provided adequate medical guidance.

Willard R. Espy, in *Almanac of Words at Play,* captured some of the inane hoopla that substitutes for medical information.

> Jogging causes heart attacks in the elderly, and slipped disks in the young; bed rest encourages blood clots . . . coffee leads to gout; tea is constipating; eggs clog the arteries. If you bib wine expect cancer of the larynx. If you sleep, you dream, and an exciting dream may wind up in coronary occlusion. To cap the climax, as advocates of birth control might put it, semen has been charged with responsibility for cancer of the cervix. . . . Living may be dangerous for your health!*

---

* Willard R. Espy, comp., *An Almanac of Words at Play* (New York: C. N. Potter, 1975).

ON DEPRESSION

The depression I encounter in the elderly comes not, William Styron states, as "a howling tempest in the brain."* Hamlet's words capture it more closely: "How weary, stale, flat, and unprofitable / Seem to me all the uses of this world." It is a form of ennui with living so subtle that at times it defeats recognition. The smile of sociability has not vanished. The mask all wear is not turned down at the mouth. Conversation is briskly engaged. No change in attitude is admitted. It is when the doctor knows the patient well that one senses attenuations. The boast is gone. The bravado isn't there. A sense of indifference or even defeat reigns around the eyes. The presence of a spouse is enormously helpful in confirming such observations. She responds affirmatively, "Yes, Charley is depressed," then details a wealth of somatic and behavioral changes.

Troubled sleep is often the first sign of depression. While the patient may sleep excessively or is unable to fall asleep, far more common is staying asleep, then waking at three in the morning, surfeited with fatigue yet certain that sleep cannot be resumed. The harder one tries, the more elusive sleep grows. In Rupert Brooke's words, "The cool kindliness of sheets, that soon / Smooth away trouble," aren't felt.** One gets up even more tired than when one went to bed, and the fatigue endures throughout the day. The palate is in a state of tedium. Usual pleasurable activities are without allure. Sex takes more energy than the pleasure it affords. Grandchildren tire one too readily, their cute expressions lacking the usual charm. Work is carried on as an unstimulating routine.

Although I encounter elderly patients who continue to be charged with life, they are the exception. The buffeting of life has left the majority invalided in spirit and morbid in outlook,

* William Styron, *Darkness Visible: A Memoir of Madness* (New York: Viking, 1990).
** Rupert Brooke, "The Great Lover," in *The Collected Poems of Rupert Brooke* (New York: Dodd, Mead, 1943).

and the future trajectory is only downward. Those who have been creative and had meaningful lives are not always spared.

I always look forward to seeing Mr. E. He enjoys vigorous health, notwithstanding twenty years of angina. In his mid-eighties, he is still functioning at full throttle as an artist, loaded down with accolades and honors. Although he has angina when walking to get his morning paper or readying for bed, he never has chest discomfort when working at his art.

"How come?" I ask. "Is it the pleasure of work?"

"It's more than pleasure, it's my life."

His life is full, he is wanted, he is applauded. A woman more than twenty years his junior is in love with him. Yet he is full of morbid thoughts and surcharged with a sense of worthlessness. The reason he has angina before going to bed, he related, is that he thinks he will not wake up in the morning.

When chided, he claims he inherited the blues from his mother. He once took her to get reading glasses. The optometrist, offering her a pair, inquired whether she was seeing all right. She responded, "What is there in life that is so good that I have to see well?"

Before he leaves, I reassure Mr. E. of the stability of his heart condition and tell him that if anything comes up he should feel free to call me at home. He looks uneasy and crestfallen, and I realize that this was the wrong thing to say.

"What do you expect to happen to me, Doctor? What should come up?"

I spend much time reassuring him again, but as he walks out the door, he asks, "You think I'll live until tonight?"

"I'm certain you'll survive at least until tomorrow night," I reply.

With a little laugh, he says, "I feel better already."

Depression is a biological problem accentuated by aging. It represents the wear and tear of life's stresses, which may exhaust specific brain neurotransmitters. It may therefore be a deficiency disease, like myxedema or Addison's disease, short-changing the body of either thyroid hormone or cortisol. Yet the word "depression" belies the bodily state. The organism is not subdued but rather agitated, which wreaks havoc on the cardiovascular system. Extensive data indicate that following a heart attack, patients who have high levels of depressive symptoms fare poorly. They have a far higher risk of recurrence and are more likely to die suddenly.

Unless the physician recognizes this condition, therapy for many complaints is invariably futile. Fortunately, neurochemistry and psychopharmacology have provided profound insights and very effective medications. There is no panacea, however. Drugs, if employed, need to be individualized and fine-tuned in dosage and may have unpleasant side effects. The biochemical abnormality may not be permanent and once the depression is overcome, drugs should be discontinued. As helpful as these pharmaceuticals are, life is far better without them.

ON WORK

In this country, a leading cause of depression relates to work or loss of it. Nothing is more taxing on the nervous system or draining of energies than being unappreciated at work or disliking one's job. I have found this cause for depression most challenging and frustrating. Loss of job is a significant factor for aggravation of heart disease and premature death at any age. Being demoted because of age is also psychologically and physically destructive. The following cases involve two patients, who, though quite unalike, had a similar problem.

Mr. W., in his early seventies, was an executive vice president of a successful furniture company. Seemingly without effort, he continued to put in a ten-hour day, six days a week, and boasted of never having taken a holiday in forty years. He worked this hard not out of necessity but because he found his work creative and rewarding. The business had prospered because of his tender loving care, and the owner was a close friend who valued the devotion Mr. W. invested in his work. When the owner died, his eldest son took charge. He was similarly committed to Mr. W., who taught him all the intricacies of running the business.

Mr. W. had come to see me several years prior to the change

in ownership because of angina pectoris, the common indicator of coronary artery disease. The chest discomfort was readily controlled by the nitroglycerin pills I had prescribed, but they were rarely necessary. His angina occurred only when he took a brisk walk after a meal, especially during winter months. Each time he visited, we spoke about his job, which was his whole life, and after the owner died how much the new administration valued his contributions. On one December visit he told me that the new president had given him a month's vacation in Florida, all expenses paid, in recognition of his invaluable service, as well as a sizable Christmas bonus and an unexpectedly generous increase in salary.

Although his next scheduled appointment was not until summer, in late February Mr. W. came to see me with increasing angina, which occurred daily within a week after he had returned from Florida. The holiday was low key and restful, spent largely in playing golf and gin rummy. "To be honest, it was boring. How long can you play golf or cards without going bananas?" A tan made him look much younger than before, yet something was missing. Prior to leaving for Florida he was full of bounce and regaled me with new ideas for the company. The enthusiasm was now gone. Something had deflated his balloon. He was thinking of retirement, even though prior to the vacation he said he planned to work until he was eighty.

I was troubled that the angina was provoked with little effort. Now he experienced angina primarily in the morning when walking from his house to the garage. Angina is more likely to occur in the early morning hours, but the walk to the garage was a short one and he told me it was downhill. Furthermore, when he carried out the heavy garbage barrels, walking a similar distance, or exerted himself later in the day, he did not experience angina.

"Is everything okay at work?" I asked.

"Oh, sure," he answered far too quickly.

"Your work is the same?"

"Yes, absolutely."

"Is your authority diminished?"

"Not at all."

I felt like a prosecuting attorney. Something had changed, but what was it? As we conversed matter-of-factly, he finally mentioned that after returning from the holiday, he found someone else occupying his office. His desk had been moved to the main floor where other executives worked. Mr. W. was still treated with respect, his salary was undiminished, and his advice was still sought and valued. He felt humiliated, miserable, and was deeply hurt, he confessed. But he had lost all interest in his work. "Doc, you may laugh. Maybe I'm making a mountain out of a molehill." I remained quiet. "They badly needed my office. What they did is good for the business." He was rationalizing.

So each day, as he walked to his car, he obsessed about the indignity of the demotion. I told him to quit. Rarely do I give such advice, but I was stricken by the thought that such men who continually have to face indignity against which they are helpless are the ones who drop dead out of the clear blue — in his case, I feared, while walking to his garage on the way to work in the morning. I was not convinced that my advice was sound and I did not press him to take my advice. He continued to work and shortly thereafter suffered a significant heart attack which forced him into retirement.

I encountered a similar problem with Y., a retired professor of mathematics whom I had been seeing for about seven years for mild, rarely troubling angina. He was normally exuberant, with a ready and winsome smile, but one day he appeared introspective. When I asked how the year had been, he hesitated and responded with a "Pretty good." When asked why only pretty good, he told me that a tendon injury had kept him from playing tennis. Somehow the answer did not ring true. We talked about his work, which he enjoyed immensely. Though Mr. Y. was retired, the university had provided him with an office, secretarial help, and recognition. Then he added, "There's a big space crunch." The way he stated it made my antennae vibrate. No doubt my experience with Mr. W. had sensitized me to the importance of retaining an office where one carried on his or her life's work. Losing such space can be tantamount to losing one's identity.

"And supposing the dean needs the space for some young and promising mathematician?" I inquired. "You must know that institutions retain few loyalties to retired personnel, whatever their contributions."

A shadow of discomfort flitted across his face, and he said, hesitantly, "I don't know what I would do if I had to give up my office."

"Does this worry you?"

"Not really."

"But what will you do if you are asked to leave?"

"I'm not sure. There's very little I can do. So far they've been very good to me."

I then expanded on the difficulty of carrying on one's work and the need to plan and prepare so that the loss of an office does not mean the loss of purpose. I told him of Mr. W.'s angina after he lost his office.

With some hesitation, the professor confessed that he was plagued by uncertainty. At any time he expected the dean to ask him to vacate his space. I asked, "Why wait? Why not prepare for it?"

He appeared puzzled, as though I were encouraging him to confront a natural, unalterable calamity.

"Start by working one day a week at home."

"But I need the library."

"How far are you from the university?"

"A ten-minute walk."

"As a mathematician, you probably could do your work and research anywhere."

"Yes, indeed. Of course, it's only a short walk," he then reassured me.

The realization slowly sank in that I was not suggesting retirement from his work in mathematics but a change of venue. We talked some more and I emphasized that as he worked at home more, the dean would become less of a threat and he would no longer seem omnipotent. In reality, Mr. Y. would be freed from the threat and thus be more empowered. I urged him to think the issue through.

He made a quick decision. "It sounds like a good idea. I'll try it," he said, then added, "I'll go back to tennis."

The connection eluded me at first. But then I realized that when one is depressed, contemplating social displacement and ensuing uselessness, why bother to keep physically fit? Nothing mattered. With affirmation that he could maintain his professionalism despite institutional displacement, he had reason to keep fit for new challenges.

When I saw him a year later, the professor was his spry and cheerful self again. His office had been assigned to someone else, but he had set up an excellent office at home and walking to the library gave him a little extra energy. He was entirely free of both worry and angina.

ON FORGETFULNESS

Bruce Bliven, one-time editor of *The New Republic,* described some of the blights of age.

> We live by the rules of the elderly. If the toothbrush is wet, you have cleaned your teeth . . . If you are wearing one brown and one black shoe, quite possibly there is a similar pair in the closet. I stagger when I walk, and small boys follow me, making bets on which way I'll go next. This upsets me. Children should not gamble.*

Few aspects of aging are more agitating than the shriveling of memory. Proper names are often among the first to go, but nothing is sacred. A former roué now in his dotage, when asked during history-taking about sexual activity, responded with a joke. "Two men, one old, the other young, are walking. The young man keeps looking around at every passing woman. The

---

* Bruce Bliven, in Lewis Thomas, *The Fragile Species* (New York: Scribner's, 1992), 74.

old man reflects, 'I remember doing this also, but I can't recall why.'"

The impact of impaired memory was brought home to me when I saw Mr. B., who in his heyday was one of Boston's leading attorneys. A fabulous memory, quick recall, a sparkling wit, and a profound mastery of the law made him highly successful. For a quarter of a century this gentle, kindly man had been my patient. Now in his mid-eighties, he had shrunk three inches, his hearing was impaired, his vision clouded, and he frequently fell. He still walked at a fast clip, leaning slightly forward and looking as if he would tumble at any second and land on his face. Despite fracturing limbs and several ribs, he had not changed his lifelong habits. Like many elderly people, his behavior had not been constrained by physical limitations. It took many months to persuade him to carry a cane.

During one medical visit, when we went into the examining room he was preoccupied with not forgetting the cane. To ensure that this would not happen, I hung the cane from a ceiling electrical fixture. We could not leave the room without bumping into it. After the examination we returned to my office and talked for about ten minutes. As we said good-bye, he panicked. "Where is my cane?"

No problem, I assured him, and searched my office, even crawling under my desk. It wasn't in the examining room either, and I went back and looked in every nook and cranny of my office again. Finally, I asked him to retrace his steps with me. Slowly we walked together the short distance between the two rooms.

"I came from the examining room into your office," he said, his voice trailing off.

"Where else did you go?"

"Nowhere else. I came directly into your office."

"Did you go to the bathroom?"

"Yes, I did go to the bathroom."

And there on the towel rack hung the handsome cane.

Mr. B. chuckled. "You have now learned how I spend my day, searching for this damn cane!"

I had learned a good deal more. It brought home that without immediate memory, human beings are completely dysfunctional. Depression, so common in the elderly, may be the result of the continuous and mounting frustration in searching for canes and their like.

ON SEX

It was not so long ago that I skipped all questions relating to sex in patients over the age of sixty-five. Even after maturing as a doctor, I was still reluctant to talk about the subject to elderly women patients. Slowly the age threshold has risen. Now even those in their eighties are not exempt from questioning or discussing the subject. Nevertheless, after more than forty years of medical practice, I am still constrained by the taboos of our society. Sex is usually associated with youth. Society takes a dim view of sex among the elderly as ridiculous, laughable, unclean, even perverse. The older the person, the more improper the act. The folk concept of the "dirty old man" doesn't help doctors in dealing with sex problems.

Is the disappearance of sexual capacity long before life ebbs a biologic law? In *King Henry IV,* Shakespeare asks the very same question. "Is it not strange that desire should so many years outlive performance?" The answer is both yes and no.

Very early in my medical career I was disabused of the preconception that sex is only for those who are young and vigorous. The patient, Mr. S., was eighty-six, stooped over, and clearly burdened by the weight of years. Mrs. S. looked even more ancient, her face a skein of wrinkled parchment. Built like a tub, she didn't move gracefully forward but wove from side to side like a Russian Maryoshka doll.

Mr. S. came to consult about occasional weak spells, and I nearly had such a spell when examining him. I put my stethoscope on his chest and heard a lub-dub, but the next lub-dub did not come for the longest interval. I looked anxiously at him and he stared straight back. His heart rate was only 28 beats per minute. This was surprising, as his sole complaint was infrequent fainting spells. He was taking no medications that could slow the heart rate, and I came up with no explanation for the block except age-induced scarring of the heart's conduction system. I urged the immediate insertion of a ventricular pacemaker.

Notwithstanding my entreaties, patient and wife categorically refused. "I have lived my life without such a contraption and I will die without it." He certainly was right about the latter conclusion, but my pleading and explanations were of little avail, and I was unable to persuade Mrs. S. when I spoke with her privately. They were unalterably opposed.

As they were getting ready to leave, the woman nudged her husband. "Ask the doctor, ask the doctor, don't be shy." I hadn't the foggiest idea what they were after until Mrs. S. finally blurted out, "Is it okay for him to have sex, considering the heart condition?" I was too speechless to respond, but nodded affirmation and admiration.

A patient's age offers little justification for a doctor to proscribe sexual or any other activity. It is best to define the broad principles of therapy and let the patient limit the patient.

Some years later I was taking care of Mrs. D. for paroxysmal atrial fibrillation. At eighty-two she retained lovely traces of her youthful beauty. She lived in Texas, but did not trust the doctors there, for they had failed to control the arrhythmia. I had prescribed amiodarone, then a new antiarrhythmic drug that worked well and obviated all attacks even though she was taking it only twice weekly. But when a new onset of shortness of breath induced a sense of suffocation, she telephoned me frequently.

The sense of suffocation was very troublesome, because one of the serious complications of amiodarone is lung disease that can cause disabling breathlessness. I was puzzled, though, that an additional amiodarone pill and a Valium gave her prompt relief. The symptoms abated within several minutes, long before either pill could have been absorbed from the gut.

After several weeks and many calls, I had her come to Boston. During history-taking, she spoke elliptically, then suggested that elderly men like her husband should find other women. "I can't take it anymore. My husband is eighty-eight. His sex drive is getting more active as he gets older, and I am unable to satisfy him. While I have an orgasm quickly, he keeps it up and up and he suffocates me. I don't know what to do, Doctor." She began to cry, then continued. "Because I can't satisfy him, he grows ill-tempered and takes it out on me and calls me a bitch, neurotic, and worse."

The conversation proved reassuring. I advised that they seek counseling.

"At our age to have counseling for sex!" She burst into peals of laughter.

This was a new twist in the sexual comidrama marking the human condition. I was reminded of a verse by Thomas Campion, a musician, poet, and physician of the late sixteenth and early seventeenth century.

> Though you are young and I am old
> Though your vaines hot and my blood is colde,
> Though youth is moist and age is drie,
> Yet embers live when flames do die.

Contrary to Mrs. D.'s case, my observation suggests that a woman's sexuality often seems to last longer than a man's. By sexuality I mean the capacity to focus on the totality of love-making rather than merely the genital component, a capacity that is more feminine than masculine. Sexuality among the aged is compelled more by recollection than by passion, and women have keener recall.

Though in her early nineties, Ms. N. loved a man half her age and he loved her. They had never gone to bed, because she thought it would spoil their love. Yet she told me that the one thing she missed most about aging was no longer making love. "It is the most difficult to live without." She woke frequently with an overwhelming sense of lust fueled by erotic memories, but the sight of her sagging breasts, wrinkled, ugly skin, filled her with shame and revulsion.

The physician is witness to a wide panorama of the human

condition. Sexuality in the aging is invariably tinctured with sadness. The loss is deeply felt and rarely mentioned forthrightly. Doctors avoid the subject, feeling helpless about a state they ascribe to the inexorability of age. Yet a sympathetic ear may still prove therapeutic. If the gods had been kinder, they would have permitted a surge of hormones at life's end. It would have enabled one not merely to caress memories of love with poetic words, but embrace one's partner with still quavering passion. In the absence of such divine restructuring of aging biology, one seeks substitutes.

ON ROMANCE

Many patients raise my spirits by the way they confront the involutions of advancing age. Mrs. E.G., eighty-five years old, had thin white hair that, like parting clouds, exposed a luminescent scalp. Her lively, darting blue eyes were encased in whorls of fine wrinkles, and she was quick and birdlike, twittery in speech, yet graceful. From the rear she could still be mistaken for what was once a coquettish young woman ambling down to meet a boyfriend. When she talked of Peter, her husband of sixty-three years, she grew bubbly as a teenager relating the wonders of first love. He was no longer doing well, was afflicted with severe emphysema and phlebitis, unsteady in gait, and largely housebound during the winter months because his slightest exposure to the cold brought a bout of pneumonia.

When I examined her, she said that what she regretted about aging was her slowing down. She hastened to add that one has to accept it gracefully. She was proud of her weight, which was exactly what it had been on her wedding day. This had required adherence to a strict diet for an entire year during which she lost thirty pounds. However, she had achieved this svelte figure at the price of aprons of hanging integument.

Mrs. G. reminisced. "My mother made an important point to me. 'You have your children, darling, but eventually they will leave the nest and find their own. You will then have only your husband. With him you have a life. If you lose him, you are left with nothing, darling. He needs you, too. That is a very fulfilling role.'" She didn't regret her role a bit and pooh-poohed modern feminism. I asked about her social life. She laughed. "Of course I have many friends. But I make it a point to be home by two P.M. in case Peter may wish to surprise me by taking off from work early. It would be too sad for him not to find me home. I would never forgive myself."

When I went in to examine her husband, his first question was "How is my girl? Have you seen her yet? Is she okay?" When I assured him that she was well, he told me that her health mattered more to him than his own. "Everything else is trivial." When they got together again in my office after the examination, they embraced as though having endured an interminable separation. "Oh, darling, we've been apart far too long," they said to each other, hugging like young lovers clinging with an intensity belying age. This act had been repeated at each annual visit for the quarter of a century that I had been their doctor.

During his examination Mr. G. had commented, "You know, Doctor, though we've been married for over six decades, I still like to look at Edith and stare at her for hours on end, she is so beautiful." When they left in late afternoon, I felt buoyed and ready for a full day's work. I, too, was walking on air.

But this type of relationship is rare. Age ordinarily diminishes the titer of romance. Far too often with an elderly patient, a doctor confronts an incurable ailment and an insoluble problem. To my mind the question in treating the elderly is how to remedy conditions that cannot be cured and how to educate such patients to live fully notwithstanding the limitations imposed by age and illness.

ON HUMOR

In our youth-fixated culture, old age is regarded as the dreary denouement to life. The elderly, if not to be ignored, are to be humored and trivialized. They have little to teach that is relevant to our racing times. I have learned the contrary. People who have reached ripe old age with intact faculties are commonly a source of great insight and instruction. I look forward to the visits of many of my older patients and linger longer at their bedside when they are hospitalized. What impresses me especially is that, unlike my younger patients who are still caught up with the chase, these elderly patients take time to reflect. Their insights are poignant and sharply targeted and they contemplate life's transience with detachment and humor.

A sense of humor is critical in making advancing age more fulfilling. An eighty-six-year-old retired businessman summarized his plight with a chuckle of amusement. "My daughters are very solicitous about me but are doing me in with their concerns — 'Dad, you mustn't eat salt, you mustn't go out or you'll slip on ice and break your hip, or you'll get a cold that will turn to pneumonia.' Food is tasteless without salt. Can't play golf because of my arthritic hip. My bowels don't function without Metamucil, Colace, and the assistance of a suppository. No alcohol or red meat because of the gout. No one with whom to socialize because all my friends are dead. Sex is too dangerous because of AIDS. So what's left? I might as well be dead."

I had followed Mrs. C. for more than a decade. I knew she was eighty-six, yet when I asked her age, she insisted she was fifty-nine. She reminded me of a tale told by theater director Harold Clurman. "A newspaper man interviews Sarah Adler, doyenne of Jewish theater, when she was in her late eighties. 'Madame Adler,' he began, 'I don't mean to embarrass you, but would you mind telling me your age?' Without blinking she replied, 'Sixty-eight.' 'But Madame Adler,' the reporter rejoined, 'how could that be? I asked your son Jack how old he was, and he told me he is sixty.' 'Well,' she responded without hesitation, 'He lives his life and I live mine.'"*

Slowly recovering from many ills, including pneumonia, congestive heart failure, angina pectoris, arrhythmias, and a painful knee infection, Mr. M., ninety-two, lay in a hospital bed

---

* Harold Clurman, *All People Are Famous* (New York: Harcourt Brace Jovanovich, 1974), 197.

looking like a small withered cherub with silken white hair, rosy cheeks, a scraggly white beard, a yarmulke on a bald pate, curled sideburns. Without his dentures, his words tumbled out in a high-pitched hiss. After a while I grew attuned to his voice and began to grasp what he was saying. My eyes were fixated on his playful, deep-set brown eyes.

"The doctors say the findings are negative but the patient is positive," he said, savoring his own words as testimony that all was still functioning upstairs. He continued. "The other day, in the foyer of the building where I live, a youngish woman threw her arms around me and tried to kiss me. I said, 'Lady, hold off, I'm allergic to tulips.'"

He bragged that many women were after him. "The janitor keeps asking, 'Why live alone when all these women are after you?' I tell him that any woman willing to marry a broken-down man like me has got to be crazy. 'You want me to be saddled with a crazy wife, do you?' That shuts him up until the next day."

As I was leaving the bedside, he inquired, "Doctor, will I live a month?"

"Why only a month?" I asked.

"I want to be alive to go to my great-granddaughter's wedding. And after that I'll find another reason." He was not at all afraid of dying, but too much was happening for him to let go of life just yet. He conveyed the sense of an old Jewish proverb, "A man should go on living, if only to satisfy his curiosity."

The next day during rounds he related that a cardiologist had told him that his heart was enlarged. "Why is that surprising, Doctor? For over fifty years people have been telling me that I'm bighearted."

Another patient I admired for his sense of humor was Mr. T.N. Shortly before his ninety-third birthday, he sat motionless in a wheelchair, eyes closed as though in deep thought or light slumber. He had pulmonary congestion and fluid at the right lung base and I told him he needed the diuretic Lasix to clear up the excess fluid in his lungs. The instant reply was "I prefer piss-tachio nuts," the first syllables emerging in a sibilant gush.

At ninety-two, Mr. N. still went to work and found humor in the daily human comedy. He had stopped driving a few months earlier after smashing up four cars while trying to park his wife's automobile. He complained that when he took diuretics, he lost control and dribbled so much that it soaked through his underwear and trousers, forming a puddle at his feet. I jokingly suggested that he wear short pants, to which he responded, "Only my breath comes in short pants."

At another visit he complained that he was so unsteady he feared moving even a few steps without a walker. "The big problem is my balance." Then he laughed, growing ever more breathless. "I told my wife, my balance isn't what it used to be. She was taken by surprise. 'Tom, how could that be? You just deposited money into your account.'"

One day he arrived unshaven, explaining that my appointment forced him to forgo a visit to the barber, whom he saw twice weekly, on Wednesdays and Saturdays. When prescribing the Lasix, I suggested that he take it on Tuesday, Thursday, and Sunday.

His wife objected. "It's easier to remember Monday, Wednesday, and Saturday." As an afterthought, she added that Tom frequently refused to take the Lasix.

I insisted on my schedule.

"But why?" she asked incredulously.

I responded, "Because then he won't wet the barber's chair."

Tom let go with a big guffaw. "From now on I take the damn Lasix."

His sense of humor did not desert him even at the very end. I asked him whether he could still do gentle calisthenics. He answered affirmatively. When asked what the exercise was, he replied, "Rolling my eyeballs."

"How is your hearing?"

"Badly impaired."

"How bad is that?"

"I can't hear the dropping of a one-dollar bill, but I have no trouble when it's ten bucks."

When I reassured him that we would assuage the excruciating pain of bone cancer he sat up more erectly, eyes no longer half closed, and grew wistful and jocular. "Doctor, I have an important question." There was mischief in his eyes. "Now that I'm stable, when can I start horsing around again?"

While I try to be evenhanded, I am partial to elderly patients who do not constantly complain, who die living rather than live dying. Mr. X., when we first met, was in his late seventies. He was short and solid, and a full head of curly white hair gave him a boyish look. This was emphasized by his laughing blue-green eyes, which emanated kindness and charm. He spoke vintage Bostonian, was extraordinarily well read, and was a keen observer of human foibles. He wholesaled furniture more as a way to meet people than as a means of making a living. He laughed uproariously when telling a joke, and he had one for every season and even out of season.

"Did I tell you this one? An old man comes to an ear, nose, and throat specialist complaining of an earache. The doctor says, 'No wonder, you have a suppository in your ear.' 'Thank God,' crows the patient. 'Now I know where my hearing aid is.'"

Some years later Mr. X., in his mid-eighties, was brought to the hospital by ambulance. He had a fractured hip and was muttering to himself, "That ends it, that definitely ends it!"

"Ends what?" I inquired.

"My sex life."

"What do you mean?"

"Definitely. That's it, no more."

"What happened?"

"We were having sex and I fell off the bed. That's it. A man should recognize the end of an affair."

Old people learn how to navigate and get around the limitations that age and society impose. Betty S. was visually impaired, but she liked to drive her BMW around the block — it made her feel in control. She would soon be ninety and dreaded going to the motor registry for renewal of her driver's license, knowing she would have to take an eye test and was certain she could never pass. She could barely make out the big stop sign at her intersection.

Nonetheless she decided to risk it. When the eye test came, she listened carefully to a woman in front of her in the line and memorized the sequence of numbers she read to the examiner. When it was Ms. Betty's turn, she put her chin on the support, peered through a binocular type of device, and saw nothing but a blur. She waited a minute, trying to focus, but to no avail. She whispered the sequence she had just heard. The examiner said, "Louder, please," and Ms. Betty repeated the letters more loudly. The examiner smiled. "Your eyesight is real good at ninety." And Ms. Betty got her new license. She rocked with laughter as she told me how she had beaten a system she maintained was biased against the elderly. She never again drove, realizing full well the hazard she presented to others, yet this act of defiance enabled her to cling desperately to her diminishing sense of independence.

ON HEALING

Mrs. K. always assaulted me with a multiplicity of complaints, so numerous that I often stopped writing them down. She arrived painted like a Kewpie doll, and when I examined her eyes, my fingers became smudged with blue-green eye shadow. I worried about her spike heels, since she stumbled frequently and had recently sustained a triple fracture of an arm. Her figure was still seductive, and she invited the appraising male eye.

Over many years she had suffered from disabling arrhythmias that were now well controlled by drugs. By nature she was a cheerful, somewhat flighty woman, but in recent years she had grown increasingly despondent, at times bordering on depression. I couldn't figure out why she was continually gloomy. Physically her situation had remained stable and she claimed that coming to the Lown Cardiovascular Group always gave her a boost.

During one visit everything seemed to be bothering Mrs. K. even more intensely than usual. Once again I reassured her. "It's very queer," she said. "You find nothing wrong with me and my doctor in Hartford finds nothing right." She went on to say how he'd warned her that, with her severe osteoporosis, any fall would result in a disabling fracture. In addition he told her that she had serious diverticulitis, which sooner or later would lead to a perforation or obstruction. Furthermore, he asked her, "How can you feel well when your thyroid is malfunctioning, you have a diseased gallbladder, and kidney stones to boot, not to mention the extensive arthritis?"

After that, whenever I emphasized how well she was doing, she would respond, "But you're the only doctor who says that. When I go to the others, they tell me I'm sick and dying. Maybe I'm so well because they've healed me by the time I see you."

Then during one visit, surprisingly, she was free of all complaints except for chronic constipation.

"How come?" I wondered.

"Because I haven't seen another doctor in a year," she told me.

The aged patient brings an abundance of historic baggage. In a brief visit, only the essential contours and binding elements can be grasped, and even this takes more time than is generally available. The first visit is critical and I therefore spend an hour or more with the patient, until I can perceive the human being behind the medical complaints. Even then my imagination has to churn disparate facts to make a coherent story. There is much guesswork. The mind looks for cogent reasons motivating human behavior, but in fact a mole on a chin may have more of an influence on someone's life than ancient childhood traumas. A doctor intent on healing must dare to dredge up material that even a patient's intimate friends do not know. A sympathetic understanding of what went wrong does not erase past hurts but can make them far more bearable.

The patient, at eighty-four, was so delicately pale she looked embalmed. I thought of myxedema, the sluggish state with a deadpan expression that is a symptom of an inadequately functioning thyroid gland. The likelihood of myxedema was rapidly belied by the stare with which she fixed me. I felt like a deer caught in the headlight of an oncoming car. There was no way to escape the searchlight gaze.

"And what brings you here?" I inquired.

"Angina pectoris, intermittent claudication, cerebrovascular disease, peptic ulcer, emphysema, kidney failure, gout, need I go on," she bellowed.

She was still attractive, very bright, and I wondered why she had never married, having instead spent her life taking care of her now ninety-year-old brother.

When I asked her directly she said only, "It could not be."

During the physical examination I was surprised at the rough stubble of hair on her arms, and when I asked about her shaving habits I uncorked a grief so utterly senseless yet so unspeakably agonizing, I recoiled at what I had done.

"Ever since I was a little girl I had these long ugly hairs. They were a constant nightmare. I could never wear short-sleeved blouses that little girls wore, no bathing suit, no exposure. It was a source of constant shame. You asked why I didn't marry?"

She had come for only a single consultation, but after I advised her about angina, she asked, "When do you want to see me again?"

"What about Dr. X., whom you've been seeing for nearly thirty years?"

"It's time for a change. You understand me better."

In subsequent visits I learned that this singular fact that so derailed her life had never been brought up, nor was the hirsutism ever noted by several physicians who had followed her.

At times when I listen to the problem of an elderly patient, I am filled with dismay for it seems insoluble. Then I break it up into little parts, separate the essential aspects, and converse with myself. "You can't solve it, but at least you can ameliorate this or that aspect." From that, a number of solutions surface.

She was white-haired, with rosy, red-apple cheeks, nice features, green watery eyes that teared a lot. Her hair was parted in the middle, like a Victorian grandmother's, her head held so rigidly it looked cemented to her body. The slightest movement provoked intense vertigo, the result of an earlier automobile accident. She came to me initially because she was misdiagnosed as having angina, and the inappropriate medications had disabled her still more. Her vision was severely impaired by cataracts. Unable to move rapidly, she had to sleep in a sitting position lest she faint or fall when she rose. She had seen numerous doctors, all to no avail.

Since she did not have angina, I stopped all her cardiac medications. All her symptoms, including the inordinate fatigue, disappeared, but her vertigo remained intractable. Not knowing what else could be done, I asked her, "What do you like to do above all else?"

"Oh, doctor dear, how I would like to return to the piano, my one pleasure in life." Having fallen off a piano stool, she gave that up, too. Now she sat in near darkness from dense cataracts, which she was too fearful to have operated. She did nothing the whole day, yet she had a happy smile and laughed readily. She had been a ravenous reader before the cataracts, but amazingly still had a rich inner life. Her doting, professionally successful daughter was a source of great and justified pride for her.

When I urged her to resume playing the piano, she said, "But I can't do that. The moment I begin to play briskly on the keys and move my head, I get so dizzy, I fall off the stool."

"If you didn't fall off your stool, would you play?"

"Of course, I would."

"Well then, the problem is easy to solve."

She looked surprised and suspicious.

"Why don't you get a swivel chair with arms so you can't fall off?"

About six months later, at her next visit, I was impatient to learn whether she had returned to the piano.

"Of course I have."

"Aren't you afraid of falling off the stool?"

"No. I immediately got the swivel chair you suggested, and now I can't fall off."

This was not a case of restoring light in the realm of darkness, but simply of lighting a very small candle. A doctor should teach acceptance of aging without accepting the consequences of thinking old. The great French poet Paul Claudel wrote on his eightieth birthday, "Eighty years old. No eyes left. No ears, no teeth, no legs, no wind, and, when all is said and done, one does without them."

ON THE AGING DOCTOR

Now that I have passed the milestone of my seventieth birthday, the subject of the elderly physician fills me with trepidation. In the words of the Czech writer Milan Kundera, "There is a certain part of all of us that lives outside of time. Perhaps we become aware of our age only at exceptional moments, and most of the time we are ageless."

Yet the signals are all about me. I must admit that there is a notable slowing in my recall of facts. It is more difficult to tap into my database. I cannot so readily dredge up the appropriate reference. Names of even intimate friends do not always surface easily. I am beginning to feel uncomfortable when confronted with basic science data or complex scientific relations, and I read more slowly. Texts that I could have comprehended at a glance I may have to read several times. Well-intentioned compliments are no longer so persuasive. Indeed, I take them as ominous warnings. "Dr. Lown, have you found the elixir of youth? Why don't you share it with me?" "You have remained the same over the last ten, fifteen, twenty, or twenty-five years." A red light flashes as a patient beseeches, "Dr. Lown, I hope you are not thinking of retiring." And of course, while retirement is remote from my mind, once the subject is raised it is all I think of the rest of the afternoon.

Still, at other times, I am convinced that I'm just reaching the apogee of my medical skills. Despite all the shortcomings, my doctoring has improved and I am a lot more helpful to my patients. My judgment is sounder, I have greater clarity in anticipating a patient's outcome, a honed sensitivity to unspoken problems, a more empathic faculty. I am less likely to imagine an esoteric medical diagnosis behind every clinical bush, and less mesmerized by the latest fad or technical wizardry. My measure of anxiety relating to malpractice, always low, is nearly zero. The older I get the less I rush to judgment. The less I rush, the older my patients get.

I am persuaded that as we age we may fail in knowledge but gain in wisdom. How could that be? Is not knowledge the foundation for wisdom? Yes and no. I can best illustrate some of these qualities with an example.

U.Q. telephoned at 10:00 P.M. A few hours earlier his wife, Olivia, had developed excruciating chest pain. He sounded panicked and I asked to speak to Olivia. She said that while talking she developed a sharp pain under the left breast and she couldn't take a deep breath. She did not sound worried, but then she generally acted blasé. I diagnosed pleurisy, advised a good night's sleep, and assured her that she would be better by morning. The next day she was free of pain and marveled at my certainty.

Olivia was a squat, obese, hypertensive sixty-year-old woman with a substantial family history of cardiovascular disease, and most doctors, suspecting either a heart attack or a pulmonary embolism, would have pursued the obvious trajectory; that is, urged her to go to an emergency ward (EW) for an electrocardiogram, chest X ray, and blood work. She would have waited around a good part of the night in a noisy EW, then been hospitalized in intensive care for several days with the diagnosis RO MI or PE, that is, "Rule out myocardial infarction or pulmonary embolism." The hospital stay would have cost more than $5,000, and it would have taken the patient more than a week to recover from the medical ordeal.

My confidence was an expression neither of callous indifference nor overbearing arrogance. The pain was in the wrong place and uncharacteristic of a heart attack. Olivia had no leg swelling, calf pain, or shortness of breath. When I had her count her pulse, it was only 72. All these facts spoke decisively against pulmonary embolism. As I talked with Olivia, I had cracked a joke and she laughed. This finally convinced me that we were not dealing with anything major warranting a trip to the hospital. My self-assurance was a product of the experience that only age affords.

Reaching a diagnostic conclusion is a process of sifting through extensive experience. The brain forms an algorithm and searches for like cases, and the emerging gestalt is increasingly relied upon. Why this complex process does not attenuate with age when so much else does is puzzling to me.

With the passage of time, I share my uncertainties with my patients. Contrary to expectation, this increases confidence and trust. The arrogance that doctors convey is a transparent cover-up for enormous uncertainty. Humility is not granted to the young but gifted to the old. Ultimately, the human organism is a beautifully organized system of chaos. The variables are infinite. In confronting them, it takes years of experience to sort the kernels from the confusing and abundant chaff. It takes a doctor nearly a lifetime to clear from his or her system the tendency, ingrained during medical education, to focus on remote and rare oddities; to think of zebras when hearing hoofbeats; to cease being on an ego trip; and to stop dreading being wrong.

With age you learn to sort out and understand that the common is what we most commonly encounter. The majority of human afflictions are self-limited; they are aggravated by the patient's imagining the worst and are consistently ameliorated or cured by unstinting and unequivocating reassurance from the physician. As I grow older, I listen differently. I hear more of the unspoken text. Facts and data slip by so rapidly, I begin to wonder, "Why invest time to acquire these gossamers?"

So what is medical wisdom all about? It is the capacity to comprehend a clinical problem at its mooring, not in an organ, but in a human being. Intuition and experience are required to grasp the subliminal and integrate it rapidly and comprehensively. The doctor as healer searches for this skill, above all others, all of his or her professional life. This wisdom of integrating fact and subliminal inputs to synthesize a holistic clinical image comes with age. The young brain craves a singular well-defined, rapidly actionable diagnosis. The conception is that what ails the patient is technologically scrutable. Yet in reflecting on what the ancient Greeks already understood about character, I wonder whether we have really advanced in our understanding of the human condition. We have certainly added a lot of details.

17

Death and Dying

In my youth I believed death was trivial, even unreal; only life laid claim to seriousness. Now, as I approach the outer boundary of living, my views have turned full circle. An old Hasidic utterance captures what I surmise to be the unvarnished essence of existence: "There is doom on either side, only life in between." A half century of doctoring suggests that nothingness rather than doom shrouds life. This possibility agitates the innermost core of everyone's mind.

The great evolutionary leap forward marked by the acquisition of self-consciousness brought with it death as the self's inseparable shadow. Rather than confronting its own end, the self attempts dissimulation and mystification. The complex rituals of diverse cults and religions are largely driven by the denial of life's inexorable finality. The powerful cacophony of denial and rejection cannot still life's ticking metronome, which every day brings death's inevitability closer. Each rhythmic tick affirms the clock's unwinding. The end is standstill. Time ceases. Life is sucked into a black hole of cold nothingness. We are not good at conceptualizing nothingness, infinity, or eternity. Beginnings and ends are within our programmed brain. Their endless extension evades comprehension. The pervading fear is not that life is far too short but that death is far too long. We choke with sorrow on the forever of our absence.

Earlier in my career I believed that the truly religious had achieved spiritual tranquillity by silencing the gremlin of doubt. Yet much experience with ultra-orthodox rabbis who have been and still are my patients convinces me otherwise. They, too, are wrestling with the serpent timekeeper permanently tenant in a hidden cavern of their minds. These rabbis, basking in piety, glorify the end as fulfillment of life's destiny. They impatiently await the final day for its blissful communion with Almighty God, but their actions belie the depth of their conviction. The luster of certainty tarnishes as they seek medical consultants, even as do those who lack persuasion of the hereafter, and struggle vainly to delay the joyous homecoming.

Much has been written about illness and dying. As an adolescent I encountered two works that made me face up to the essentiality of death, Tolstoy's *Death of Ivan Ilyich* and Thomas Mann's *Magic Mountain*. These books left an enduring imprint of sadness on me, a melancholy related not to the emptiness of death but to the solitariness of dying. The last steps are trudged utterly alone, witnessed only by the naked, ever diminishing self.

Socialized humans poorly tolerate the thought of journeying alone. We try to convince ourselves that life is a gift forever. Death happens to others. Our logical brain notwithstanding, we are hidebound in denial. Yet not coming honestly to terms with mortality detracts from the intensity of living. In the words of Albert Camus, "If there is a sin against life, it consists not so much in despairing of life as in hoping for another life and in eluding the implacable grandeur of this life." Paradoxically, preoccupation with or denial of death ultimately ill prepares us for its inevitability. To turn again to Camus, "There is only one liberty, to come to terms with death. After which everything is possible."

While the public expects them to address the question of death sagely, doctors are no more profound or insightful about this subject than anyone else. Experience with death does not lend wisdom to physicians any more than to undertakers. To explore life's meaning or death's mysteries we can learn more from poets, philosophers, and theologians. Doctors, however, are experienced in observing the process of dying, and indeed, they frequently shape the traverse of the final denouement, either as chief perpetrators of a technologic obscenity or as orchestrators of a serene passage.

My entire professional life has involved caring for critically ill cardiac patients. Far too often, having to rub shoulders with death, I gained intimacy with the many apprehensions burdening the very sick and the elderly. These do not relate to being dead, but rather to the torment of dying. I am persuaded that the medical profession has unmatched power to diminish the misery and fear of dying for the majority. It can humanize and lend a dignity that is absent for most in this very last stage of life.

Many factors shape the act of dying. Essentially, it is either prompt or delayed. Instantaneous death presents no problem for the victim. Nearly two thirds of patients with coronary artery disease die unexpectedly, many in their sleep. For a quarter of those who die suddenly, death is the first symptom that the victims had been afflicted with a serious cardiac problem. This type of final passage is wished by most. I am not persuaded, however, that this is the best way of dying for everyone involved. Death is far too integral to life to be so cavalierly short shrifted. Sudden death does not prepare those who are left for the totality of the loss. The insensate corpse is not the key actor in the drama of death, it is those who remain, the survivors who experience death's hurt and are compelled to continue along life's path. As the German philosopher Ludwig Feuerbach perceived, "Death is death only for the living." Indeed, death is the price paid for virtually all the properties we value in life. As one of my patients who had liver cancer phrased it with detachment, "We owe to the gods a death for the debt of life."

Sudden death, which seems such an easy passage, leaves a terrain strewn with unexploded emotional mines that cannot be swept away. They are durable and episodically discharge shrapnel, inflicting pain and provoking remorse. The sudden death of a spouse, parent, sibling, or friend is an unanticipated destination undertaken without the preparatory journey. Such deaths leave an unfinished life, a lingering ghost long remaining unexorcised to haunt the living. I am not convinced that sudden death is a fair deal for everyone.

Human beings are enormously adaptable psychologically, but adaptation is warped when death is instantaneous and unexpected. To adapt requires the balm of time. Sudden death removes the emotional space for coming to terms with loss. Fiscal affairs, wills, bequests, have not been arranged. More important, human relations have not been brought into any semblance of order. One need not harbor illusions that the last few days can miraculously remedy festering problems and deep hurts accumulated over a lifetime. Death has no such magic power. Nevertheless, any talk, even fragmented and inadequate, heals. The mere show of concern and affection is a beginning of absolution, lessening the burden of pressing guilt. A last goodbye is emblematic of communion, a terminal reconnection that has enduring meaning for the living.

Certainly sudden death is to be preferred to a slow and painful one, which is a reality for most people who die in institutional settings. At least 80 percent of Americans die in seclusion, away from their homes, their beds, and their loved ones. The dying person struggles above all else to cling to a human identity, but the struggle is a losing one. Even the best of hospitals is an environment organized to depersonalize, infantilize, and disempower. The patient is detached from all that is intimate, familiar, and kindly. Adding to the disintegrating image of self is the usurpation by anonymous others of decisions about life's ultimate fundamentals. Life's essence is further expunged when basic functions such as breathing and eating are surrendered to mechanized devices. Under such circumstances one is decoupled from life.

Dying in small steps while one is still very much alive stokes seething but unvoiced anger. In the modern hospital, far too many specialists flit about; the patient rarely knows who shoulders responsibility for his or her care or who can make a difference. Even our own doctors are frequently strangers, unfamiliar with who we are, how we lived, and how we wish to die.

We may also have an uneasy feeling that raising difficult questions or expressing protest would compromise care. Not knowing to whom to turn, sensing helplessness against a towering bureaucracy, fosters self-directed anger. The result is that every discomfort associated with illness is amplified, and painkillers stupefy rather than ameliorate. This hastens a ghastly process of psychological and spiritual dying. For some, the last days can only be described as a time of unrelenting torment, a veritable descent into hell.

DYING IN AMERICA

American culture has approached death not in a sensible manner but with a schizophrenic mix of denial and morbid preoccupation. A Frenchwoman told me, "Americans are the only people who think that death is an option." This stems in part from the American glorification of youth. But in my mind the paramount factor is hospitalization of the dying with the pervasive idea that death is somehow indecent and to be avoided at all cost. This is a precept to which physicians contribute mightily. Medical school and hospital training prepare doctors to become journeymen in science and managers of complex biotechnologies. Little of the art of doctoring is imparted, and doctors are taught little about dealing with a dying patient. From the beginning, a young doctor is conditioned to view death as the mark of failure, the ultimate sacrilege in the temple of science. The doctor, trained as a problem solver, is led to believe that this is the basis for the greatest challenges and the source of the deepest professional satisfaction. The paradigm that all problems are soluble is doomed to fail in the face of nature's immutable law of death. Time and again when I ask a young house officer why extraordinary measures are being taken for a dying patient, the answer is a challenge: "What if this new antibiotic or this new whatever promotes recovery? Do we have the ethical right to deny someone the one chance in a hundred of surviving?" And of course even the youngest doctor will have stored in his read-only memory a recollection of some terminally ill, moribund subject whose death was postponed. Belief in miracles is the sustaining power of unarguable religious convictions. The result is that physicians are increasingly ill prepared for one of their most challenging tasks, allaying the misery, pain, and psychologic stress of dying, for both victims and their families.

Yet a doctor is not a free agent. Even when aware that it may be improper to inflict pain in order to postpone the inevitable, the physician is shackled by cultural and societal constraints. A hallowed medical tradition charges the doctor with a singular mission, to cure illness and thereby prolong life. To achieve this mission, all available resources must be employed. While this central charge is noble, and undebatable in the abstract, it is detached from new realities. The most essential reality is the biotechnological revolution that enables one to prolong the act of dying interminably. This near-godly potential is a source of hubris for the doctor and inspires patients with unreal and unrealizable expectations. The barrage of public relations hype about this or that miraculous cure fosters the illusion that doctors are able to offer reprieve from nature's death sentence. Norman Cousins addresses this matter in *The Healing Heart*.

> The physician is not just a prescriber of medicaments but a symbol of all that is transferable from one human being to another short of immortality. We may not be able to live forever, but we persist in the notion that the physician possesses the science and the artistry that will provide us with endless deferrals. He seems to be in command of those fastnesses where the secrets of life are stored.*

Before utilizing this new, death-defying technology, numerous questions need to be answered. If death can be postponed, how long is the deferral? Will the extra time be a mere extension of misery? Will living remain purposeful? At what individ-

---

* Norman Cousins, *The Healing Heart: Antidotes to Pain and Helplessness* (New York: Norton, 1983).

ual, social, and economic cost will the extra time be purchased? In the daily calculus of clinical decision making, the medical specialist relegates these questions to ethicists or health economists. The physician deals with cold facts in making therapeutic decisions, rarely considering what genuinely matters to the individual patient. Furthermore, in any individual case, the physician can rarely predict the likely outcome of a particular therapeutic option. While the statistical prognosis for those with a similar disease is known, the distribution is invariably Gaussian, namely, some profit from the intervention, some show no change, and some are made much worse. From my observation, doctors have a penchant to emphasize the successes and downplay the possible aggravation that may make one's remaining days a veritable living hell. With emphasis on a possible reprieve, the patient grasps at the slimmest statistic. Generally what is offered is not a cure but a brief remission, at times so short as to be meaningless.

In my experience, oncologists are the worst practitioners of intervention at whatever the human cost. They have never refused to treat any of my patients. They have been truthful in defining the small chance of gaining a postponement, but less than forthright in portraying all the miserable consequences of engaging death in unequal battle. Death comes in any case, but its arrival is encrusted with untold woe. When death is the inevitable result of a chronic and incurable disease, it is often kinder not to impede it with heroic measures but to manage its approach with common sense and compassion.

Life-sustaining biotechnologies have advanced so miraculously that it is no longer easy to recognize the boundary between life's presence and absence. The hum of respirators, the silent pulse of pacemakers, the pumping of cardiac assist devices, and the tangle of lines delivering nutrients or removing secretions and excretions can make the demarcation invisible until these devices are silenced. In intensive care units, I commonly see intubated bodies bereft of those qualities that define a living presence. The surviving artifact is only the shadow of a life that has already vanished.

To sustain life against its will is both enormously costly and extraordinarily profitable. A substantial percentage of a hospital's revenues derive from prolonging the act of dying. Ironically, death constitutes the most lucrative part of the health care business and end-of-life expenditures are disproportionately large. For example, approximately one third of Medicare disbursements each year are for the 6 percent of beneficiaries who die in that year. Payments for dying patients increase exponentially as death approaches. The last month of life claims 40 percent of the payments for an average patient during the last year of life.* The health care system is structured to torment the elderly, not because of intrinsic malevolence but because it is a program based on reimbursement rather than on what is best for the individual patient.

The pornography of death derives largely from an amalgam of five factors: a technology that makes it possible to prolong life almost indefinitely, a medical profession that has declared war against death, a hospital that has a vested interest in extending the usually futile battle, a patient who is ignorant of his or her rights and conditioned to suffer, and a public that has been led to expect only victory from the medical profession.

For those who subscribe to conspiracy theories, there appears to be one huge conspiracy in American society in favor of slow dying. The bottom line is that scientific medicine has lengthened and improved life but, by the same token, worsened death.

The ugliness of death is largely of our own making. My first encounter with it was a horrid shock which nearly persuaded me that I lacked the stomach for medicine. It occurred during my initial week at Johns Hopkins Medical School, while

* J. D. and G. F. Lubitz, "Trends in Medicare Payment in the Last Year of Life," *New England Journal of Medicine* 328 (1993): 1092.

we were being given a tour of the facilities. It was a hot, sultry midsummer day, before the introduction of air conditioning, and we happened to be in the pathology department. Ambling aimlessly, I observed, protruding from an adjoining room, a pair of shapely young legs, toes manicured with red nail polish.

Curious, I moved closer and peeked around, unprepared to be staring at a patch of dark, curly pubic hair. I was embarrassed at intruding on a young, naked woman, but my eyes were drawn irresistibly upward — to the belly, which was slit wide open and packed with sawdust. The woman's arms hung over the sides of the narrow gurney, her eyes were bulging and contorted into a fixed gaze, her swollen tongue protruding through a half-open mouth. Stifling a scream and engulfing nausea, I raced away, but the stench of formaldehyde would remain in my nostrils for several days. Every time I smelled it, the whole horrid scene flashed before my eyes again.

There was no mystery to death, only ghastly horror. I came to medical school to learn about life, how to make living better, not to confront the sordid ugliness of death. With the passage of time I came to appreciate that a dead body has only a remote connection to a living person. The body is merely a dwelling place for a human mind, the miraculous embodiment of a living brain. When the brain ceases, the miracle ends, leaving behind an inanimate object that should provoke neither fear nor dread.

Inanimate death has little meaning. I don't feel with John Donne that "any man's death diminishes me, because I am involved in mankind; and therefore never send to know for whom the bell tolls; it tolls for thee." The death of a stranger is an unreal cipher in the march of life. It evokes little emotion, does not choke us with grief, does not ruin the taste of our morning coffee or affect the day's schedule. In the process of becoming a doctor one continuously brushes by anonymous deaths as remote as those in Rwanda or Bosnia. Extensive exposure tends to trivialize death and does not prepare a doctor for dealing with the complex act of dying.

My first involvement with a death that "mattered" came several years after medical school while I was still in hospital training. I cried when the patient died and was left seething with anger, frustration, and helplessness. I had encountered Mrs. D. while working at the Montefiore Hospital in the Bronx as a junior resident. She was critically ill and I struggled alone the entire night, with only occasional help from a single nurse, to reduce her fulminating congestion. Mrs. D. had tight mitral stenosis obstructing the entry of blood in her left ventricle. This caused blood to back up and drown her lungs with fluid, thereby choking off the exchange of oxygen. The medical name for her condition was pulmonary edema, lethal unless promptly reversed. The excess fluid was bubbling from her mouth in an orange froth. This was several years before the popularization of mitral valve surgery to correct this condition and I futilely tried oxygen, tourniquets, digitalis drugs, aminophylline, and mercurial diuretics.

I still see her large, dark green Irish eyes as she stared at me like a frightened elf. She was in her mid-thirties and had three small children. "Doctor, I don't want to die," she implored between sobbing gasps for air. "My children desperately need me." Then she would grow quiet, the stillness even more oppressive than her anguished pleading.

There were no phlebotomy sets, no washbasins, no buckets. It was one of those nights when an overloaded emergency room was disgorging into our overtaxed ward numerous critically ill patients. In a desperate effort I placed tourniquets on her upper arms, cut her elbow veins, and let her bleed into the bed. Draining off blood lessened the engorgement in her lungs, and as the bed was filled with blood her breathing grew less labored. She was responding to the morphine, and her waxen pretty face grew tranquil, the furrows around her mouth relaxed as she rested. I changed the bedding, raised her to a near sitting position, exchanged the pillowcase soaked with sweat, and made her comfortable. As dawn was breaking, she slept in the oxygen tent, with the peaceful repose of an angel.

Bleary eyed, I was writing up the night's events and inscribing orders when I was interrupted by a heavyset and balding Irish priest who came in, puffing. He had learned that his congregant, Mrs. D., was critically ill, and he had to see her immediately. I told him that she had just fallen asleep, her first rest in twenty-four hours, and explained her precarious medical condition. "That is the more reason for me to see her," he retorted. I pleaded with frustration and no doubt irritation. I was ready to go on my knees, go to church, contribute to a Catholic charity of his choice. He grew increasingly incensed. He said something to the effect that I should not be permitted to practice on Catholic patients because I lacked understanding of their culture and their psychology. Catholics rejoice and gain spiritual sustenance from seeing their pastor, and pointing to his breast pocket, he announced emphatically, "I carry with me her passport to heaven!"

With those words he stalked past me, hurrying to her bedside, and I followed close behind. She was asleep, still peaceful, her breathing unhurried. The priest's presence roused her abruptly. She opened her eyes wide, fearful, uncomprehending. He began to intone in Latin and waved a crucifix over her body. She let out a painful sob, and bloody fluid once again poured from her mouth, accompanied by a wheezing loud rattle. Within twenty minutes she was dead.

The priest angrily upbraided me for trying to interfere with a holy mission, pointing out that in the nick of time he had succeeded in easing the final journey to the hereafter for one of his flock. He reported me to the hospital administration for trying to impede a priest in performing an essential religious function, and the administrator of this Jewish hospital gently reprimanded my behavior.

Reflecting over this experience, I sense a certain arrogance on my part. Mrs. D. was terminally ill, and nothing then available would have prolonged her life even for several weeks. More likely she would have succumbed within the ensuing twenty-four hours anyway. For the family to know that she had received last rites and sacraments assuaged the enormity of their loss. The tragedy of her death was magnified for me, however, when, within the year, Dr. Dwight Harkin in Boston and Dr. Charles Bailey in Philadelphia introduced the mitral valvulotomy operation to open a tightly stenosed valve. It would have saved her life.

In those early years, each of my experiences with death was a near calamity. I had just begun to practice clinical cardiology and waited futilely for patients to knock at my door. As few came, I would see a patient anytime or anywhere, which is how I happened to be at my office, without air conditioning, on a sweltering late Friday afternoon. It was July 3, and my secretary was unhappy at having to hang around just before a long holiday weekend, but a patient had telephoned earlier that day about a problem that sounded urgent.

At three o'clock that afternoon I encountered a tall, distinguished-looking, white-haired man of seventy-five. My first black patient, he was a retired physician who proudly told me that he was among the first of his race to have graduated from Harvard Medical School. The history he presented was a classic case of recent-onset angina pectoris. The rapid progress of symptoms and the fact that the chest discomfort was now occurring at rest and awakening him from a sound sleep suggested that he was in the throes of a heart attack. As he spoke, my disquiet communicated a growing concern to Dr. J. He reassured me with these words: "I am a deeply religious man without any fears of dying."

I showed him into the examining room and told him to disrobe. Just before I left him for a moment to write some notes and arrange for his admission to a hospital, he abruptly turned about. Looking me straight in the eyes he intoned in a deep timbre, "Dr. Lown, I want you to know that I am ready to meet my maker. Oh, Lord, I am ready to go!"

A few minutes later there was a loud thump. I raced in to find the doctor, totally nude, lying stretched out on the floor, body twitching, eyes staring fixedly at the ceiling, harsh gasps coming from his mouth. Detecting no pulse, I straddled his body to provide mouth-to-mouth respiration and began systematic pressure over the lower sternum. At the same time, I shouted at the top of my lungs for my secretary. She rushed in, took one look, and raced out of the office. I screamed for her to return, explaining that the man was dead. Reassured that she was not witnessing a homosexual assault, she sheepishly came back and called the police.

An electrocardiogram showed the straight line of cardiac arrest. Dr. J. was beyond resuscitation. Being inexperienced, I pronounced him dead, and when the police arrived they berated me for being so stupid. The dead body could not be moved until the coroner had examined it. The enormity of my calamity began to sink in. This was Friday of a Fourth of July weekend and the coroner was not likely to come for at least four days. Meanwhile the body would be speedily decomposing in an overheated office.

My secretary left, and I was alone with the body of a total stranger. Then I recalled that I had once done a medical favor for the medical examiner of Boston. I located him that evening in New Hampshire, and he released the body with an admonition never again to pronounce anyone dead. "Pretend they are in extremis, have them rushed to a hospital, let the hospital declare them DOA."

These three experiences with death at the very outset of my medical career left me feeling that dying was something to be avoided at all costs. Yet the trajectory of my professional work constantly brought me into death's orbit. Work on coronary care, defibrillation, and cardioversion exposed me to the critically ill and dying, and I intimately witnessed the death of many hundreds of patients.

In patients who die of illness, the underlying disease shapes the course of dying. The final act is less difficult in the case of heart disease, and the precise time of death is unpredictable when compared, for example, with the inexorable advance of cancer. While each disease has its own rate of progression and a defined set of symptoms, certain broad generalizations can be made. The fundamental truth is that the way we die is shaped by the way we have lived. Death is confronted with less anguish when a person feels that he or she has lived a full life. As James M. Barrie wrote in *Peter Pan*, "The life of every man is a diary in which he means to write one story and writes another; and his humblest hour is when he compares the volume as it is and what he vowed to make it."* That humblest hour often comes at life's end. The person who does not fear death is one who can look back without serious regrets, who has retained self-respect, who has stretched to the marrow of possibility the potential of innate endowments. While these attributes cannot empty death of its attendant discomforts, they make it bearable and do not quench our sense of dignity. While even mild pain can be intolerable when associated with guilt and amplified by anxiety, excruciating pain can be borne if one is not burdened with negative emotions.

One need not live dying. Nor does the act of dying need to be surfeited with horror, pain, and misery, as is the case for many. Indeed, one can live well until the very minute of death. There are no sharp biological boundaries demarcating the process of dying from that of living. In fact, like all biologic phenomena, death is an ongoing process that begins at birth and proceeds at various tempi until the end. For most patients, death is preceded by a chronic, long-lasting illness. Many live for decades thus afflicted. It would be improper to refer to them as dying people. In cardiology especially, a doctor's prognostication about survival is most accurate as a statistical generalization. It is woefully inept when applied to an individual patient. I frequently see patients who have survived for decades after having been told that they had months to live. If pressed to prognosticate, I always try to err on the optimistic side, since optimism is often self-fulfilling.

What I have learned during my years of caring for dying patients is that the quality of one's life helps determine the

* J. M. Barrie, *Peter Pan* (New York: Charles Scribner's Sons, 1929).

course of final passage. What is most important are close and affectionate relations with other people, particularly family members. To have a storehouse of fond memories and family present in the final hours eases the trial and tribulation of dying. Having been successful in one's work, whatever the occupation, is a staunch pillar of support at life's end. A life of self-preoccupation leaves one emptied of the emotional capital to navigate the shoals of the final journey. Those who have given most to others generally have the easiest time in dying. As the Talmud has taught, "A person possesses what he gives away."

THE NATURE OF DYING

People increasingly wish to gain control of their end-of-life decisions and die with dignity. However, Dr. Sherwin B. Nuland, in *How We Die*, maintains that death cannot be dignified because the very nature of dying constitutes a physical and psychological disintegration that dissipates dignity. The classic image of dying with dignity, according to Nuland, is best discarded.*

For Nuland, death is bereft of dignity because dying is an ugly, putrid event that should not be prettified. The challenge for medicine is to improve the quality of life for older people and for persons with terminal illnesses, "not to prolong its duration." Since there is no dignity in death, the public, in order to be prepared, had better be informed. Nuland's text leaves little to the imagination as he touches on most of the excruciating miseries accompanying life's final passage. The sole way of purchasing a reasonable death, according to Nuland, long antedates the act of dying. "The dignity that we seek in dying must be found in the dignity with which we have lived our lives."

Underpinning Nuland's argument is a broadly humanitar-

---

* Sherwin B. Nuland, *How We Die: Reflections on Life's Final Chapter* (New York: Knopf, 1994).

ian, biologically anchored philosophic stance. Death is intrinsic to life, he argues, and necessary to clear our species of those burdened by the biologically imposed infirmities of age. Far from being irreplaceable, we should be replaced. "Better to know what dying is like," Nuland writes. "We may thus be better prepared to recognize the stations at which to ask for relief, or perhaps to begin contemplating whether to end the journey altogether." But in my experience, a knowledge of the morbid details of dying does not better prepare one for confronting death with equanimity, although it may lower a patient's expectations, making it less likely he or she will fault the doctor for not performing a miracle. Moreover, even if the patient is knowledgeable about death, the way he or she dies is not up to the patient. In the words of songster Joan Baez, "You don't get to choose how you are going to die. Or when. You can only decide how you're going to live." Modern medicine shapes the contemporary mode of dying in which doctors make each patient another battleground in their unceasing struggle against death.

I believe that the image of the physician has been tarnished by the way doctors approach the act of dying. A vast apparatus is deployed to service death instead of life. Biotechnology defines the rules of the road, with the possible determining the necessary, and the doctor follows these absurd rules rather than focusing on the well-being of the patient. The madness of the system is illustrated by my mother's death.

Mother was in her ninety-sixth year. Although she was intellectually sharp and had a rich storehouse of memories, she frequently expressed dismay at her visible physical dissolution. As the love of books was one of her supreme joys, the loss of vision was the deprivation she found hardest to bear. Her hearing was impaired, too, but she was far too proud to wear a hearing aid. When I probed how she felt, no joint seemed to be spared excruciating pain. She was embarrassed by a substantial shrinkage in stature, by wrinkles, by false teeth, by thinning hair, and by numerous infirmities. Though shriveled, she enjoyed being complimented on a youthful demeanor, and people generally thought she was in her late seventies rather than her mid-nineties.

Fluent in at least five languages, she was catholic in her interests. Agnostic in religious outlook, she nonetheless cherished tradition and liturgy and to the end remained committed to Yiddish culture. Having experienced a life of poverty and deprivation in the old country, she was strong in character and without illusion about the benisons of a full life. She loved company, beaming when visitors came, especially grandchildren. Mother made a point of telephoning her thirteen grandchildren every week, and my wife, Louise, and I visited her daily and frequently more often. Still, she missed no chance to complain about how rarely she saw her family. She relished being a matriarch and the hub of the family wheel, and her longevity was largely nourished by the intensely reciprocated affection of a doting family. She was also determined to live until she had completed and published her autobiography, which she did.

As Mother became increasingly limited, Louise and I hoped she would move in with us, but she was adamant about not burdening her children in any way. But when asked what troubled her most, she would confess it was loneliness, to which her diminished vision and hearing contributed substantially. She was the last survivor of a large circle of close friends. The Roman philosopher Lucius Seneca commented, "Death is sometimes a punishment, often a gift, and to many a favor." Mother, in her final year, began to welcome death as a favor. Mere survival she regarded as a worthless exercise. She craved to die, fearing not death but dying.

Thirty years earlier she had experienced a significant heart attack from which she had fully recovered. During the last five years of her life she was at times afflicted with angina, assuaged by nitroglycerin. If family provided Mother the sustenance to forbear, her long life was also supported in no small measure by a group of sensitive and very competent physicians who lavished enormous attention on her. These were mostly geriatricians, impeccably well trained in the science and competent in fully engaging the humane art of their profession. They responded with frequent house calls, as though she were their own mother. Never once did they try to hospitalize her, even for the heart attack, in large measure because they knew she would have refused.

During her final two months she began to fail visibly, and I could see that she would not live long. A major problem was intractable arrhythmia; her pulse never slowed to less than 120 beats per minute and was unresponsive to therapeutic measures. Fully aware that the end was near, she would go to bed at night hoping she would not wake in the morning. But on festive occasions, such as her ninety-sixth birthday, she joked that she would surprise us by celebrating the one hundredth milestone. Increasingly she spoke about how much she would welcome departing, though she regretted not knowing what would happen in the world and especially in the lives of her family.

In the final few weeks it was clear that death was imminent. Her congested lungs were impervious to strong diuretics, making every breath an effort. Oxygen afforded respite from the air hunger and her lucidity was undiminished, but while comfortable, she grew increasingly impatient for the ordeal to be over. On her very last day, Mother awakened with a start at about 3:00 A.M. and asked the nurse who was staying in her apartment around the clock to help her shower. When my wife and I arrived some hours later, she was fully dressed, her hair nicely set, a dab of makeup livening her still pretty face. She was lapsing in and out of consciousness, and we told the nurse in attendance not to call emergency services. At about noon my wife and I stepped out to have lunch. We were away about forty-five minutes, and on returning to her apartment saw a hospital ambulance outside the building. With trepidation we raced up to find a hubbub of voices and shouting within her small flat.

The sight I encountered was unbelievably ghastly. My mother

was lying on the floor completely nude, a tracheal tube stuck in her mouth, her chin covered by a white froth, her face puffed with purplish suffusion, both hands swollen from intravenous infusions going nowhere, her skin already submitting to death's waxy pallor. Hefty robust men were compressing her chest and discharging a defibrillator against her dead heart. It was a spectacle of utter obscenity, a kafkaesque nightmare. I screamed and tried to push the men away, but they shoved me out of the room, ignoring my shouts. "This is my mother. Don't you see she is dead? I am a doctor." I pleaded between sobs, "I am her son."

Regaining my composure, I asked who was in charge and was given the name of a physician at one of Boston's leading hospitals. When I called and identified myself, the doctor was full of apology and immediately ended this hideous travesty.

That morning, a new nurse had been in attendance, and the moment she saw her patient expire, she panicked and called 911 — despite our instructions. No doubt each member of the emergency squad and the doctor in charge were upstanding, well-meaning people, who would have been appalled to be regarded as storm troopers. Nevertheless, our carefully laid plans for allowing my mother a humane ending to a well-lived life were short-circuited by a sick, robotized system that wages mindless battles against death. My mother was beyond pain, her death was peaceful and dignified. While she was spared suffering, the indignity was inflicted on the living. The memory of her death evokes pain and tears, but I weep more for what is happening to my profession.

Although the sorry spectacle surrounding my mother's death could be explained as an emergency service response to an unknown, similar incidents happen in hospitals where the same excuse cannot be made. Fixated on monitors and laboratory data, doctors frequently seem oblivious of the tormented human reality. The doctors in the front line are the young, largely inexperienced house staff, not seasoned by experience to distinguish when the struggle against death must be made without quarter and when it is an exercise in demeaning futility.

I recall a confrontation with house staff that indicates how much we need to change our attitude toward dying. Mr. I., a seventy-four-year-old retired businessman, arrived at the hospital with a heart attack, his sixth. In the past year he had been completely disabled with congestive heart failure and experienced numerous life-threatening episodes of ventricular tachycardia. His lungs were filled with rales, his blood pressure barely measurable. He had a huge ventricular aneurysm, an immobile outpouching of dead heart muscle. When his pain and anxiety were promptly controlled with morphine and oxygen, the house staff began mobilizing all the technologic resources. The monitor had begun to intone a staccato rhythm, while the scopes were full of neon-lighted electrical signals. The respirator and intubation were at the ready, the defibrillator was wheeled in. The room was getting crowded with equipment and attendants, leaving little room for family members. One could feel the excitement of a medical challenge rather than respect for the completion of a human destiny. A careful examination clearly indicated that he was irreversibly afflicted.

Mrs. I. was beseeching us to do everything possible to save him, while her eldest son, a man in his early forties, unavailingly tried to calm her. I took the son aside and outlined the options, conveying my opinion that we could prolong his father's dying but not his life. The son listened carefully and then responded, "Do what you would have done for your own father in similar straits."

"But what about your mother?" I inquired.

"She will listen to common sense and will agree to what is in Dad's best interest."

I instructed the staff that Mr. I. was to receive only oxygen, morphine, and anything else necessary for comfort. All other procedures were to be discontinued. The room quickly emptied out. An eerie silence prevailed. The tension, as well as the excitement, abruptly dissipated. The wife and son sat in silent vigil where previously they had been excluded. No one entered the room, neither nurse nor doctor, as though the patient was under quarantine. I pondered sadly how lonely is the final journey of life when one is hospitalized. I sat down by his bed and held his hand. He was in full possession of his faculties. We chatted about trivia and reminisced about our long relationship. I felt a stab of remorse and guilt as he commented, "There are advantages to dying. I get to spend a good deal of time with my doctor." He fell asleep and passed away peacefully in the following hour.

Immediately thereafter, I assembled the entire medical staff and asked why no one else had come to provide comfort for this dying man. "Had we decided to balloon pump him or called the shock team or considered him a candidate for bypass, you would have been hopping around the bed." Ten people, young doctors and nurses, clearly pained, stood with heads bowed. I kept intoning, like a priest in a hushed church, that life is robbed of meaning when human beings avoid confronting the inexorable certainty of death. For those of us in the healing profession, our failure to accept death as life's ultimate destination made a mockery of our vaunted humanitarian commitment. We continually assaulted patients who should have been allowed to die peaceably because we saw death as a professional failure. We put technology between us and our patients, to spare us the grief of failing to confront our own mortality. I spoke without rancor, almost pleading. Several weeks later I received from Mr. I.'s widow a thoughtful letter full of commendation for my staff and myself for affording her husband the dignified death that was a deserved culmination of a fulfilled life.

Medicine has been programmed to resist giving up the ghost. Is it conceivable that we can be reprogrammed? I am persuaded that the act of dying can be humanized and the suffering attenuated. My optimism derives from the number of "good" deaths I have witnessed. The patient I am about to describe taught me much about how to die.

A GOOD DEATH

Mr. Y., a distinguished writer, had a shock of white hair, a round, smooth baby face illuminated with the bluest azure eyes, a ready shy smile, and a forceful manner of speaking. I first met him when he was transferred to my service at the Peter Bent Brigham Hospital with what was diagnosed as intractable terminal congestive heart failure. He continued as my patient for a decade and lived a productive life, able to complete several important books while afflicted with end-stage cardiomyopathy. When he was hospitalized for the last time, his heart's pumping of blood was so low that one could imagine each cardiac contraction propelling only a pitifully few forlorn red corpuscles forward, releasing but a meager supply of oxygen to suffocating tissues. He was breathing rapidly and shallowly. His body had wasted from about 150 pounds to less than 80. Subcutaneous tissues and fat had long ago melted away, and his wrinkled skin was a mummified sallow parchment tightly hugging a skeleton. While he spoke deliberately, each word was uttered in a whisper, cushioned by hesitations. His mind, however, remained crystal clear.

We discharged him to his home on Cape Cod in late July, and I did not expect him to last until Labor Day. As I was giving him final instructions about medications and diet, he suddenly looked up and asked whether he would see me again. "Of course I'll see you. I still make house calls." He offered a wan smile as the ambulance drivers moved the stretcher out of the room.

The following November I received a call from Mrs. Y., who told me that her husband was asking when I was going to make that promised house call. On Thanksgiving weekend I took a small commuter plane to the Cape. Mr. Y. was in the very end stage of multisystem failure. His stertorous breathing was interrupted by pauses that seemed permanent — until they were interrupted by deep, protesting, loud gasps or rapid breaths. The white snowy frost of uremia coated his lips, making them look as if they were smudged with shaving cream. A skein of purplish veins added a dab of color to his deathly pallor.

To celebrate my presence, Mr. Y. sat at the table for lunch, which he never touched. His wife, Augustine, looked wretched, the embodiment of exhaustion after endless nights of bedside vigil to attend to his every wish. I took her aside and urged that she take a weekend off to catch up on sleep and recoup her utterly spent resources. "Never, never," she exclaimed. "That is completely unthinkable!"

"You think he's going to die while you're away and you won't be with him?" I questioned. She did not respond, but her dread-filled eyes affirmed that possibility. "This will not happen," I assured her with more conviction than I really felt.

I went into the bedroom to speak to Mr. Y., telling him that I needed his help to persuade Augustine to take a few days off. For the first time since my arrival, he beamed. I could once again see the smiling eyes that I remembered so well, their stark blue not yet glazed by advancing dissolution.

"Doctor, I've been worried sick about Augustine doing too much for me and neglecting herself totally," he replied. "It's not fair. It would make me very happy to have her take off for a few days."

When Augustine was persuaded to take a weekend off to visit a son in New York, Mr. Y. looked triumphant. Augustine was at last convinced that her husband of sixty years would not die in her absence. She returned invigorated. About a week later, in early December, a light snow was dusting the denuded trees. Mrs. Y. dressed her husband warmly and pushed his wheelchair out on the small veranda. Looking up at her with deep affection, Mr. Y. said, "The trees are so pretty, it brings memories of my boyhood in New Hampshire." His head abruptly sank and he was dead.

This was a dignified death at the end of a fulfilled life. Norman Cousins wrote, "What I have learned is that the tragedy of life is not death, but what dies inside of us while we live."* Nothing of Mr. Y.'s spirit died during his struggle with prolonged congestive heart failure and a trying illness. He spent ten years at death's door but never yielded to despair or permitted illness to erode his humanity.

My role as Mr. Y.'s doctor was to diminish symptoms, to improve cardiac function to the limits that science and technology permitted, constantly to devise ways to enhance his comfort, and to impart optimism to his caregivers. Perhaps most challenging was spurring his prodigious creativity when it appeared he might not live to complete a task. When the end was near, the medical strategy was to cease supporting his physical existence, which had become life's counterfeit coin. I look back with pride to having been able to exercise both the art and the science. A doctor has the power to make a dignified death possible for many patients.

Each of us resists becoming an inanimate glob of aching flesh. Not unreasonably, and for as long as possible, we crave to hold fast to that speck of uniqueness that endows each of us with a self-image of godliness. A good death should be our inalienable right. Most people don't ask for much except a brief final illness free from unbearable pain, the presence of family and friends, enough time and energy to tidy up affairs, and above all, avoidance of an embarrassing loss of control — in short, not to deplete in one's last days the dignified sense of self that took a lifetime to cultivate. We want to be remembered kindly, a very modest wish that should be within the reach of most. While a good death cannot be guaranteed to all, it seems certain that nearly everyone can be spared an agonizing one. The medical profession already possesses the know-how to assure such a benign transit.

---

* Cousins, *The Healing Heart.*

DIGNIFIED DEATH

Not everyone can have a good death, but most patients crave far less. They wish to receive palliative care and not to be abandoned. Now that the dying process can be extended interminably, it is all the more important that doctors know how to care for the dying patient. Patients wish physical ease, relief of symptoms, and a sense that their unique defining psychological and spiritual qualities are recognized and respected. Anxieties about being left alone can amplify symptoms and make bearable pain intolerable agony, so an essential element in caring for the dying is to assure them that their doctor is unequivocally available.

This, like many other important aspects of healing, was brought home to me by Dr. S. A. Levine. When he was dying of stomach cancer, he asked me to be his doctor. Stopping in to see him nightly after work, I found the visits emotionally draining, because he was not only my teacher but as close to me as a parent. After each examination I would offer an upbeat pronouncement, which was the most difficult part of the visit. From our long association, I knew that SAL did not tolerate cant and abhorred deception, yet he plainly welcomed an optimistic message. Asking me whether he should give up his private office, he seemed pleased when I advised that he need not rush.

Eventually it became an ordeal for him simply to move in bed. He had been reduced to a mere assemblage of bones and a bizarre patchwork of thin venules that ran helter-skelter across his thin parchment-like, taut, yellow skin. I could already visualize him enshrined in a sarcophagus, yet his eyes never lost their vital sparkle.

One evening I decided not to burden him with the charade of physical examination. As I was leaving, he whispered, "Bernie, do you have a minute? I am reminded about a tale that may interest you. When Sir Clifford Albutt was dying, he was attended by Sir William Osler. One day as Dr. Osler was leaving his sick chamber, Sir Clifford called out, 'Sir William, what should I do about my decubitus ulcers?' Osler did not recall any pressure sores. With consternation he turned to the nurse beside him and whispered, 'What about the decubitus?' She responded, 'He doesn't have any!' Sir William, who was at the door, returned, examined Sir Clifford, and reassured him that the skin was healthy."

Of course I immediately found a reason to examine Dr. Levine more thoroughly than I had hitherto done. The lesson had been learned; thereafter, until SAL's death, I examined him carefully at every visit. No one accepts abandonment.

SOME REMEDIES

Reflecting on a life of dealing with death and dying, I am persuaded that death's anguish is, in no small measure, man made. It is a product of Western culture, which denies death its due and foolishly allocates mammoth resources to prolong the tormenting act of dying. This is a contemporary phenomenon and therefore not immutably fixed. But it is difficult to foresee any change in hospital structure or in physician thinking that will humanize institutional death. The economics of dying are too great, and doctors too deeply fixated on proving their power over death, for the system to yield readily to what is socially appropriate. Furthermore, the romance of saving a life, even when it is an exercise in futility, will not be easily abandoned by youthful house staff who are the ultimate guardians of the hospitalized patient.

Any melioration of the problem has to face up to the fact that the contemporary hospital functions most efficiently when patients are infantilized and disempowered. There can be no dignity to death when the patient lacks control over the vital decisions concerning how to die. Death with dignity is meaningless when life has been robbed of it. To change our cultural approach will require the deinstitutionalizaton of dying, a prerequisite being that hospitals no longer serve as the place to die. The empty spouting about "lending dignity to death" will not be realized until hospitals are decoupled from the act of dying.

Each person will have to die in his or her unique way, reflecting the life one has lived. Dying therefore will have to move back to one's home, where it has been throughout human history until the last few decades. For many, to enable the family to cope, a hospice should be a way station between hospital and home.

The growing hospice movement provides a ray of hope. It is estimated that by 1992, the last year for which figures are available, 246,000 people had chosen hospice care.* In the hospice philosophy, death is not viewed as an event that has to be delayed at all costs. The person is comforted physically as well as psychologically, while the family is involved in ministering to the dying loved one. The fact of death no longer hidden, dying gains full disclosure. Helping the dying face up to the inevitability of the end becomes an act of healing. The aim of the hospice movement is to provide a modicum of dignity for the dying.

Studies of hospice deaths contravene the notion that dying has to be an ugly and miserable end of life. Dr. Loring Conant, medical director of Hospices of Cambridge, has estimated that "well over 60 percent of people in hospices have good deaths with their symptoms addressed appropriately, allowing for the patients and significant others, friends or family, to achieve closure that may not have been fully identified up to that time." According to Conant, the good death has three elements. The first is the palliation of symptoms and alleviation of suffering, which have become increasingly possible by growing scientific understanding of the pathogenesis of pain and by the introduction of new and powerful analgesic drugs, as well as by innovative drug delivery systems. The second involves helping the family come to terms with the death of a loved one. Finally, there must be an effort to discuss the vexing matters and

* J. Foreman, *Boston Globe,* March 7, 1994.

bring to the surface concealed problems, perhaps never hitherto addressed. Even if such conversations remain uncompleted, the mere beginning is therapeutic. Lessening the burden of such unresolved issues frequently enables control of intractable pain.

In the final analysis, a good death is a mirror of a life well lived. In July 1776, James Boswell paid a visit to the dying David Hume, British philosopher and leading humanist of his day. Now that Hume was nearing his grave (indeed, he died seven weeks later) Boswell was curious to discover whether the notorious nonbeliever would recant. Boswell inquired if the thought of annihilation gave him uneasiness. No more uneasiness, Hume replied, than the thought that he had not existed before birth. Hume looked forward without fear to a speedy dissolution. The serenity of Hume's final hours haunted Boswell and left a deep impression on contemporary Britain.*

Twelve days before his death, that remarkably creative physician and brilliant essayist Lewis Thomas was interviewed by *New York Times* correspondent Roger Rosenblatt. Thomas said,

> When death was regarded as a metaphysic event, it commanded a kind of respect. Today when the process is long protracted it seems as evidence of failure. A dying patient is kind of a freak. It is the most unacceptable of all abnormalities, an offense against nature itself . . . In a sense quite new to our culture, we have become ashamed of death, and we try to hide ourselves away from it. It is, in our way of thinking, failure. . . . There is really no such thing as the agony of dying. I'm quite sure that pain is shut off at the moment of death . . . Something happens when the body is about to go. Peptide hormones are released by cells in the hypothalamus and pituitary glands. Endorphins. They attach themselves to the cells responsible for feeling pain . . . On the whole . . . I believe in the kindness of nature at the time of death.

* Michael Ignatieff, *The Needs of Strangers* (New York: Viking, 1985).

When asked what it felt like to die, Thomas answered, "Weakness. This weakness. I am beginning to lose respect for my body."

"Is there an art to dying?" Rosenblatt asked him.

"There is an art to living," Thomas replied.*

* Roger Rosenblatt, *New York Times*, November 21, 1993.

V

The Rewards
of Doctoring

18

A Modern Hasidic Tale

DESPITE more than forty-five years in medicine, I still feel like a student struggling through a tough curriculum at a demanding university. The teachers are not august scholars but the patients I encounter daily. Many instruct me about the manifestation or progress of a disease. Some provide understanding of the ups and downs of fickle fortune or the bad hand dealt by an indifferent fate. A number inform me about the ineluctable tragedies that affect nearly everyone's life. A small group of patients, like closely passing comets, have permanently altered the trajectory of my life, the powerful gravitational field of their personalities displacing my own traverse into a new orbit.

My most enduring memories are of illnesses that posed impossible challenges, the resulting intense human interactions, and the enduring friendships wrought thereby. Such experiences have stretched me to the outermost limits and taught me that knowledge of the human condition is not to be derived from books but from intimate engagement with other human beings. No book knowledge equals what one may glean from patients who have permitted a doctor to look deeply into their eyes.

Rereading the earlier chapters of this book, I am left with an aching frustration at my inadequacy in communicating the complexities of the healing process. I want to write, therefore, in far greater detail about one patient who shook me up, educated me about issues remote from medicine, provided me with unusual psychologic insights, and deepened my art of healing. Long ago I realized that the teaching which endures tells memorable stories. From the haze of distant medical school memory, few facts persevere, but many of the instructive stories persist with diamond luster.

There is a more compelling reason for my sharing the tale of the patient, S.V. His story launched me into writing this book. Reflecting on my relation with S.V., I realize it represents a caricature of the healing process. But like any good caricature, it conveys a deeper truth; the seeming exaggeration and distorted perspective brings into focus what is truly relevant. S.V. was seemingly a very humble and ordinary man, but he made the deepest of impressions and left me utterly mystified and long grieving after his death. He looked puzzled when I indicated my wish to write about him someday.

"Why about me? Do you find me so interesting? I should be honored. No doubt I will be in very distinguished company. Although I am not sure you will tell the whole truth since you have so little sympathy for my perilous state of health." After this conversation, however, he often urged me to tell his story.

It all began in December 1974, when my wife, Louise, and I took a trip to Sicily with a brief interlude in London to go to the theater and museums. I had promised Louise a real holiday free of medical diversions, but during our brief stay in London I was asked to consult on a most complicated and unusual medical problem at the National Heart Hospital, and I could not refuse.

The patient, S.V., had had his mitral and aortic valves replaced the previous year by a leading London cardiac surgeon; since then he had suffered very rapid heart action that kept him in intractable cardiac failure. He had engaged the best possible consultant, a highly respected doyen of British cardiology, and every conceivable measure had been tried without success.

At the hospital I found the patient to be an unprepossessing middle-aged man, short in stature, broad shouldered, and ruggedly put together. A pair of slightly protruding, large blue eyes gazed out in awed astonishment from a head that seemed too large for his body. His demeanor conveyed childhood innocence, but the voice, with a clipped British accent, was larded with adult cynicism. He looked remarkably intact, notwithstanding the ordeal of a year of recurrent hospitalizations following a grueling operation marked by numerous complications, including several small strokes. He was evidently in both right- and left-sided heart failure, with swollen, cordlike jugular veins and crepitation at the very lung bases. The immediate explanation for his difficulties was not hard to find — his heart was in perpetual tachycardia, racing nearly three times normal at a clip of 180 to 200 beats per minute without respite, even during sleep.

I carefully examined the thick clinical chart for some clue to account for the heart's fibrillating at such an extraordinary rate, but every possibility had been entertained and bizarre diagnoses had been ruled out. In despair I let go with a consultant's ploy: "If only Mr. V. were in my clinic at the Peter Bent Brigham Hospital in Boston, we would resolve the problem." The moment these words were uttered I felt ashamed at my stooping to such hogwash. Clearly the British cardiologist rounding with me saw through my pretension but was too much the English gentleman to ask precisely what I had in mind. Even modest inquiry would have exposed this pretense as mere legerdemain. S.V. was completely unimpressed with the promissory note and had but one request, that I meet with his mentor, a leading London rabbi, F.G. With some reluctance I agreed, although I hoped that this was the first and last time I would lay eyes on S.V., whose problem seemed insoluble.

The next day I met with Rabbi G., a distinguished-looking, bearded man in his early seventies, impeccably attired in a long black caftan, gracious in solicitude for my well-being. He spoke mellifluously without a wisp of foreign accent. I asked the rabbi how he was involved with S.V., hoping for a brief explanation. He warmed to the subject with zest. "As you are the man who will save the life of my ward," the rabbi articulated emphatically, "I shall begin at the very beginning.

"As a boy of twelve, he already foresaw the Holocaust and extinction of the Jews. Young S. urged his parents to leave Germany while there was still time. They ignored him, but he beseeched them relentlessly. By mid-1939 the parents were becoming persuaded. Kristallnacht and mounting Nazi strictures against Jews proved the truth of their son's jeremiads. The family agreed to leave Germany after the High Holidays. S. would not hear of this, convinced that it would be too late. On September first, taking a small suitcase of belongings, this slight boy journeyed by himself to England, arriving in London the day war was declared. His family perished without a trace."

Being remotely related to S.V., the rabbi took charge and placed him in an orphanage outside London. In late 1944, S.V. contracted bacterial endocarditis engrafted on the mitral valve previously scarred by rheumatic fever.

Knowing no cure for this illness, the doctors did not expect him to survive, but the rabbi did not accept their verdict. "How," he asked, "could one make sense of this? The Lord is not capricious in his actions"— a remark not unlike Einstein's, that God did not play dice with the universe. "After all," the rabbi continued, "the Lord intervened directly to spare this boy's life. He endowed him with immense prophetic power for a purpose. It is not God's will for him to die without reason in this wonderful free land of England."

The rabbi badgered the physicians with the same question over and over. "Are you sure there is no cure for this infection?" One doctor told him that there was a new miracle drug, penicillin, effective against endocarditis, but as the drug was in very short supply, it was restricted to use for military personnel. The rabbi inquired into the dispensation of penicillin. When informed that it came bottled as a powder which was poured into a large container of saline solution and then administered intravenously, he had an inspiration. The rabbi suggested that the hospital send telegrams, at his expense, to all British military installations, requesting the discarded bottles of penicillin. "What shall we do with the many empty bottles?" asked the puzzled doctor. "All you do," the rabbi replied, "is rinse them with a few milliliters of saline and inject the solution into my ward." He reasoned that a few crystals would adhere to the glass and the washout from thousands of such containers would provide enough penicillin to save the boy's life. The doctors did exactly as the rabbi prescribed, and S.V. made an unprecedented recovery.

S.V. remained well until 1970, when his heart valves began to deteriorate, leading to ever more disability and invalidism. His cardiologist urged valve replacement, but the patient demurred. One day the cardiologist announced with pomp that the eminent London surgeon Sir Donald Ross was prepared to do the operation. S.V. was unimpressed and said that he would decide for himself who was the right surgeon. Thereupon he sent letters of inquiry to many of the great cardiac surgeons worldwide: Michael DeBakey and Denton Cooley in Houston, Norman Shumway at Stanford, Christian Barnard in Capetown, John Kirklin in Birmingham, R. Barrat-Boyes in Auckland, and Gerald Austen in Boston.

S.V.'s British cardiologist had suggested that none of these eminent physicians would respond to his ignorant and arrogant missive, but S.V. received detailed answers from nearly all of them. None satisfied, however, and after much thought, deciding to have the operation in London, S.V. selected a young and outstanding Egyptian surgeon. A year later, S.V. showed me the responses from the cream of the world's cardiac surgeons. Most remarkable was that each had responded not only in substantial detail but tried to entice S.V. into becoming his patient.

Sometime later, when I questioned S.V. about his choice of cardiologists, he explained that he had refused to accept plastic valves in his heart, and only a very few surgeons had expertise with tissue valves. The most competent was Barrat-Boyes in New Zealand, which was too far away. Indeed, S.V. was prescient; if he had had plastic valves, he would not have tolerated the arrhythmia. The plastic prostheses could not have kept up with the ultra-rapid heart rates and most probably he would have died. As for his choice of the Egyptian surgeon, S.V.

reasoned that an Egyptian surgeon in London would have to make damn sure that his Jewish patient survived, especially after having been selected in preference to the distinguished Sir Donald Ross. Once again S.V. was correct. His hospital course was stormy, complications stalked one another, and the cardiac surgeon saved his life numerous times, going so far as to move a cot into S.V.'s room, where he slept for several critical postoperative nights.

"But why have you called on me?" I asked the rabbi. He indicated that S.V. had carefully researched this question, too, and concluded that there was only one doctor in the world who could correct his rapid heartbeat, namely, me. I persisted. "On what did he base this conclusion?" The rabbi became elliptical and asked me what portion of the Torah was being read that week. I had no idea. He elaborated. "The portion being read recounts how Joseph, not having seen his father, Jacob, for twenty-two years, meets him at last. And the Torah says Joseph cried, but Jacob was elated. Pray tell me, Doctor, why these varied responses of father and son during this joyous get-together?"

I shrugged my shoulders, once again at a loss.

The rabbi continued triumphantly. "The Talmud provides a profound psychological explanation. When Joseph met up with Jacob, he immediately realized the great wisdom of his father, and he cried for the years of lost opportunity for study and growing spiritually by exposure to this sage. But Jacob, having cried every day over those many years for his absent son, could now indulge in the joy of long-hoped-for reunion."

Still bewildered, I asked, "How is this relevant to me?"

"Like Joseph, you meet up with Jacob," the rabbi replied.

"Who then is S.V.? Is he some sort of *Lamedvovnik?*" I asked.*

---

* *Lamedvovnik* comes from the Cabala, an ancient rabbinic teaching which asserts that the earth is sustained by thirty-six righteous men chosen by God. In the Hebrew alphabet, letters have numeric equivalents, "lamed" corresponding to "thirty" and "vov" to "six."

"Could be, could be," the rabbi responded in a mystifying whisper, "but we would not know it; we could not know it. Indeed, S.V. himself would not know it. Only the Lord God would know. Mortal human beings can never fathom those secrets hidden away in the *Zohar* [the most important book of the cabalistic movement] which sustains the universe."

Many months elapsed and I put S.V. out of my mind. I had reasoned that he was too sick to undertake a trans-Atlantic journey, but hadn't fully appreciated his determination. On April 13, 1975, a London cardiologist flew with S.V. to Boston, where he was met at the airport by a New York rabbi who checked him into the Peter Bent Brigham. The experience of the next several weeks was rather painful, for I still had no solution to the problem. S.V. sat in his bed day after day, waiting for me to perform a miracle.

He knew not a soul in Boston, had no visitors, and as a vegetarian did not enjoy his meager hospital fare. I presumed his dietary restriction was related to his being kosher. His only diversion was to study the Talmud. As S.V. wore a yarmulke, I thought he might appreciate some spiritual consolation and informed an orthodox rabbi of S.V.'s plight. The next day, S.V. was incensed that I had breached his privacy. "Why do I need these religious fanatics?" he inquired angrily. He rebuffed many invitations from Hasidim, and though I encouraged him to leave the hospital for a few hours now and then, he was adamantly against it. I was at a loss to know what to do for him.

During S.V.'s long stay in the hospital, I began to gain some psychologic insight into this strange character. His conversations were frequently so outlandish that I thought his tongue permanently glued to his cheek, but S.V. rarely joked. On the contrary, there was a brooding and morbid seriousness about him, yet he was not depressed. He laughed readily, but with embarrassment, as though it were sinful. He was a committed hypochondriac with multiple system complaints, and answering his questions was as futile a task as severing a Hydra head — two more would sprout as soon as one had been cut off. He had a ready smile and seemed cherubic, yet, while smiling, he spoke of the tragedy of his current plight. Morbidly fascinated with the medical profession, he obtained the birth certificate of every physician who attended him and knew intimate, at times disconcerting details of their lives. He would flaunt these tidbits at appropriate moments.

Because of the persistent rapid ventricular rate in atrial fibrillation, I became suspicious that S.V. was not taking his digitalis drug, which was intended to slow the heartbeat. I questioned him carefully on this, but he answered evasively. He did relate that at the National Heart Hospital in London, he so distrusted the doctors that he would not take the prescribed medications. When he finally decided to try some, he first ran a screening test for drug safety. Many pigeons nested on the ledge outside his London hospital window. He mashed a quinidine pill into a powder, mixed it with bread crumbs, and placed it on the windowsill. After a pigeon pecked at it and shortly thereafter fell over dead, S.V. never took that particular medication. After learning of this practice, I made sure that a nurse was always in attendance when he took his drugs.

As weeks passed, I grew more despairing of ever finding an answer to S.V.'s problem. Late one evening I telephoned Boston's famous rabbi Joseph Soloveitchik. I didn't know him, but the great rabbi listened carefully to my presentation of the clinical facts and commented, "Doctor, this is a medical, not a theological problem."

S.V. was on my mind morning, noon, and night. I considered every possible permutation. I began to dislike him passionately. My sleep became restless. But as I awoke with a start at three o'clock one morning, the answer was staring me in the face. I could barely wait for dawn. When the hypothesis was tested, it worked. We were able to lower the heart rate drastically, to 70 beats per minute, by a combination of drugs administered intravenously. Now, would it work with oral medication? Indeed it did. S.V.'s heart rate remained slowed for twenty-four hours.

I entered my patient's room the next morning, feeling triumphant, expecting hosannas of praise and gratitude. None were forthcoming. Instead, with the grim visage that greeted me daily, S.V. stated, "I must admit not feeling too well."

"Why?" I asked sternly.

"Because of my rectal itch that you have ignored for months" was the unexpected answer.

I was about to commit mayhem, but confined my rage to stalking out of the room. After several hours I returned with an entourage of doctors and told S.V. that he was one of the more ungrateful characters it had been my ill fortune to encounter. "I long ago learned in doctoring that one cannot cure someone of the itch who loves to scratch," I continued. "Furthermore, many years of illness have so conditioned you to its secondary gains that you now dread being well. You will no longer be able to exploit many well-meaning people with your kvetching. Your ingratitude dwarfs an Alp." And having let go with the meanest diatribe I ever directed at a patient, I left the room without waiting for an alibi. The doctors accompanying me were astonished at my outburst. They had known me to be diplomatic even with the most difficult and provocative patients. Where was my tact, equanimity, and charity? I could sense them wondering.

The following day, S.V. was like a kitten. He apologized as he recalled a somewhat similar reaction from a British physician several years earlier. The doctor told him that he was uninterested in being further involved in S.V.'s care until he received a written explanation of the reasons why S.V. desired to get well.

Notwithstanding the newly won insight, and though he was now totally asymptomatic, S.V. refused to leave the hospital. He resumed his theatrical insistence that he was a dying man. Finally, I sent a cardiac fellow to pack S.V.'s belongings and move them to a nearby hotel, the Children's Inn. S.V. sheepishly followed, protesting all the way that this was no way to treat a critically ill patient.

His sojourn in Boston seemed interminable. S.V. insisted on frequent, if not daily, examinations, and a good part of my staff seemed to be in his employ. He brought chocolates, flowers, and perfumes to the secretaries on birthdays and in anticipation of birthdays. He took them to the Ritz, where they dined sumptuously. He showered some with expensive gifts. He knew all my plans and prided himself on intimate insight into my family life. He had become a bore and a grand nuisance.

When asked his plans for returning to London, S.V. responded that this would depend on my readiness to accompany him. I told him categorically that there was no likelihood of my ever doing so. He responded philosophically that he was ready to wait indefinitely, and it soon dawned on me that he was serious. When he learned that I was to lead a cardiologic delegation to Moscow, he urged me to book flights through London. However, the trip had already been arranged through Copenhagen, which was the assemblage point for the National Institutes of Health–sponsored delegation. S.V. kept droning on that London is on the way to Copenhagen, and nearly every other place on the globe.

I finally succumbed to his pleading, largely because of the intolerable thought that he might otherwise become a permanent fixture in my clinic. The change of flight plans was embarrassingly difficult to explain to the sponsoring agency that was picking up the tab. S.V. then struck again. Once the decision of traveling through London was secure, he launched his next demand in the form of a question. "What, pray, will I be able to do for twenty-four hours at Heathrow Airport, unless, of course, your intent is for me to desecrate the holy Sabbath?"

"What do you mean?" I asked, irritation dripping from every syllable.

He responded that since I had booked a day flight, we would be arriving Friday evening after sunset. Orthodox Jews are not permitted to travel or engage in any weekday activities for the twenty-four hours following sunset Friday, and he was not about to profane the holy Sabbath. He claimed he could not leave the airport, he could not buy food, he wasn't sure he could go to the bathroom since the toilet doors required coins, so he would be forced to sit quietly, starving throughout this long interlude. S.V. had turned my noble gesture into an ignoble sacrilege. Already having yielded on the fundamental demand of flying to London, I gave in once more and rebooked us on a night flight leaving Boston a day earlier.

On the eve of our departure, S.V. was driven to Boston's Logan Airport by the same New York rabbi who had accompanied him to the Brigham several months earlier. The rabbi appeared breathless and fatigued; apparently S.V. had demanded that they visit all the sights in Boston that he had so far missed. They went to the new aquarium, where S.V. insisted they climb to the very top rather than riding an elevator. Yet the rabbi was filled with gratitude for the privilege of being a sightseeing guide for the former invalid!

At the airport, Louise, my wife, took S.V. aside and suggested that he urge me to sleep, for "Dr. Lown has been up several nights in a row with sick patients and is bone weary." On the contrary, he told her, he planned to keep me awake the entire flight. "Thereby," he suggested in punctilious King's English, "Professor Lown will be afforded the opportunity to redress his dereliction in answering many urgent questions about my survival so far ignored." He thereupon pulled out a large three-ring, loose-leaf notebook "loaded with questions for the professor." As we were embarking, Louise informed me of S.V.'s plans for the trans-Atlantic crossing.

As soon as we were seated on the plane, I dramatically pulled off my wristwatch and held it close to S.V.'s eyes. "This is a stop watch," I said, enunciating every syllable. "I am starting it now. You have exactly one hour. If during this hour you repeat even a single question, your inquisition will be abruptly terminated."

S.V. appeared frantic. "You can't do this to me. I have waited weeks for this occasion. One of the major reasons for our flying together is for me to obtain answers vital for my survival. At least you must give me two hours to reorganize my questions." I agreed. He puttered for the two hours and when he indicated readiness, I started the stop watch. His questions were the very ones I had answered numerous times previously. When the hour was up, I turned my back to him, ready at last to catch a few winks of sleep. S.V., an insomniac, was not about to be left companionless. He tapped my shoulder and inquired whether I was ready to vindicate the honor of the medical profession. "It does not need vindication," I replied.

S.V. persisted. "Oh yes, it does."

"How so?"

"A doctor has never defeated me in chess," S.V. proclaimed.

"But I will," I blustered. I had not played chess for decades and my game, never very good, was rusty. He whipped out a chess set and we began. Within thirteen moves I had mated him. Claiming this was a fluke, he demanded a rematch. I agreed, and I mated him in eleven moves. When he insisted on another game, I indicated that I would savor this victory for the rest of my life and never give him the satisfaction of another game. He responded, "It is well worth my losing to have exposed a brutal facet of your personality. You are a tiger disguised as a caring physician."

There was no longer time to catch any sleep, as the sun peaked over the horizon, flooding the flight cabin with the bright morning light. The pilot announced that we would be landing at Heathrow in one hour. S.V. was wide awake and as energetic as though he had just been roused from a restful sleep. He alerted me to a new development: a luncheon had been arranged for me with some of S.V.'s London physicians at the Carlton Towers at about 12:30 P.M. that day. I could not bring myself to tell my supposedly disabled patient that I was too tired to join him for lunch, so I merely insisted on an hour's postponement, to which he magnanimously agreed. He was now in total command.

At 1:30 P.M., S.V. was waiting in a chauffeur-driven Bentley he had hired to transport us to the restaurant. The table was bedecked as for a banquet with mounds of food: caviar, sturgeon, fowl, beef, and other goodies, as well as wines that included Château Mouton Rothschild and great Burgundies. Disappointingly, none of S.V.'s London doctors inquired how his remarkable recovery had been brought about. There was great interest, however, in some new technologic advances emerging from the Brigham Hospital at the time. At the end of the luncheon, S.V. urged a walk to aid digestion. He himself had barely touched any of the food.

We walked, seemingly for hours. I felt drugged. When we reached Harrod's department store, S.V.'s favorite haunt in London, clerks and saleswomen greeted him warmly. They were aware that he had just returned from the States and complimented him on his robust appearance. He consistently responded that appearances were deceptive, declaiming, like a refrain from Gilbert and Sullivan, "But I am a very sick man." As we ambled through the huge department store, S.V. announced loudly to everyone we met, "This is my American doctor, Professor Lown from Harvard." Late in the afternoon I was finally liberated. I had been with S.V. almost continuously for twenty-four hours. It would take me more than a week to recover.

On August 10, 1975, S.V. wrote to me.

Boston was an eye-opener and indeed most refreshing. To have had the opportunity to observe you in action at close quarters, seeing a far more scientific approach to cardiology than what I had become used to, leaves me standing in awe of and respect for your immeasurable accomplishments.

I have had opportunity to observe many cardiologists in my life, but never experienced the personal interest, humanity, and warmth which I received from you and — through your influence — from your team. My gratitude is greater than I can adequately express.

Earlier that June, he had written to my secretary.

Traveling back with Dr. Lown was a very nice and interesting experience. . . . None of us got any sleep. . . . Poor man, he really went through a Gestapo type of an interrogation, and with nowhere to escape to. I questioned him about his family, parents, uncles, brothers, wife, children, and went to his views on religion, or lack of it, politics, where he does hold strong views, etc. . . . and then I made a big mistake, by asking him to play chess . . . It was interesting to watch this kind and gentle man suddenly become transformed. . . . He plays a fast, strong, sharp, gambling, ruthless type of game . . . I must admit the guy made mincemeat out of me.

S.V. made several trips to Boston over thirteen years. He required numerous adjustments in drugs, but perhaps the main reason for these costly visits was to receive counsel on a host of personal issues. He acted like an obedient teenager seeking parental advice. Above all else, he needed assurance that he would survive. However unhesitating my encouragement, the certainty of my words dissipated over the course of several months. We conversed frequently by telephone, and when I tried to discourage a visit, he would begin to talk of my wishing to be rid of him since his prognosis was now so bleak. He kept this up with increasing stridency until I relented and agreed to see him.

I avoided informing S.V. of my visits to London, but each time he found out. When he had enough advance notice, he would plan some lavish entertainment. Once it involved the opening season of the opera, a formal and splendid event. We had a box in the royal circle close to the Queen Mother accompanied by Prince Charles. I later learned that this was a benefit with the least expensive seats going for £100, then about $180. S.V. had booked a box with ten seats. Where he got his money was a tightly held secret.

Several times I tried to keep my secretaries in the dark as to my travel plans to London or where I would be staying. It did little good — he always found me. I recall one night arriving in London and switching hotels at the last moment, feeling that at last S.V. had been outfoxed. On entering the room, I saw, with a sinking feeling, a vase with elegant roses with S.V.'s embossed greeting card. Spooked, I spent a sleepless night with the light on, feeling as though S.V. was in the room watching me.

Thirteen years after I had first encountered S.V., he continued, against all medical odds, to do well. His survival was no small miracle and I was mystified by it and by everything else about him. Who was S.V.? Where did he derive his abundant resources without ever working? Why did people always come to his rescue? What constituted his power over others? Why were so many people deferential and fond of him? Was he indeed a *Lamedvovnik,* one of the holy Thirty-six for whom nothing was impossible?

Sometime in late January 1987, while hectically preparing for a major trip to Moscow in February, I felt compelled to write down S.V.'s story. No sooner was it finished than I received a telephone call from S.V.'s cardiologist in London. On February 1, S.V. had felt unwell and experienced a high fever during the night. He was seen immediately. There was nothing to suggest bacterial endocarditis, but blood cultures a few days later grew staphylococcus. He was hospitalized and promptly started on intravenous and intramuscular antibiotics. The next day, however, he was in septic shock and kidney failure and required a circulatory assistance device to maintain a semblance of blood pressure. In an emergency heart operation, his Egyptian surgeon found serious valve disruption from infectious endocarditis. Both mitral and aortic valves were replaced with appropriate prostheses. S.V. went off bypass readily but then developed rapid atrial fibrillation, the very arrhythmia that was the basis for my initial consultation. With the onset of rapid heart action, his precarious clinical condition rapidly unraveled. He was given a large dose of an antiarrhythmic drug intravenously, but died almost instantly thereafter.

S.V.'s death left me with a gnawing ache, a feeling of emptiness, of something ill defined but essentially missing. I had lost a point of eccentric reference that had punctuated my life with inexplicable unpredictability and yes, security. Why, though I was dreadfully busy in mid-January, had I felt compelled to draft S.V.'s story? Why at that time? Why could it not wait? Was I writing because I "knew" S.V. was sick, which he must already have been, even before he sought medical help? By writing his story did I terminate S.V.'s life, because *Lamedvovniks* can never be exposed?

His life in England had ended the way it had begun, with bacterial endocarditis. The immediate cause of death was uncontrolled atrial fibrillation, the very arrhythmia that had brought us together thirteen years earlier. The number 13 is holy and charged with cabalistic significance for orthodox Jews.

My secretary, who knew him well, had kept S.V. informed of my whereabouts. When I tried to talk with her about S.V., she would only say, "He was a very mysterious man."

To this day I continue to puzzle at the seismic effect he exerted on me and others. It reflected a complex interaction residing in a province where science has little dominion. His story is an example of the extraordinary relationships a doctor weaves with some patients and how drastically life is thereby transformed.

VI

The Art of

Being a Patient

§

19

Getting Doctors to Listen

A DOCTOR MUST rely on the art of human understanding to amplify the insights provided by science. A patient likewise must cultivate a special art, that of dealing with a physician. Whereas the medical transaction is largely concerned with curing a disease, the patient craves to be healed. The object of the patient's art is to have the doctor incorporate healing in the process of curing.

To heal requires a relationship marked by equality — a key element in a sound doctor-patient relationship — and reciprocal respect. This is not automatically granted by either; it needs to be earned. Without respect, a doctor cannot gain a patient's trust. Respect is not the mush of language. As the essayist Anatole Broyard, dying of cancer, commented about his doctor, "I don't trust anyone who tells me that he loves me when he doesn't even know me." The patient desires to be known as a human being, not merely to be recognized as the outer wrappings for a disease. Only the patient is capable of widening the doctor's focus to encompass the larger domain of the person who is ailing. Therein resides the art.

While doctors differ from one another as much as individuals do, there are nonetheless some principles that are broadly applicable to the art of being a patient. First, in my view, is the need to lower expectations of what medicine can do without reducing respect for the medical practitioner. While miracles have been wrought by scientific medicine, it is important to understand that science, while seemingly unbounded, will always be constrained in dealing with the human condition. Irrespective of the expansion in medical knowledge, there will always remain huge lacunae of ignorance. Medicine will never be able to prevent death, or the deteriorations of age, or fully repair the consequences of severe traumatic accidents, or totally correct some birth defects. Many other conditions will long evade definitive cure.

At present, scientific medicine, even in a narrower sense, lacks precise solutions to most chronic ailments such as arthritis, heart disease, neurodegenerative disorders, autoimmune disease, and most cancers. While the scientific pace is quickening, we have a long way to go before these major disorders are fully understood. In the absence of a cure, these diseases require management, usually over a lifetime. The only available medical approach is to assuage symptoms, to slow and where possible halt a downhill course, to help the patient maintain a positive outlook, and to prevent the disease from taking charge of his or her life. These goals can be achieved only when patient expectations are narrowly focused on the attainable.

An exaggerated attitude toward the potential of medicine proves self-defeating. In this age of hype, patients come to expect the impossible. They are not readily satisfied with mere abatement of symptoms but frequently demand nonexistent cures. Pretensions of the health care industry and the godly posturing of some doctors contribute to such unreasonable expectations. Theatrical illusions are promoted by an unwholesome dynamic between hyperbolic professional claims and the public's inflated hopes.

Unreal expectations heighten dissatisfaction for many who find that their conditions are not diagnosable, yet in my experience the vast majority of symptoms lack exact explanations. The medical community has partially resolved this problem by devising a host of meaningless diagnostic labels that mask ignorance rather than illuminate an underlying cause.

In *The Doctor's Dilemma*, George Bernard Shaw generalized that "all professions are conspiracies against the laity." Deliberate deception is not the basis for these charades, however. Denial is humankind's defense against the ubiquity of ignorance. For example, when a doctor affixes the name essential hypertension to an illness that afflicts an estimated 50 million Americans, the patient presupposes it to be a specific, well-defined, fully understood disorder. Alas, the word "essential," in the peculiar medical parlance, means "I don't have the foggiest notion of the cause." Doctors frequently grope in the dark, not because they are delinquent in learning, but because the science is not there.

The weaker the science, the more creative the diagnostic labels become. There are fashions in medicine as in clothing. For example, people from time immemorial have experienced such constellations of symptoms as weakness, constant exhaustion, low-grade fever, sore throat, arthritic pains, memory deficits, headaches, and sleep disturbance. At present a patient with these symptoms is often diagnosed as having chronic fatigue syndrome, or CFS. However, CFS is merely an arbitrary descriptor rather than a well-defined entity. The symptoms probably arise from a host of diverse diseases, including viral illness as well as immunologic, neuroendocrinologic, psychologic, and psychiatric disorders. Placing such heterogeneous symptoms, stemming from a diversity of unrelated conditions, under one rubric does not advance understanding of the pathophysiology of the illness. On the contrary, the designation fosters confusion and retards the possibility of a cure. Worse still, the afflicted person is left in limbo. In the absence of organically identified illness, doctors tend to convey the impression that the patient harbors a character disorder rather than a disabling, tormenting disease.

Cardiology, the discipline I have practiced over a lifetime, is full of such imaginative diagnostic designations. When a patient who has an innocuous heart murmur experiences palpitation, chest discomfort, and various expressions of anxiety, the current fad is to diagnose mitral valve prolapse syndrome, or MVP. The association of these symptoms is not new. One hundred and sixty years ago, a Nottingham, England, physician, John Calthrop Williams, described the very same entity as "nervous and sympathetic palpitations of the heart." During the American Civil War, it became identified by the eponym DaCosta's syndrome. Over the ensuing decades, a similar symptom complex was successively designated as irritable heart, soldier's heart, neurocirculatory asthenia, hyperventilation syndrome, and hyperkinetic heart.

With the advent of the powerfully insightful technique of ultrasonography, it was observed that in some of these patients the mitral valve billowed during the heart's contraction, and this entity took off. Hence the new diagnosis, mitral valve prolapse, was launched; the physiologic deviation was presumed to be an abnormality and was promptly transformed into a disease. All types of malign outcomes were ascribed to MVP, thereby justifying medical intervention. The fact that 99.9 percent of patients with MVP lived long and normal lives was ignored although the condition was no more hazardous to one's health than freckles.

This is but another example of a fashion carrying the day, driven in part by the fact that the human brain does not tolerate incomprehension of causality and invents the spurious to avoid a vacuum. A poor explanation is considered preferable to confessing ignorance. In reality, a designation of MVP, like DaCosta's syndrome more than a century ago, is a meaningless diagnostic wastebasket.

The same compulsion to provide an explanation accounts for the prevalent medical practice of ascribing any odd symptom to a viral or postviral illness, a hardy diagnosis. It is unassailable, not readily disprovable, reassuringly benign, and sooner rather than later symptoms disappear without a trace. Such sleight of hand, when not harmful — as it would be in the case of essential hypertension, which if untreated results in a host of life-endangering cardiovascular complications — is not without some redeeming social value. In fact, both patient and doctor may gain from the gamesmanship of diagnostic labeling. For the patient who receives such a nonsensical diagnosis, there may be the satisfaction that being pigeonholed is but a short step from being cured. It is also psychologically valuable for the doctor, who, in rendering a diagnosis, generates respect and remains in unquestioned control. Of course, if the condition continues unrelieved, the patient's dissatisfaction focuses on the physician. When endless tests and costly technologic probing do not offer an instant cure, the failure is blamed on the physician rather than on a deficiency in scientific understanding.

The patient has to understand that many discomforts stem not from disease but from the rough-and-tumble of living. In our death-denying culture, individuals are grimly determined to purchase happiness at any cost. The sooner patients understand that doctors are not in the happiness-promoting business, the greater their likelihood of being helped. The psychiatrist Viktor Frankel, a former Auschwitz inmate, proposed that there is such a reality as negative happiness; it is the freedom from suffering. Competent doctors are more in their element in relieving suffering than in purveying happiness.

We also turn to medicine to repair what essentially are tears in the social fabric wrought by violence, economic oppression, class ostracism, racism, sexism, and a host of other factors. In a consumer culture, in which nearly everything is treated as an article of consumption, medicalization is the response to mounting social frustrations. Dissatisfactions with one's job or marriage or children, or with one's lot in life, are not uncommonly somaticized. Most doctors do not have the time, patience, training, or incentives to become involved in these societal quagmires, and their inattention leads patients to shop around for a quick fix. Unless they encounter an empathic physician who helps assuage symptoms, focuses on the potential source of the problem, and teaches them how to endure life's constraints, these troubled people increasingly turn to alternative medicine, with many falling prey to charlatans.

The sophisticated patient, who is neither taken in by the hype nor succumbs to medical fads, can, I believe, master the art of navigating through our far from perfect health care system. The chronically ill patient should question the doctor, not with the intent of mastering the rudiments of physiology or biochemistry of an illness but to gain clarity in coping with a chronic problem that requires highly personalized answers. The doctor should be able to answer the following six questions in a straightforward way that provides the patient with substantial insights on how to live with an illness:

1. Are the symptoms from a precisely understood medical entity for which a definitive cure exists?
2. If the disease is not curable, can symptoms nonetheless be ameliorated?
3. If a disease is life threatening, what is the approximate life expectancy?
4. If not life threatening, is the disease likely to plateau or progress? If so, over what time frame?
5. Are there attendant complications and how are these to be mitigated, or better still, prevented? If that is a possibility, at what compromise in living?
6. Will a change in one's lifestyle make a substantial difference in outcome in relation to well-being and survival?

The doctor may not be able to provide exact answers, but even approximations are valuable. In this respect, it broadens understanding to appreciate that while a doctor's knowledge may be extraordinarily precise for predicting what would happen to a thousand patients with a given condition, as the denominator becomes smaller, accuracy in prediction attenuates exponentially. It nearly disappears when the sample size recedes to unity, namely, when the doctor is called to prophesy outcome for a single individual. It is difficult to apply statistics to an individual patient. The unique challenge in doctoring is to determine where, if anywhere, a particular patient fits on the Gaussian distribution curve derived from a larger population. The decisive factor is the physician's breadth of clinical experience. If a patient's problem remains unresolved after many months, it is worth seeking a physician who has more experience with that particular diagnostic problem.

With a wealth of medical experience, the doctor develops a complex template in higher centers of the brain. Comparing each patient to that template, largely subconsciously, the doctor engages in an act of discovery, at times extraordinarily creative, which may expose approaches that permit previously unattainable and seemingly miraculous outcomes.

My argument has now come full circle. In typically human fashion, I seem to be contradicting what I argued at the outset. While I began by emphasizing the need to lower medical expectations, I have come to embrace the possibility of miracles. The contradiction is more apparent than real. Even when cure is impossible, healing is not necessarily impossible. While medical science has limits, hope does not. I believe the maxim proposed by Dr. Edward Trudeau about a century ago: "To cure sometimes, to relieve often, to comfort always." The miracles reside in the capacity for comforting and healing.

This was brought home to me by Mrs. J., a well-composed, articulate woman in her mid-seventies. Over the preceding five years, she had become increasingly disabled with weekly paroxysms of atrial fibrillation, although a multiplicity of tests revealed a structurally sound heart. Several drugs tried singly or in combination were largely unavailing, and a number of them caused troublesome complications. The episodes of arrhythmia left her drained for days, and fear of unpredictable recurrences circumscribed her activities and kept her homebound. As I listened to her problem, it was eminently clear to me that no stone had been left unturned. I could think of no easy measures to effect a cure, and I was therefore astonished to hear myself express a certainty of resolving her problem. I did, however, leave a clever escape hatch by indicating that it would take time.

When Mrs. J. returned some months later, the problem was largely ameliorated. I was impressed with this remarkable turnabout, though the basis was self-evident. I had reassured her that the arrhythmia, while troubling, was not dangerous, and I had discontinued many of the drugs that were responsible for a host of symptoms previously ascribed to the heart. She was now able to sleep through the night, and with more sleep, arrhythmic recurrences were reduced in severity. I had prescribed a larger dose of digitalis whenever a paroxysm did emerge, so that her heart rate during the arrhythmia was slowed and the bout became more tolerable. While the fundamental problem remained unresolved, she was able to resume a normal lifestyle.

Yet I could not give myself credit for the outcome. The patient herself had largely effected the extraordinary change. She could be helped because she had become reconciled to an improvement rather than a cure. She welcomed small changes for the better and was ready to exploit these to the hilt. I could expeditiously come to grips with essentials because she was sharply focused and not hypochondriacal.

If a patient is ready to be helped, even a little, and grateful for the marginal, it enhances the doctor's commitment to fostering a relationship between equals. Only such a relationship, bonded by understanding and respect, can deepen into a true healing partnership. This encourages, in the words of Lewis Thomas, "the capacity for affection," the essential element for healing.

Ludwig Mies van der Rohe said of architecture, "God is in the details." This is true of medicine as well. One may, with good reason, feel helpless when confronting a medical care juggernaut, and indeed it would be foolhardy to expect a human dimension from a heavily bureaucratized system. To navigate successfully around the shoals of the health care system demands extraordinary insight, skill, patience, and forbearance. In the present environment of managed care, even these admirable qualities may not prove sufficient. The focus of the system, as it has become an industrial behemoth, has shifted from attending the sick to guarding the economic bottom line, putting itself on a collision course with professional doctoring. Defining individual medical and human problems requires time, but in a counterproductive effort to contain costs, the doctor is pressured to minimize the time invested with each patient. Giving precedence to profits sacrifices both physician autonomy and the patient's right to know and to exercise available therapeutic options. It also makes for more expensive health care in the long run.

The monumental transformations occurring in health care have been accompanied by a cacophony of discourse purporting respect for patient autonomy and commitment to patient empowerment. Frequently these are spelled out in patient's bill of rights documents. The high-sounding rhetoric goes hand in hand with the actual attenuation of these hallowed rights. Hospital ombudsmen and medical ethicists are recruited to buff the jagged edges of an impersonal system.

The foremost objective of the system is cost containment, and to accomplish this, hospitals create vast bureaucracies of economic managers, accountants, and lawyers, now grown more numerous than the health care providers. Efficiency becomes the byword dictating homogenization in dealing with any and all patient problems. Standard clinical guidelines and computer-driven algorithms define automatic courses of action for specified diagnostic categories. Such standardization, driven largely by economics, has other putative though ancillary objectives, such as improving quality of health care delivery, reducing costly medical errors, minimizing unnecessary procedures, and creating uniform databases for assessing and comparing clinical outcomes. Physicians who do not adhere to the guidelines are disciplined by economic disincentives and threats of job loss. In this environment, doctors increasingly become technicians leashed to assembly lines, the aim of which is to maximize patient throughput.

While indeed difficult, it is by no means impossible for an informed patient to obtain better personal care by exploiting the contradictions inherent in the system of managed care. First, the fact that doctors still have a central role as gatekeepers provides some latitude for maneuver. They are the triage officers directing the flow of human traffic to diverse procedures, to other specialists, and to hospitals. These professional sentinels generally are uncomfortable with the system and have been educated, if sometimes imperfectly, to address the individuality of each patient. They are ill prepared to view patients as an assemblage of clones. The majority of doctors take pride in being competent and deeply crave recognition as dedicated professionals. Some mileage can therefore be derived from playing on these qualities.

Another factor is that, in a market environment, the system is eager for the public to view health care as a service industry which considers customer contentment as paramount. The capacity to attract new subscribers to a health maintenance organization (HMO), an overarching goal of management, depends on a reasonable level of satisfaction among existing members. Those in command devote mammoth resources to being perceived as dedicated to the greater good. The HMOs' allergy to poor publicity affords patients leverage for manipulating the system.

Within this new framework of health care, the initial visit assumes even more decisive importance than in the past. Doctor and patient are afforded their first opportunity to take a measure of each other. At the outset, both must be committed to building a solid and enduring relationship. The doctor needs to come rapidly to terms with what ails the patient, to define the procedures and tests required to confirm a presumptive diagnosis, and to set a therapeutic course promptly. It may lead to referrals to other doctors, to invasive interventions, and possibly to hospitalization.

The launching of the diagnostic trajectory is stirred by the patient, who is the only repository of all relevant information. Whether a sound or hasty judgment is rendered depends on how the patient informs the doctor during the initial visit. The patient is better served when he or she is clear on the objectives of the visit and presents them lucidly. Simply stated, the purpose of the first visit is generally twofold: to focus the doctor's attention on the correct medical problem and to engage his or her sympathy for the sick person. The latter is all important. The ease of such engagement is a litmus test for the compatibility of personal chemistries and indicates whether a relationship of reciprocal respect is possible.

In this first encounter the patient is well served by being exquisitely attentive to the preciousness of time. Many elderly retirees, accustomed to a great deal of free time, are unable to function well in a time-intensive environment. Some do not fully comprehend the pressure cooker atmosphere of a modern clinic, which is overbooked with patients and constantly urged to increase "productivity." While the patient can hardly alter the system, attentiveness to conserving time at least serves to gain the doctor's sympathetic attention immediately.

Much experience teaches me that a doctor's initial assessment is contoured not by the medical problem alone but by indefinable qualities of either annoyance or gratification in dealing with a particular individual. The doctor's emotional reaction is not formed by insights into character but is shaped by trivial, even superficial impressions relating to whether the patient is long-winded, tiresome, meandering, and repetitious or direct and well-organized. In no small measure, these have bearing on the time factor and the doctor's constant disquiet about disrupting an already overstretched schedule.

Since first impressions are enduring, it is not a good idea to ensconce oneself in a chair in a doctor's consultation room as though invited for a leisurely cup of afternoon tea. If the doctor gets an inkling that a long séance is in the offing, much of his or her thinking becomes preoccupied with short-shrifting the visit rather than solving the medical problem. What immediately puts the doctor on a counterproductive alert is a relaxed patient clutching a thick sheaf of notes. Much is to be gained by an initial wholesome impression. Entering the room briskly without loitering to examine diplomas and the knickknacks invariably cluttering a doctor's desk, or indulging in small talk, sets the proper stage for a serious discourse. It begins to shape the ambience in which a relationship of mutual respect can be forged.

The unfocused patient fares poorly. The worst effect is being pigeonholed into one or another diagnostic category that bears little relevance to the actual problem. The consequences can be tragic, leading to the prescription of inappropriate drugs, to being tracked to unwarranted investigations, and worse still, to being subjected to unnecessary life-threatening invasive procedures. It is sinful to hold the victim accountable; the misdemeanor, exclusively the doctor's, is unjustified whatever the circumstances. Yet no amount of moral indignation will rapidly alter the present health care system. A patient's awareness of the potential mayhem affords some insurance against being thus victimized.

Let me stress once more the critical importance of the patient's focusing precisely on the essential problem. Such concentration is facilitated by thinking through the specific reasons for seeking medical help, what doctors refer to as the chief complaint. It is best to develop a clear description of the primary bothersome symptom before, rather than during the visit. Frequently the lists of complaints are a hodgepodge of trivia, huge haystacks in which are hidden but few needles of relevant information. It is understandable that having waited weeks for an appointment, one is eager to unburden totally, but in my view this is a serious error. If the complaints are multiple, especially when they seem unrelated, one is in danger of being categorized as a hypochondriac, or as having a "psychosomatic" problem, or worse, being labeled with a pejorative term such as "turkey" and the like. From the moment a patient's problem is trivialized it grows intractable.

Conserving time requires thinking through the essential problem and how it can be most succinctly presented. This is frequently difficult even for the most articulate and intelligent person. The language of dysfunctional organs is not readily translatable into English or any other spoken tongue. Adjectives fall far short in conveying bodily sensations. Patients frequently offer a presumed diagnosis suggested by a neighbor, or more often, by a health report in the media. The patient's motivation — aiming to help a doctor come quickly to terms with what is wrong — though sound, is nonetheless mistaken. The patient may be ill served as a result. The harassed doctor, pressured to shorten the time spent with the patient, may accept a self-diagnosis without further analysis.

One experience illustrates the mayhem wrought by self-diagnosis. Mrs. T., a woman in her mid-eighties, had been completely crippled by postural hypotension for the past five years. Each time she stood, dizziness and light-headedness caused a near faint. She became bedridden, burdening family and growing depressed as a result. She was on a bevy of drugs for angina that indubitably contributed to the drop in blood pressure when she stood.

Initially I did not question the appropriateness of the prescribed medicines, since she had been seen by an experienced cardiologist. On careful discussion, however, it was evident that this woman did not have angina; her chest pain was caused by arthritic and musculoskeletal problems.

I tried to determine how the diagnosis of angina had been arrived at, and the patient admitted to having suggested it to the doctor. Comparing notes with a friend who had experienced a recent coronary heart attack and suffered thereafter from angina pectoris, Mrs. T. grew convinced that her problem was identical. After further discussion with her sick friend, she absorbed some of the appropriate descriptive terms. On the initial visit she told the cardiologist that she was certain her condition was due to angina. The doctor, without questioning this intelligent woman, prescribed the usual antianginal fare. Since none of the medicines helped, more drugs were added on many subsequent visits. When she became totally disabled, Mrs. T. sought a second opinion from me. When all medicines were discontinued, the vertigo and the other symptoms disappeared, except for the chest pain, which she now took in stride.

Many patients have lost their lives by ascribing their rectal bleeding to hemorrhoids because an unwary doctor accepted this diagnosis instead of identifying a colonic cancer. The most common self-diagnosis, however, is the more harmless hiatus hernia, a ubiquitous, exclusively benign condition. But even this diagnostic designation may be far from innocuous, as it may misdirect the doctor from seriously lurking problems that should have been more fully investigated. There is no excuse for a doctor's not going beyond a patient's labeling of a problem. Nonetheless, it is worth paraphrasing a common warning, *caveat aeger*, "let the patient beware." Avoiding the role of accomplice in self-victimization is a modest first step.

The patient is far better served by presenting the doctor with an accurate description of symptoms, detailing their time of occurrence, indicating their duration, describing the possible precipitating factors and the measures that afford relief. Such sharply presented facts are likely to put the doctor quickly on the right road.

Another ploy to avoid is having a doctor adjudicate between different opinions of several specialists already consulted. Some patients begin a visit by asking whether one agrees with doctor one or two, or even three. I have often been asked, "Would you please explain why Dr. A totally disagreed with Dr. B?" as if resolving the presumed contradictory counsel would illuminate the patient's problem. It is frequently difficult enough to explain why one reached a particular judgment without second- and third-guessing other doctors' conclusions.

As the interview proceeds, the doctor tries to fathom what exactly is going on. The task is challenging and demands the patient's straightforward, succinct responses. But often these are not forthcoming. "How many pillows do you sleep on?" is a simple question amenable to a single-word answer. Yet circumlocutions such as, "When I had my retinal operation I had to sleep flat, that was ten years ago. Later when I suffered from hiatus hernia, I used three."

"What about now?" is the tired follow-through.

"I use one."

At times the journey to the correct answer is far more circuitous. Clinical narratives are best avoided, as are disquisitions about the remote past. Not everything that happened is worth remembering and far less is worth repeating. The shorter and more direct the answer, the less likely the patient is to be subjected to an assault of mindless technology. Doctors have learned, I believe incorrectly, to regard technology as a cost-effective substitute for time spent with patients.

The patient should also avoid posing general medical questions that have little bearing on the problem at hand. If one wishes to enrich one's understanding of medicine, it is preferable to take university extension courses or read medical textbooks. Even then it is better to avoid becoming a minidoctor. A prevailing misconception is that mastering the rudiments of anatomy or endocrinology, or whatever medical subdiscipline, prepares one to deal more intelligently with a physician or better defend oneself as a patient. Both suppositions are wrong. Being tutored in the anatomy of the coronary circulation does not enable one to cope more effectively with ischemic heart disease. Such ideas are promoted by medical industrial complexes which, whether by intention or happenstance, promote medical consumerism by breeding unbridled hypochondriasis.

In a sense, minidoctoring and promoting such avenues of questioning express distrust for the medical profession and are so perceived even if the intent is completely innocent. Physicians, even when surcharged with ample Samaritan virtues, take unkindly to such distractions. The art of being a patient involves eschewing such cul de sacs.

Patients should take their medicines with them. It is better still if, when asked what drugs are being used, a patient can reel off the exact medical names, the precise dosages, and when during the day they are consumed. The doctor then concludes that the patient is either intelligent or potentially litigious. In either case the result will be salutary and treatment will be far more respectful than it would have been otherwise. Being well informed about the prescribed medication protects the patient from receiving the very same class of drugs produced by some other pharmaceutical company but bearing a different name. The patient's interest is further protected when he or she keeps a detailed record of adverse drug reactions encountered. This diminishes the chance of being prescribed a similar drug with potential serious toxicity.

To get the most out of the system, a patient should always be accompanied by a significant other or family member, preferably a spouse. The other person helps the patient remember what has been discussed, concluded, and prescribed. The presence of a family member or friend gives the patient more courage to question the doctor about the rationale for procedures, tests, and the like. In this respect a few fundamental questions are always in order.

1. Is the test or procedure indispensable to confirm or disprove the diagnosis the doctor has already reached? Or is it merely a preliminary reconnoitering that will require many more such tests?
2. Whatever the findings of the testing, will they alter the way a disease is managed?
3. Finally, how expensive are the tests and will they be reimbursed by insurance?

For example, if a doctor suggests a cardiac catheterization, or whatever, one should not waste time with whys. The doctor has precooked standard answers, generally intoned with near-ecclesiastic authority, that in a scientific age, "medicine must be guided by precise information." A more relevant question is whether the condition can be effectively treated without the anatomic information provided by the costly invasive procedure. If the answer is no, the doctor does not know how to treat one adequately without information about the anatomy of the coronary arteries, that doctor, in my view, is usually either a poor clinician or an overspecialized technician. In either case one should seek a second opinion. Whether to pursue another judgment depends on the seriousness of the suggested intervention. For example, if a large lymph node is discovered or the patient has blood in the stool, it would be reasonable for a doctor to recommend a biopsy for the former or a colonoscopy for the latter. However, it would merely waste time and increase cost to run tests to confirm the obvious and the necessary. In the case of a cardiac catheterization, this test is invariably the first in an inexorable cascade of invasive approaches involving potentially life-threatening procedures. Moreover, coronary heart disease can be effectively treated by a host of benign noninvasive methods that do not require knowledge of the precise coronary anatomy.

In today's technology-driven health care system, a patient cannot passively accept a doctor's decisions. A full partnership is the objective, but with rights come duties. A paramount obligation is adherence to the agreed program. A patient's careful records of what happens informs a caring physician whether the medical agenda is sound or requires course corrections.

CHOOSING A DOCTOR

There are a few practical guidelines to follow in finding a good doctor. Obviously, one wishes to choose a physician well trained in medical science who keeps informed about the latest advances. Any graduate of a first-class medical school should be well versed in the fundamentals, skilled in recognizing a curable illness, and knowledgeable about how best to effect a cure. But that is hardly adequate. Some doctors may have great names but rub one the wrong way. The chemistries between doctor and patient must be compatible. The patient must feel as at ease with the doctor as with an intimate friend.

A few small clues can help to decide whether a doctor is one with whom a patient can be comfortable, can grow to respect, and in time learn to trust on matters of life and death. When meeting a patient, does a doctor shake hands? This gesture is a small first sign that the doctor wants to reach out to the patient. The lack of a handshake may not justify a loss of faith, but it would earn a negative value in a checklist. Punctuality should be a serious determinant of a physician's human qualities, for it fundamentally signals respect for another person. Respect for a patient's time is a significant indicator of qualities required for a partnership in healing. Being consistently late is generally attributable to managerial sloppiness, poor planning, excessive overbooking, unwarranted indifference to the time of others, and an expectation, common among doctors, that the patient will assume the doctor was unavoidably detained by a far sicker patient. True emergencies are rarely the cause for doctors' habitual lateness.

One also has to look askance at a doctor who allows an interview to be interrupted by telephone calls. I have forbidden my secretary to interrupt me except for a dire emergency. Interestingly, months can go by without a single intrusion. There is ample time to respond to genuine emergencies between patient visits.

A doctor's disposition and demeanor, in my mind, should be a decisively important factor in selecting a physician. The doctor should radiate affirmation and optimism. Three centuries ago, Jonathan Swift advised, "The best doctors in the world are Doctor Diet, Doctor Quiet, and Doctor Merryman." One should expect affirmation even when no cure is in sight and the trajectory is worsening deterioration. At all times there remain interventions that can lessen the intense ache of a terminal illness. The very sick, while not taken in by phony optimism, are eager for a warm touch and the caress of human concern.

An important factor is whether a doctor is ready and able to listen. Several studies have shown that physicians typically interrupt their patients every fifteen to thirty seconds. The message conveyed is of impatience, of time pressure, or of lack of interest in what is uppermost in the patient's mind. Open-ended questions indicate a readiness to explore pressing concerns. The physician who repeats and summarizes what has been said confirms that he or she is a well-tutored and good listener.

Trust in a doctor is also fostered by the thoroughness of history-taking, by questions about work and other relevant social issues, by commiseration with minor losses, and by expressions of genuine solicitude for serious problems. The doctor should win points for acting as though he or she has all the time in the world, even though the patient will surely be aware that many other patients are waiting to be seen.

One should be wary of a doctor who, at the very outset, puts a guilt trip on a patient by such locutions as, "Why did you wait so long?" "If I only had seen you earlier," and so on. One could justifiably harbor reservations regarding such a doctor's aptitude to heal.

A doctor who employs words that maim, even in jest, should receive a low rating. Mrs. N., nearing ninety, was usually jovial, but one day, for the first time, she appeared in my office in a state of depression. She had just visited a gynecologist.

"Did he find any serious problem?" I asked.

"Oh no," she replied, "it was merely what he said." She elaborated. The doctor had asked what she was doing there, to which she inquired, "Where should I be?"

He answered, with a laugh, "At your age, you should be dead."

A doctor who has a patient disrobe totally is probably superior in thoroughness. When the examination includes viewing eye grounds and the arterial pulses in the feet, with a pause on the way to palpate and auscult other organs, the physician is probably a competent practitioner. But a quality more valuable even than thoroughness in the physical examination is a doctor's readiness to acknowledge error without equivocating. It should be evident to an intelligent patient that the practice of medicine is not an exact science. Mistakes are inevitable even among the most conscientious professionals adhering to the highest of standards. The public admission of mistakes is the best way to minimize their recurrence and is usually a sign of a capacity for first-rate doctoring.

The problem of frequent referrals to specialists also deserves comment, for it is not a recent issue. A century ago, Dostoevski complained, in *The Brothers Karamazov,*

> And then they have that way, nowadays, of sending you to a specialist: "I can only diagnose your trouble, but if you go to see such and such a specialist, he'll know how to cure it." I tell you the old doctor who could cure you of every illness has all but vanished and you find nothing but specialists these days, and they even advertise in newspapers.

If the problem was then in its infancy, it has now grown out of bounds. When a doctor is sparing in the use of procedures and refrains from multiple referrals to subspecialists, yet is ready to acknowledge the limits of his or her own knowledge, a high rating is in order. The modern physician, being superlatively trained technically, should not function merely as a policeman for directing patient traffic to diverse specialists. Most problems are common and readily manageable by a primary care physician.

When should one seek a specialist? Clearly when a trusted primary care physician recommends that a patient would profit from someone with greater expertise. When the patient has an identified disease that requires long-term care, a specialist is generally better tutored in its management than a general physician. A referral is warranted when the patient continues to have unabated symptoms that undermine life's quality and the internist or primary care physician has not resolved the cause after an adequate period. Certain problems, such as those in the domain of dermatology, gynecology, neurology, ophthalmology, orthopedics, and urology, profit from being attended to by specialists in these areas.

In the last analysis, one searches for a physician with whom one feels comfortable in describing complaints without worrying about being subjected, as a result, to numerous procedures; a doctor for whom a patient is never a statistic; a doctor who does not recommend measures that compromise life in order to prolong life; someone who neither exaggerates the hazards of minor illnesses nor is overwhelmed by major ones; and above all else, a fellow human being whose concern for patients is actuated by the joy of serving, regarding it as an incomparable privilege.